1 ^{50}

P 153

CONSCIENCE AND SOCIETY

CONSCIENCE AND SOCIETY

A study of the psychological prerequisites of Law and Order

by

RANYARD WEST

M.D.(LOND.), D.PHIL.(OXON)

METHUEN & CO. LTD. LONDON

36 Essex Street, Strand, W.C.2

TO

MY MOTHER, MY WIFE AND MY FATHER

WHO BETWEEN THEM PROVIDED THE
CONDITIONS WHICH ENABLED THIS
BOOK TO BE WRITTEN

First published . . *September 17th 1942*
Second edition . . *1950*

CATALOGUE NO. 5307/U

PRINTED IN GREAT BRITAIN

PREFACE

I AM indebted to Prof. J. C. Flugel of University College, London, for reading the psychological chapters and to Prof. C. A. W. Manning of the London School of Economics for reading the chapters on law and international law. Each of them has made acceptable suggestions which I believe to have improved the book. Prof. Manning adds certain " fundamental " criticisms which it has been my responsibility to withstand. To both I am very grateful for placing their expert technical knowledge of the two diverse subjects concerned at my disposal. I also wish to thank Sir Walter Langdon Brown, the first of my teachers to interest me in psychological medicine, and my friends Dr. R. A. McCance and Mr. A. L. Lamaison for their helpful comments upon the manuscript as a whole. Mr. Lamaison has very kindly read the proofs as well.

Readers familiar with the literature will be aware how heavily I have leant upon certain standard works—of J. L. Brierly, W. A. Dunning, L. T. Hobhouse, H. Lauterpacht, R. Pound, J. Vinogradoff, and others—in the subjects with which I was less familiar. I have tried to mark my debts by appropriate references in the text of the book.

I wish to thank the Institute of Medical Psychology of London (the ' Tavistock Clinic ') for access to my case notes at the Clinic, from which nearly all the clinical material of Chapter IV is derived.

RANYARD WEST

June 1942

Thus they in mutual accusation spent
The fruitless hours, but neither self-condemning,
And of their vain contest appear'd no end.

MILTON : *Paradise Lost*, Book ix. 1187–9.

CONTENTS

PART II

PART III

INTRODUCTION

MEN like to be able to give reasons for their own actions, and to explain and forecast the actions of their fellows. And so there has never been a dearth of theories about human motivation and of generalizations about human behaviour. Nowhere, perhaps, in human thought has the power of pure theory to give emotional satisfaction been so striking as in this field of behaviour and its mental concomitants. In the realm of the mind man has always suffered from a positive dearth of facts in the face of an overwhelming desire to know. In consequence there has been a peculiar readiness to accept theoretical explanations. And theories about mental processes and the sources of human behaviour once formed are not readily abandoned. Their purpose being to account for phenomena for which explanations are felt to be necessary, they tend to be held tenaciously by minds of a certain type until new theories will acceptably replace them over the whole field.

But, where human conduct is concerned, not only are our minds open to theory and very anxious to have theories presented to them; our behaviour itself is capable of being greatly modified by the theories we adopt. And the success of a theory depends not less upon its presentation than upon its content. The remark, attributed to Carlyle, that the social theories of Rousseau resulted in the skins of aristocrats being used to bind the second edition of his book was an extravagance. But there is little exaggeration in Lord Bryce's [1] statement that Rousseau fired a thousand for one that Bentham convinced, or in his emphasis of the influence of the vivid French idealist upon the forms both of the Declaration of American Independence and of the French Declaration of the Rights of Man. [2] Again, it is to doctrines of Hegel that many people have ascribed modern nationalism, particularly in the form which it has taken in Germanic culture. According to Hobhouse, it was Hegel who ' turned the edge of freedom by identifying it with law, of equality by substituting discipline, of personality by merging the individual with the state, of humanity by making the state the supreme form of

[1] Bryce, *Modern Democracies*, vol. i. p. 51. (Macmillan. 1921.)
[2] ' We hold these truths to be self-evident, that all men are created equal, that they are endowed by their Creator with certain inalienable Rights, that among these are Life, Liberty, and the pursuit of Happiness, that to secure these rights Governments are instituted, deriving their just powers from the consent of the governed.'—American Declaration of Independence (1776).
' Men are born and continue equal in respect of their rights. The end of political society is the preservation of the natural and imprescriptible rights of man. . . . The principle of all sovereignty resides essentially in the nation.'—Declaration of the Rights of Man. French National Assembly (1791).

2

human association'. In England, we shall find Hobbes and Locke good examples of philosophers who presented political theories of wide scope and great influence which were built upon a limited basis of fact.

G. D. H. Cole,[1] 'first setting aside the psychologists', describes two schools of political theorists. 'One school, by collecting facts, aims at broad generalizations of what happens in human societies ; the other tries to penetrate to the universal principles at the root of all human combinations.' Rightly claiming Rousseau for the latter school, he adds that for them, 'facts may be useful, but in themselves they can prove nothing. The question is not one of fact, but one of right.' If we accept Cole's two categories of political theorists (which we may), and reintroduce the psychologists (which we must), we shall find that the latter fall sometimes into one of these two groups and sometimes into the other. There are psychologists whose chief concern is observation and measurement—they fall into the first category. There are others who bring psychological conceptions based on limited experimental observations which admit of only a limited inference, into contact with wide introspective philosophical speculations, in Rousseau's hope of penetrating to universal principles of conduct. There is, however, a third category of psychologist in respect of their reliance on facts, a class which hovers between the other two. For them, certain phenomena are observable so consistently that in formulating the laws which govern them they feel entitled (and observers concede their right) to place themselves in Mr. Cole's group of fact-finders. But facts require interpretation. And psychologists have not lost man's desire to press his interpretations as far as he feels he legitimately can. Thus a psychology which starts by demonstrating and classifying repeatable observations, and proceeds to legitimate generalizations from them, may end by postulating theories of which one can only say that they 'claim to penetrate to the universal principles at the root of all human combinations'. In so doing they transgress every rule of scientific inference. The reason for this is that the psychologist is trying to be at once a scientist and a philosopher. As a scientist he must not be content until he has observed and measured. Where he attempts philosophy he is forced, like other philosophers, to resort to distant inference and speculation. Now, rightly or wrongly, the critical public sets itself a different standard of credulity when it is dealing with men who claim to have observed and measured, than it does with those who claim merely to have 'thought out' their answers. A result of this is that the modern psychologist, who has observed much and measured a little, is liable to carry a certain prestige which he has acquired as a scientist into the realm of his philosophical speculations. And

[1] Preface to Rousseau's *Social Contract*, in Everyman, No. 660.

the prestige of a philosopher should come from the force of his reasoning alone.

There is another community of men who study the nature of society and the relationship of individuals and groups within it —the lawyers. Like psychology, jurisprudence has in the past been more closely bound up with political philosophy than it is to-day. But, studying as it does rules for the guidance of human conduct and their application, legal theory has had throughout the ages its peculiar terms of reference. While psychology is virtually a new development, branching out from philosophy to study human nature by new approaches, jurisprudence has since Roman times marched by the side of political philosophy, observing both it and the phenomena of human conduct which it sets out to explain, developing the while its own theories about one particular aspect of organized human life, namely the restraints which society puts upon its individual members. From that prime study of the lawyers have sprung legal theories of moral obligation and much speculation as to how it is that people have in fact managed to live together in relatively stable communities. In addition to being a student of laws the legal theorist has thus become in part a philosopher and in part a student of psychology. In so doing he has built into his systems of legal theory conceptions of human nature which require recognition and study in any attempt we may make to collect and correlate and improve man's various theories about himself.

It is from this classification of the students of human nature into the three groups of political philosophers, psychologists, and lawyers that we shall proceed to our study of what man has thought of himself, what he ought to think, and how in certain important respects he ought to act. Members of these three learned faculties have not yet sufficiently absorbed each others' thought. Each faculty has made difficulties for the others by its rigidities, its technical language, and its high self-esteem. Each has presented to the outside world as valid, conclusions which may be questionable to a painstaking critic. The political philosopher suffers the least from jargon, the least perhaps from self-confidence, and, in the confusion of his theories, presents the least effective façade of omniscience to the outside world. The psychologist has recently become a great offender in respect of jargon. And with the confidence which thousands of practitioners have acquired from the successful manipulation of the mysteries of psychoanalysis in medical treatment, there is a growing tendency towards undue presumption, particularly with regard to much of the unproven theoretical assumptions of its founder, Freud.

With all these matters we shall deal as we attempt to follow our own threads of theory and of fact through the various opinions of all these faculties. I believe that there are certain simple facts of human nature which can be inferred from the assembled contributions to knowledge and thought of the philosopher, the lawyer, and the psychologist, but which we have hitherto failed fully to interpret. To my mind that failure is the chief reason why we are shunning as difficult or impossible the very necessary and waiting task of building, upon our common human nature, our total human society.

Though one vital need of enlightenment inspires it throughout, convenience of presentation divides this book into three parts.

Part I (Chapters I to IV) is a study of ' human nature ' in its social relationship, and in particular the nature of the misunderstanding which we men and women have entertained about both the place and the significance of aggressiveness in our social lives. As for the place, we shall find it in ourselves. And as for its significance it is that it is a disturbing minority influence in our social life and so is controllable by our own ' best selves '.

Part II (Chapters V and VI) thus becomes a study of the control of human nature by law, and of how law can secure a maintenance of the ascendency of man's Social Instinct over the socially inimical tendencies of his Self-assertive Instinct, and thus act as a necessary supplement to his moral self-control.

We shall find that the reason why ' International Law ' has so conspicuously failed to give us an effective alternative to war is that instead of regulative law it gives us a system based upon promise and moral obligation alone, and thus ignores a vital need of man's nature, the external control of his aggressiveness.

Part III (Chapters VII to IX) applies our present knowledge of man's social nature to our present problems of social organization and world order. A study of the emotion of loyalty, its sources and its manifestations, added to our knowledge of the inevitable limitations of man's judgment and the consequent requirements of effective law, enable us to forecast the essential structure of that World Order which mankind now seeks but has yet to find.

PART I

I

THREE PHILOSOPHIES OF HUMAN NATURE

AMONG the many men who, at various stages of civilization, have been impelled to write down their opinions upon the ordering of society, there have occasionally been individuals who were in actual possession of political power. But more often such writers have not been notable practical administrators, but have stood aside, watching the behaviour of men, examining themselves, and brooding over how society works and how it could be made to work better. In the latter half of the seventeenth century and the first half of the eighteenth century, three contemplative philosophers, whose lives practically overlapped, looked out upon a not very rapidly changing European society.

Hobbes, *Locke*, and *Rousseau* were three very different men. In some ways they were obviously influenced in their general theories by contemporary events and their attitudes to them. Hobbes was a Caroline, Locke—perhaps by the accident of his personal appointment as physician to Lord Shaftesbury and the odium this brought upon him—was not. Rousseau was born in Geneva, and lived in the later stages of the French monarchy, a generation after William III became settled on his throne. But they were all men of education and leisure, affiliated to the upper rather than the lower classes of society. They were all men of letters. They all met famous men of their time, had knowledge of history, recent and remote, and knew something of governmental institutions. Yet their views of society, of the fundamental relationships between man and man, of 'human nature', were very different. And, in considering the needs of seventeenth- and eighteenth-century Europe, they came to very different conclusions.

THOMAS HOBBES (1588–1679)

Thomas Hobbes was the son of a country clergyman who was apparently of violent habits. When Thomas was still an infant his father had to flee his home as a result of having struck a man, 'being provoked'. Brought up thereafter by an uncle, Hobbes went to Oxford (Magdalen Hall) and became tutor and companion to the Earl of Devonshire till he was forty and his employer died. After an interval he returned to the same (Cavendish) family. Twelve years later (1640) he wrote a treatise in support of the sovereignty of Charles I at the time of his conflict with his Short Parliament. Then he fled to Paris where he was first popular with the exiled English court, but later was 'banished' from it, apparently more for his unorthodox religious than for his political views. He was allowed to return to England, where he remained unpersecuted either by the Commonwealth Government or by the returning Charles II. He published his famous political and theological treatise the *Leviathan* in 1651 when he was sixty-three years of age. At the time his intentions were variously thought to be to support the Stuarts, to flatter Oliver Cromwell, and to justify the transfer of allegiance from the losing to the winning side. Actually he appears to have been a lover of law and order who thought the English Civil War a tragedy, wars in general the curse of civilized life, and the prime need of a society (of whatever size) to be the centralization of adequate force to protect good men against bad.

Hobbes was in search of a fundamental grounding for law and government for the people of his own time. The seventeenth century was a time of re-examination of first principles in sociology. The stability of society had seemed in the past to be based on some sort of contract or understanding between peoples and their governor, which secured peace, order, and justice to them, in exchange for wealth and power to him. With the rise of national states, temporal power in the sovereign had become limited less by the power of his subordinate princes and nobles than by a sense of 'natural justice', of which the custodians were the subjects themselves, together with the organized and disciplined Catholic Church, which received the allegiance of ruler and subject alike. By the end of the seventeenth century the second of these restraints upon absolute sovereignty had become generally weakened, and, in Protestant England, largely lost. Hobbes, as others in his time, was concerned to recreate the weakened control over the sovereign power, at the same time retaining a strong government in an unstable and revolutionary age, steering as he says in his dedication of the *Leviathan* between 'too great Liberty' and 'too much Authority'. This he attempted to do, first by deriving the government (whatever it turned out to be) from a mutual contract between men for their own security, and secondly by basing the civil laws which were enacted upon fundamental 'laws of nature' which must not be violated. It was in the former of these two exercises that Hobbes came to set down his views of human nature and the sort of way men had come together to form social groups and national states.

Hobbes has been both praised and upbraided for being a 'realist'—meaning by the term that he does not invent human nature but observes it. In the *Leviathan* (or 'Discourse of Commonwealth or State—which is but an Artificial Man') he first sets out some views of the physiology of sensations and movements of the body which are difficult to make sense of in terms of modern knowledge and modern views of these matters.

Then he proceeds to a discourse of social custom and human nature which does not seem quite so archaic to the twentieth-century reader, although it may well do so to the reader of a little later time than ours. Under a schematic representation of human qualities with headings such as ' Power ', ' Worth ', ' Dignity ', ' Honour ', and ' Worthiness ', he considers, first, the different dispositions which occur in men, and then their common dispositions. He considers ' Vain-glorious men enclined to rash engaging ', men who ' distrust their own subtilty and so are in tumult ' ; men with ' strong opinion of their wisdom of government and so disposed to ambition ' ; the effects too of curiosity, ignorance, and credulity in forming character : [1] ' When he cannot assure himself of the true causes of things, man supposeth causes of them, either such as his own fancy suggesteth, or trusting to the authority of other men. . . .[2] But *in the first place I put, for a general inclination of all mankind, a perpetual and restless desire of Power after power, that ceaseth only with death.* And the cause of this is not always that a man hopes for a more intensive delight, or that he cannot be content with moderate power, but also because he cannot *assure* the power and means to live well which he hath, without the acquisition of more." [3] He then goes on to consider man's fundamental relationship with his fellows in the following terms : ' *Nature hath made men so equal in the faculties of body and mind . . . that when all is reckoned together, the difference between man and man is not so considerable as that . . . one can claim any benefit to which another may not pretend.*' But ' such is the nature of men . . . that they will hardly believe there to be many so wise as themselves. For they see their own wit at hand and other men's at a distance . . . and each is contented with his share !—From equality of ability arises equality of hope of attaining our ends. And therefore if any two men desire the same thing, which nevertheless they cannot both enjoy, they become enemies . . . and endeavour to destroy or subdue one another. . . . And so men have no pleasure, but, on the contrary a great deal of grief, in keeping company, where there is no power able to overawe them all. For *every man looketh that his companion should value him at the same rate he sets upon himself ;* and upon all signs of contempt or undervaluing endeavours as far as he dares to extort a greater value from his contemners.' [4]

' So that in the nature of man we find three principal causes of quarrel—Competition, Diffidence, and Glory. The first maketh man invade for gain, the second for safety, and the third for reputation. The first use violence to make themselves masters of other men's persons, wives, children, and cattle ; the second to defend them ; the third for trifles, as a word, a smile, a different opinion, and any other sign of undervalue. . . . Hereby it is

---

[1] *Leviathan*, p. 51. (Everyman, No. 691.)
[3] Ibid. p. 49.
[2] Ibid. p. 54.
[4] Ibid. p. 63.

manifest that *during the time men live without a common power to keep them all in awe they are in that condition called War . . . a* war of every man against every man. For war consisteth not only . . . in actual fighting, but in the known disposition thereto, during all the time there is no assurance to the contrary.' And in such a state of war ' *wherein men live without other security than what their own strength and their own invention shall furnish them . . . there is no place for industry . . . no culture of the earth, no navigation, no more use of the commodities that may be imported by sea . . . no arts, no letters, no society ; and, which is worst of all, continual fear, and danger of violent death ; and the life of man, solitary, poor, nasty, brutish and short.'* [1]

But, ' the desires and other passions of men are in themselves no sin. Nor more are the actions that proceed from those passions, *till they know a law that forbids them : which till laws be made they cannot know : nor can any law be made till they have agreed upon the Person that shall make it.'* [1]—Here Hobbes excludes moral laws dictated by conscience from within, and also the possibility of men making their own laws among themselves directly. The reason for both exclusions is that he believed man to be guided by solely selfish motives—' laws of nature '—and that these enable him to sacrifice his own immediate interest and pleasure only by one supreme abnegation of sovereignty over his own life. To this man is impelled both by his feelings and his intellect, when he contemplates or experiences the actualities of the state of war described above. It is true, he says, that probably at no time was the whole world in such chaos as having ' every man's hand turned against every other '. But that is what human nature produces if there is no over-ruling power to fear. He cites the deterioration occurring in individuals when orderly government is abrogated, for instance, in civil wars. ' Force and fraud are in war two cardinal virtues.' There is ' no propriety, no dominion, no mine and thine distinct, but only that to be every man's that he can get and for so long as he can keep it '. He concludes this section with the comment : ' This much for the ill condition which man by mere Nature is actually placed in, though with a possibility to come out of it, consisting partly in the Passions, partly in his Reason '.

Thus for Hobbes man's passion for power is corrected somewhat by his ' passions enclining to Peace '—which are ' fear of Death, desire of such things as are necessary to commodious living, and hope by industry to obtain them '. These are aided by his reason which is capable of finding out the ' laws of nature '.[2] A ' law of nature ' for Hobbes is not a law instinctively obeyed, but a method of self-preservation discovered by the intellect, a general rule forbidding man to do anything ' which is destructive of his life or taketh away the means of preserving the same '.[2]

[1] *Leviathan*, p. 65.   [2] Ibid. p. 66.

These laws of nature are golden rules for self-preservation. Hobbes lists them as a classical series of homilies—on pardoning past offences, accommodation to others, keeping faith, etc.—but prefaces two cardinal rules of his own—(1) 'That every man ought to endeavour peace as far as he has hope of obtaining it, and when he cannot obtain it that he may seek and use all helps and advantages of war.' (2) 'That a man be willing when others are so too, as far as for Peace and defence of himself he shall think necessary, *to lay down his rights to all things and be contented with so much liberty against other men as he would allow other men against himself.'* [1]

As he derives all his social arrangement from man's self-preservative and selfish instincts, Hobbes naturally concludes that it would be useless to bind men against their own interest ; and in particular—' a covenant not to defend myself from force by force is always void '.[2] For when the time comes, ' man by nature chooseth the lesser evil ',[2] i.e. he instinctively defends his own interest. By the same token, it will be useless to allow a man to decide for himself in the matter of this laying down of liberty, when in fact he has given others as much liberty as he allows himself. Consequently no man can be a judge of his own cause. Men anxious to implement these ' laws of nature ', or rules for self-preservation, will be willing to renounce and transfer their rights of self defence, and will submit to have their causes heard by an independent judge.

Hobbes' ' realism ' next considers the *keeping* of covenants. First ' the force of words being too weak to hold men to the performance of their covenants, there are in man's nature but two imaginable helps to strengthen it. Those are . . . fear of the consequences of breaking their word, and glory or pride in appearing not to need to break it.' (This latter, he adds, ' is a generosity too rarely found to be presumed on, especially in the pursuers of wealth, command or sensual pleasure, which are the greatest part of mankind '.) ' The passion to be reckoned upon is fear ', either of ' the power of Spirits invisible . . . or of those *men* they shall offend '. And ' though the former be the greater Power, the fear of the latter is commonly the greater Fear '. Hobbes puts as his third law 'that men perform their covenants made '.[3] But he clearly does not believe they will generally do so. And here again is the striking point in Hobbes' theory. *He does not trust Man's nature to keep any of these rules.* If men were ' reasonable ' enough to keep his first rule—to seek peace, they might keep the second—to sacrifice ' liberty ' for ' security ', and so build up a less drastic system of government than he is led to advocate. Perhaps they might even learn to keep their covenants, accommodate themselves to others, pardon past offences, and so on, down the scale of social virtues which he lists. Hobbes in

[1] *Leviathan*, p. 67.　　　　[2] Ibid. p. 72.　　　　[3] Ibid. p. 73.

fact is analysing a society of men who are still partly in the anarchic ' state of nature '. Many of them are governed by a lust for power which outweighs any fear of retribution, and most of them dwell in mutual distrust and danger. All are inspired primarily by self interest. In such a world kings and sovereigns mobilize their forces, and, inspired by similar motives themselves, ' because of their independency, are in continual jealousies and in the state and posture of gladiators, weapons pointing, eyes fixed on one another . . . a posture of war '.[1] It is in such a state of affairs, that Hobbes calls on reasonable men to observe and follow his precepts for turning a theoretically free life into a practically good one, whether it be for individuals or princes. He does not believe that a strong enough central power can be built up if men are left free to keep order by a system of mutual obligation. Self interest will always frustrate any such plans. What he hopes is to get *enough* men to see *the advantage of giving up their freedom in cold blood*, so that the superior authority which they can build out of such a renunciation will be able to give them, in time of stress, order, security, justice, and peace.

Hobbes' object then is to get liberty- and power-loving men out of that ' miserable condition of war '. In hot blood they will not be able to obey those sensible ' laws of nature ', which are ' contrary to our natural passions that carry us to Partiality, Pride, Revenge and the like '. There must therefore be found enough wise men to recognize this ahead and make the renunciation of freedom of action necessary to the constitution of a ' Power ' which will keep them all in order. That this ' Power ' shall be strong enough to fulfil its functions is vital. For ' *covenants without the sword are but words, and of no strength to secure a man at all* '.[2] The criteria of adequate strength in the central authority are two. It must first be judged ' by comparison with the enemy we fear '—adequate in fact to prevent the odds in favour of an aggressor from ever becoming such as ' to move him to attempt '.[3] Secondly, it must be a power secure against the weakening influence of divided counsels within. Strength can easily be ' reduced by mutual opposition to nothing ' so that the community is ' not only subdued by very few that agree together, but also, where there is no common enemy, they may war upon each other for their particular interests '.[4]

For Hobbes, man's nature is such that self interest, lust, and fear will always keep men from achieving a secure communal life except where reason enables enough men to see two things : first that self interest is served by union in an ordered and peaceful social life ; and second that that union will be opposed and weakened by their own natural passions, of immediate self interest

[1] *Leviathan*, p. 65.　　　　　[2] Ibid. p. 87.
[3] Ibid. p. 88.　　　　　[4] Ibid. p. 97.

and immediate fear, if they do not anticipate trouble by a cold-blooded renunciation—a handing over of their weapons for safe custody.

Hobbes' final concern is for the competence of the ruling power so constituted. On its maintenance all order depends. Between ' Monarchy ', ' Aristocracy ', and ' Democracy ' (and with humour that rises above the conflicts of our own day, he offers the alternative titles of ' Tyranny ', ' Oligarchy ', and ' Anarchy ' respectively), the difference is not of power but of convenience. His own feelings for contemporary events enter into his own choice, as also into the subsequent description of a ' Christian Commonwealth ' in which he likens the Catholic Church to the ' Kingdom of the Fairies ' ! Hobbes himself chooses a single governor. And the government, whatever it is, is to be erected on a semi-permanent basis, so that events like those of the decade before the publication of Leviathan shall not recur.[1]

JOHN LOCKE (1632–1704)

When Charles I was executed in Whitehall Palace Yard in 1649, John Locke, the son of a Somersetshire lawyer and volunteer captain in Cromwell's army, was at Westminster School nearby. He went up to Christ Church, Oxford, in 1652, the year after the publication of Leviathan. He studied metaphysics for a time, then turned to medicine, and at thirty-four became physician and subsequently advisor to Ashley Cooper, later Lord Shaftesbury. He gained some experience both of administrative government and of law-making ; for he assisted in drafting a constitution for the government of Carolina for Shaftesbury, and held minor administrative posts during his Lord Chancellorship. He fled to Holland after his patron became involved in the Monmouth rebellion of 1685 and stayed abroad till after the ' glorious revolution ' of 1688. Under William III he refused an ambassadorship and became Commissioner of Appeals. His two chief works, Essay Concerning Human Understanding and Two Treatises of Government, were both published in 1690, when he was fifty-eight. But the fundamentals of his theory of government were written down when he was about thirty-five.

In a sense Locke starts where Hobbes leaves off. He admits that men living together need government ; but he begins at once to consider how much they need and how much their liberty has to be interfered with. He lays it down as axiomatic that ' the whole trust, power, and authority of the magistrate is vested in him for no other purpose but to be made use of for the good, preservation, and peace of men in that society over which he is set, and therefore that this alone is and ought to be the standard and measure according to which he ought to square and propor-

[1] Leviathan, p. 97.

tion his laws, model and frame his government. For, if men could live peaceably and quietly together, without uniting under certain laws, and growing into a commonwealth, there would be no need at all of magistrates or politics, which were only made to preserve men in this world from the fraud and violence of one another.' [1]

Between the publication of the *Leviathan* and the writing of this essay less than twenty years—the period of the Commonwealth and the Restoration—had passed. Yet while Hobbes concentrated all his attention on snatching power out of the hands of individuals and small groups to concentrate it in a central authority, and his one fear was that that authority might not in fact be strong enough to control the unruly and selfish passions of men, Locke started off to limit the functions and power of the government *to a minimum*. The reason lies principally in the difference between the views which the two philosophers took of human nature. In his last sentence quoted above, Locke speaks of magisterial and political power as only necessitated by the ' fraud and violence ' in the world. Hobbes had spoken of the state to which man is reduced in ' mere nature ' as being one in which ' force and fraud are the two cardinal virtues '. The ' state of nature ' and the ' state of war ' are one. For Locke, on the contrary, fraud, violence, and a ' state of war ' are not synonymous with the ' state of nature '. It is quite otherwise. Men in that state are in ' perfect freedom to order their actions and dispose of their possessions and persons as they think fit, within the bounds of the law of nature ; . . . it is a state also of equality '.[2] But, further, quoting Hooker, it is a state in which ' my desire to be loved of my equals in nature, as much as possible may be, imposeth upon me a natural duty of bearing to themwards fully the like affection '.[3]

This start is very different from Hobbes'. While the latter emphasizes aggressiveness and distrust, and his ' natural ' man thinks of securing material things and being respected, Locke and Hooker lay stress on natural man's desire to be approved, to be loved. Hobbes proceeded to the task of controlling the ' force and fraud ' of a majority by bribing their own long-sighted self-interest. Locke is concerned to secure the functioning of their good co-operative qualities by controlling the force and fraud of a minority. For him, man's first duty is not to get out of the ' state of nature ' but to learn the ' law of nature ' which governs it, and ' teaches all mankind who will but consult it, that, being all equal and independent, *no one ought to harm another in his life, health, liberty, or possessions* '. The execution of this law of nature is at first ' put into every man's hands '. Each should obey it himself. But each is also charged with the punishment of

---

[1] *Essay on Toleration.* See Everyman, No. 751, p. xi.
[2] *Second Treatise of Government.* p. 118. (Everyman, No. 751.) [3] Ibid. p. 119.

offenders who break it. 'Thus in the state of nature, one man comes by a power over another . . . but only to retribute . . . so far as calm reason and conscience dictate what is proportionate to the transgression.' He who transgresses the law of nature, with its demand for respect for the interests of others, ' declares himself to live by another rule than that of reason and common equity ', to have committed ' a trespass against the whole species ', and ' himself to quit the principles of human nature and to be a noxious creature '. Also ' there is commonly injury done '.[1] It becomes necessary to punish such bad men effectively. And that is not easily done in a ' natural ', unorganized society, where men are judges in their own causes, where ' self-love makes men partial to themselves and their friends, and where ill-nature, passion, and revenge will carry them too far in punishing others '.[2] Civil government is the proper remedy for these *inconveniences* of the state of nature. But the form of government is vital. ' For ', says Locke, ' absolute monarchs are but men ! . . . How much better is it than a " state of nature ", where one man commanding a multitude has the liberty to be judge in *his* own case, and may do with his subjects whatever he pleases ? ' [2]

The ' state of nature ' for Locke ' has inconveniences ' ; but it is poles apart from the ' state of war '—' as far apart as a state of peace, goodwill, mutual assistance, and preservation, and a state of enmity, malice, violence, and mutual destruction, are from one another '.[3] We find such an extreme antagonism between the states of ' nature ' and ' war ' in this description because Locke treats the good and co-operative in human nature as ' natural ', and excludes as unnatural the aggressive and evil breakers of the law. In contrast to Hobbes', Locke's ' state of nature ' is in fact a state of good-nature. It is on this altered state of nature that Locke proceeds to build his conception of what is required of a well-organized society, and how such a society is constructed.

For Locke, then, the majority of men start in his state of nature, full of goodwill, co-operation, and respect for each other's interests. The bad men are a minority who ostracize themselves. What is required is means to give minimum regulation to the lives of the majority and to provide adequate power to deal with the law-breaking minority. And all government is in the interests of those governed—' *Salus populi suprema lex* '. Hobbes had presumed that the individual could succeed in living a satisfactory life on his own once he was adequately protected. But Locke supports Hooker in looking to government to enrich men's lives by securing for them ' such a life as our nature doth desire, a life fit for the dignity of man '.[4] This is done, however, simply by making easy their free association in a community. His political society

[1] Locke, loc. cit. p. 121. [2] Ibid. p. 123.
[3] Ibid. p. 126. [4] Ibid. p. 124.

begins when man leaves the inconveniences and risks of the
' state of nature ' ' by agreeing with other men to join and unite
into a community for their comfortable, safe, and peaceable living
one amongst another in secure enjoyment of their properties,
and a greater security against any that are not of it '. They
' make one body politic wherein the majority have a right to act
and conclude the rest '.[1] This voluntary subjection to majority
rule would appear the greatest sacrifice which is entailed in
entering Locke's political state.

In Locke's proper political society, formed by the simple
process of voluntary association of men for their own good, each
.must give up all the power necessary to the ends for which they
united to the majority of the community (unless they ' expressly
agree ' to a larger number being required, for it is a free association from the first). All they need to do is to ' barely ' 'agree.
That is the beginning of all lawful government.[2] Men so united
can bring order and secure justice by establishing ' settled known
laws ', independent judges, and power to back sentences.[3] Each
man admittedly has his liberty curtailed, e.g. he gives up all
power of punishing directly ; that Society does for him. ' And
whoever has the legislative or supreme power is bound to govern
by established standing laws, promulgated and known to the
people . . . to employ the force of the community, at home only
in the execution of such laws, or abroad to prevent or redress
foreign injuries. . . . And all this is to be directed to no
other end but the peace, safety, and public good of the
people [4] . . . to preserve the members of that society in their
lives, liberties, and possessions.' [5] As for despotical power,
' this is a power which neither nature gives nor compact can
convey '.[5]

Though Locke's chief concern is to safeguard the individual,
he does a little to secure stability in his society and its government,
though always with an eye open against tyranny. He does not
approve of contracting out of a society : power once given can
' never revert to the individuals again, as long as the society lasts '.[6]
Legislative power vested in an assembly cannot revert to the
people ' whilst that government lasts. . . . But if they have set
limits to the duration of their legislative . . . or else when by
the miscarriage of those in authority it is forfeited . . . it reverts
to the society, and the people have a right to act as supreme, and
continue the legislative in themselves or place it in a new form
or new hands as they think good '.[6]

Finally, Locke held that freedom given developed the best
co-operative responses in return. In his plea for religious toleration, which was to extend to Dissenters—' who would soon cease
to be accused of faction and sedition if all churches were obliged

---

[1] Loc. cit. p. 164. [2] Ibid. p. 166. [3] Ibid. p. 180.
[4] Ibid. p. 182. [5] Ibid. p. 205. [6] Ibid. p. 242.

to lay down toleration '—he asserts that there is ' only one thing which gathers people into seditious commotion, and that is oppression '.

What are the essential differences between the political philosophies of Hobbes and Locke ? First there is the division of opinion upon fundamental human nature—individualistic, aggressive, and selfish for Hobbes, co-operative and friendly for Locke. Hobbes' state of nature, which was also a ' state of war ', deteriorates further with actual war, so that force and fraud, always well to the fore, then become ' two cardinal virtues '. He held that the laws of nature must be allowed to guide men through their intellects into the joint renunciation of immediate freedom and self-seeking in exchange for the greater security of law and order. In doing this their intellects are aided by their fears. The cardinal rule of order is that, because of his natural violence and selfishness, no man can be allowed to judge his own cause, because no man can do so without prejudice. That granted and secured by force deposited with an external authority (preferably, but conditionally, a single governor), man's individuality could develop freely, secure from his ' natural passion to partiality '. For Locke, the inconveniences of the life of nature do not include man's fundamental selfishness. The first problem is that of the evil minority, best to be dealt with collectively. But secondly, even co-operative men have occasional problems with the ' fraud and violence of one another '. The following of the restraining ' law of nature ' is a duty ; but as such it requires self-control. And Locke admits the prejudices of normal men, where ' self-love makes them partial to themselves and their friends, and ill-nature, passion, and revenge will carry them too far in punishing others '. So that in the end Locke's human nature is both better and safer in a society than in a state of freedom. His kinder view of the majority of men makes him able to suggest an easier and a democratic association of men collectively self-governing through magistrates. In fact *where Hobbes sees an anarchy unless men give up self-government, Locke sees a natural community which will improve its condition by careful self-government, and run no risk in the process.*

We must note another point. Locke's society is a limited one. Throughout, he is legislating for the ' comfortable, safe, and peaceable living ' of a given community. Its force is to be used against ' those not of it ' and ' to redress foreign injuries '. The bad men, though always present, are essentially *outside* the democratic community, either ostracized by breaking the kindly laws of co-operative human nature, or initially so as foreigners. His advice is for the better regulation of a society of good men. This is in strong contrast with the conviction of Hobbes that he could not rely upon good men. His recipe is for ending the state of war between bad men, and bringing order among men made worse by strife. Hobbes claims that his social order can be built, not merely between men who ' barely agree ' and subsequently continue (precariously, he would hold) to rule each other by majority vote thereafter, but between men who selfishly distrust each other, and have been proceeding against each other by force and fraud, demanding each of them to be valued too highly by his fellows.

The two philosophers see human nature very differently. Does one at least of them see it wrongly ? Or are they legislating for two types of men, those who are fit for democracy, and those who are not ? Or else, again, are they describing two stages, or two phases, or even two aspects of human nature ? At any rate Hobbes claims what Locke never attempts, a sovereign cure for the conflict between human nature at its worst, spontaneously initiated by the contestants. *Locke legislates out of goodwill for the organization of communities which already exist in substance : Hobbes for creating a first association out of the ill will of distrustful and aggressive men.*

JEAN JACQUES ROUSSEAU (1712–1778)

Locke died in 1704 after fourteen years of quiet retirement in East Anglia. In 1712 Rousseau was born in Geneva. His mother died at his birth. His father, like Hobbes', had to flee after a quarrel. But Hobbes, after the regular education of a gentleman of the seventeenth century, held posts as tutor and companion in one aristocratic English family for practically the whole of his working life, while Rousseau, after a perfunctory and erratic private education, led a most contrary life, from society's ordinary point of view. He undertook, or was put to fourteen distinct occupations before he was forty, in all but one of which—that of writing—he seems to have failed. From nine posts he either fled or resigned or was discharged. Alternately he wandered the countryside, and took those chance appointments (as lackey, secretary, music teacher, ambassador's secretary, etc.) in the towns of Switzerland and France. Occasionally he went further afield. By temperament he was passionate and unaccommodating, ill at ease in society, suspicious, perverse. His chief human relationships failed tragically, and so constantly as to indicate an internal reason in Rousseau himself. Indeed he lacked the ordinary principles of honourable behaviour which societies, urban or rural, of princes or of peasants, demand. He dealt selfishly and artificially with things present, and retired physically into the countryside which he loved, and mentally into a distant world where things were different. From time to time he was stirred to a warm sympathy with real oppression as he saw it, for instance when he chanced upon a peasant hiding his better food and wine in fear of the exciseman. He does not seem, however, to have deliberately studied the social conditions in which he lived, but rather to have been stimulated by isolated incidents, while he was always more ready to indentify himself with suffering than with happiness. Always he felt himself to be the greatest sufferer of all, misunderstood, denied sympathy, forced to behave under evil or fantastic compulsions when good and natural impulses should have come in their place.

Rousseau's social and political theories are much more obviously related to the peculiarities of his own mental life than are those of Hobbes or Locke. It will consequently be necessary to refer to his life while we are discussing his theories rather than to be content with a prefatory outline alone. Of his chief works one, *Emile*, deals with education. Of the other three—*A discourse on the arts and sciences* (1750), *The origin of inequality among men*, and *The Social Contract or Principles of Political Right* (1762)— the first was written when he was thirty-eight, the last published when he was fifty years old. From a psychological viewpoint Rousseau's *Confessions* are an indispensable commentary on his other works. They were published posthumously only shortly before the French Revolution, among the causes and developments of which *The Social Contract* has been considered to have played such an important part.

Like Hobbes and Locke, Rousseau starts his political theory with his own peculiar ' state of nature '. And like those of his predecessors, it is an abstraction, a fantasy. Locke's ' state of nature ' exists wherever men are living peaceably together before organizing a society, and in the absence of the bad men who would turn it into a state of war. Hobbes does not pretend that his ' state of nature ' ever existed universally. It is horrid : men are placed in it by ' mere nature ', with a ' possibility to come out of it ', which possibility wise men will seize. Rousseau's ' state of nature ' is an imagined state which he doesn't pretend ever existed at all ! It purports to be, as Cole has it, ' what man would be like if stripped of all that society confers upon him '. It is a very vague state, for Rousseau knew man's constant need of the society of his fellows. It has merely reality enough to enable him to agree with Hobbes that it is a state to get out of. He borrows Locke's analogy of a child just fledged from the home, and ' at last the sole judge of the proper means of preserving himself . . . his own master '.[1] So that any association he forms thereafter will be ' voluntary '. Rousseau wishes men to associate in an orderly and happy society, and come under the laws necessary to that end, without losing this original imagined freedom. The problem he sets himself is ' to find a form of association which will defend and protect with the whole common force the person and goods of each associate, and in which each,

[1] Rousseau, *Social Contract*, p. 6.   (Everyman, No. 660.)

3

while uniting himself with all, may still obey himself alone, and remain as free as before '.[1] To make such a thing possible he introduces his conception of a ' General Will '. ' Each of us puts his person and all his power in common under the supreme direction of the general will, and, in our corporate capacity, we receive each member as an indivisible part of the whole.' [2] The ' body politic ' thus formed is ' *sovereign* '-—can neither bind itself to an outsider nor alienate any part of itself nor do anything derogatory to the original act. The *social contract* thus made must be kept.

Like Hobbes and Locke, Rousseau then surveys the advantages man gains through entering into society by this particular form of social contract. He has lost ' natural liberty and an unlimited right to everything he tries to get and succeeds in getting ; what he gains is civil liberty and the proprietorship of all he possesses '.[3] This language is reminiscent both of Hobbes and of Locke. But ' his faculties are so stimulated, his ideas so extended, his feelings so ennobled, and his whole soul so uplifted...'[4] Rousseau is master of phrases that fly high. Indeed, throughout his work it is not the cogent argument which attracts, but the startling phrase. There are phrases which unfold profound truth never to be followed up by any argument : ' The strongest is never strong enough to be always the master ' ; [5] phrases of bitter sarcasm : ' Tranquility is found also in dungeons ' ; [6] of intuition into human nature : ' Slaves lose everything in their chains, even the desire of escaping from them ' ; [7] of hopeful idealism : ' Individuals are enemies only accidentally ' ; [8] infectious defiance : ' To renounce liberty is to renounce being a man ' ; [9] and compensatory self-deception : ' Obedience to a law which we prescribe to ourselves *is* liberty '.[3] The last two of these quotations are the key to what Rousseau believed to be his great discovery, and a justification for the profound submission which he demands that the individual shall make to the ' sovereign ' community. The problem can be restated : ' Tyranny is intolerable ; liberty is vital to life. But human associations accompanied by government and law are necessary, and should be good and pleasant things. Reassure me that by entering your society I do not lose my freedom, and I enter willingly, enthusiastically.' The assurance is found as follows : Society is based on a freely entered contract between its members for the exclusive benefit of themselves (as Hobbes). They collectively form its ' sovereign ' (as Locke). But, more than that, this ' sovereign general will ' is a common pool of the ' best ', and therefore the ' freest ' of the wills of the individual members. In ' nature ' man was selfish. But when he enters into properly organized

[1] *Social Contract*, p. 14.   [2] Ibid. p. 15.   [3] Ibid. p. 19.
[4] Ibid. p. 18.   [5] Ibid. p. 8.   [6] Ibid. p. 9.   [7] Ibid. p. 7.
[8] Ibid. p. 11.   [9] Ibid. p. 10.

social relations with his fellows, ' a remarkable change takes place, by substituting justice for instinct and giving his actions the morality they had formerly lacked. Then only, when the voice of duty takes the place of physical impulses and right of appetite, does man, who so far had considered only himself, find that he is forced to consult his reason before listening to his inclinations '.[1] In this way he loses ' natural liberty ', but gains ' civil liberty ', and more, ' moral liberty, which alone makes him truly master of himself '.[2] Rousseau holds that by entering this elementary society, man has *become* both moral and reasonable, where Locke would be content to have him *show* these qualities *in* society, as he showed them in the state of nature. Hobbes and Locke both held that social man had *lost* freedom (and Locke that he must take care not to lose too much). Rousseau claimed that man *gained* freedom by his submission to the general will.

This reference to ' moral liberty '—' the law we prescribe to ourselves '—is very important to the understanding of the development of Rousseau's theory. Both Hobbes and Locke recognized that evil, non-co-operative impulses against society may arise in unexpected quarters. Hobbes' concern was against the bad man, whom he seems generally inclined to suspect to be his neighbour, and would admit that his neighbour will be inclined in return to be suspicious of him. Locke drew attention to the possibility of the bad man being the sovereign to whom Hobbes and all his friends had handed over their power irrevocably. Locke knew too that he could appear not only in sovereign princes but also in sovereign parliaments, who could thereby forfeit their lives. But Rousseau knew good and bad to be inherent in the human soul. For he had found them in his own. As his *Confessions* clearly show, he was concerned to prove the good to be fundamental, and the bad to be incidental, explicable, or provoked. So he searches for the *conditions* which produce, for each man, the good life or the bad.

Rousseau could not find the ideal society, which freed man from the ' mere impulse of appetite which is slavery ',[2] in that elaboration of society which greeted him in eighteenth-century France, and in which he did not believe his social contract could be at work. In 1750, when he was thirty-eight years old, he was attracted to the question, ' Has the restoration of the arts and sciences had a purifying effect upon morals ? ' He answered it in a brilliant, extravagant prize essay, and the answer was an emphatic negative. ' Before art had moulded our language our morals were rude but natural. . . . In our day . . . there prevails in modern manners a servile and deceptive conformity. . . . Sincere friendship, real esteem, and perfect confidence are banished from among men. Jealousy, suspicion, fear, coldness, reserve, hate, and fraud lie constantly concealed under that

[1] *Social Contract*, p. 18.   [2] Ibid. p. 19.

uniform and deceitful veil of politeness. . . . We do not grossly outrage even our enemies, but artfully calumniate them.'[1] Egypt, Greece, Rome, and Constantinople had decayed through a dissoluteness of manners produced by the progress of the arts and sciences, and China for all its learning is ' peopled by a race of scoundrels and slaves '.[2] In contrast he cites the early Persians, the Scythians, the Germans and the early Romans. He continues : ' It is not through stupidity that the people have preferred other activities to those of the mind. . . . They noted the morals of these learned people and so knew what to think of their learning. . . .'[3] Astronomy was born of superstition ; eloquence of ambition, hatred, falsehood, and flattery ; geometry of avarice ; physics of an idle curiosity ; and even moral philosophy of human pride. Thus the arts and the sciences owe their birth to our vices. . . .'[4] And ' being the effects of idleness they generate idleness in their turn. . . . To live without doing some good is a great evil. . . . Useless ? Would God they were ! . . . These vain and futile declaimers go forth on all sides, armed with their fatal paradoxes, to sap the foundations of our faith and nullify virtue. . . .'[5] He thinks of the corruption caused by arts and letters, of the ' thousand prizes for fine discourses and none for good actions. . . . We have physicists, geometricians, chemists, astronomers, poets, musicians, and painters in plenty, but no longer a citizen among us, or if there be found a few scattered over our abandoned countryside they are left to perish there unnoticed and neglected. Such is the condition to which we are reduced, and such are our feelings towards those who give us our daily bread and our children milk '.[6] He deplores printing— thanks to the art of which ' the pernicious reflections of Hobbes and Spinoza will last for ever '.[7] And, after a passing tribute to the Academies of Science for trying to control the morals of their members, he imagines posterity praying : ' Almighty God . . . deliver us from the fatal arts and sciences of our forefathers ; give us back ignorance, innocence, and poverty, which alone can make us happy and are precious in Thy sight '.[8] The greatest exponents—such as Bacon, Descartes, Newton—will survive. ' Those teachers of mankind had themselves no teachers. . . . Let us, instead of envying them, endeavour to make between them and us that honourable distinction . . . which was formerly seen to exist between two great peoples, that the one knew how to speak, and the other how to act, aright.'[9]

In this essay Rousseau contrasts the acceptable simple life with the passions he sees active in sophisticated society, and which he wishes to repudiate in himself. In consequence we are to have no learning except among the greatest geniuses.

---

[1] *Social Contract*, p. 132. [2] Ibid. p. 135. [3] Ibid. p. 136.
[4] Ibid. p. 140. [5] Ibid. p. 142. [6] Ibid. p. 149.
[7] Ibid. p. 151. [8] Ibid p. 152. [9] Ibid. p. 154.

The rest of us will be happier doing simple things than thinking complicated things. There should be room for Bacon, Descartes, and Newton, and very naturally perhaps in his mind there would be a place too for Rousseau's best work. But not for Spinoza and Hobbes, who had painted mankind ill and so had made them worse. For the most part Rousseau is for the simple life. He had hated Paris from the memory of his first entry to it : ' Dirty and stinking little streets, ugly black houses, a general air of slovenliness and poverty, beggars, carters, menders of old clothes, criers of decoctions, and old hats. . . . The whole time during which I afterwards lived there was employed solely in trying to find means to enable me to live away from it '.[1]

But it was not only thoughts of decadent artists and of town life which troubled Rousseau. He was ill at ease in most society. Clever people always upset him. He never grasped conversation at the time, always in retrospect ; ' then from what people have said or done I discover what they have thought : I am rarely mistaken.' [2] In tête-à-tête, ' for fear of making those who are talking to me impatient, I pretend to understand them. . . .' [3] And ' I find no compulsion more terrible than the obligation of speaking continuously and on the spur of the moment. I do not know whether this has anything to do with my *mortal aversion to constraint of any kind* ; but to be absolutely obliged to speak is enough to make me infallibly talk nonsense. . . .[2] I should be as fond of society as anyone else, if I was not sure of appearing in it not only to my own disadvantage, but quite a different person from what I am. My resolution to write and live in seclusion is exactly what suits me.' [4] His native Geneva he loved. ' I have never seen the walls of this happy city, never entered its gates, without feeling a certain heart-sinking, the result of excessive emotion. While the noble image of liberty elevated my soul, thoughts of equality, union, and gentleness of manners moved me even to tears, and inspired me with a lively regret at having lost all these blessings. How mistaken I was, and yet how naturally ! I thought I saw all this in my native land, *because I carried it in my heart.*' [5]

The mortal terror of constraint only left Rousseau when he was in the country. Over and over again it worked the same miracle of healing upon him. ' The sight of the country, a succession of pleasant views, the open air, a good appetite, the sound health which walking gives me, the free life of the inns, the absence of all that makes me conscious of my dependent position. . . . All this sets my soul free, gives me greater boldness of thought, throws me into the immensity of things. . . . I have never thought so much, existed so much, lived so much, been so much myself, as in the journeys which I have made alone

---

[1] *Confessions*, vol. i., p. 144. (Everyman, No. 859.) [2] Ibid. p. 103.
[3] Ibid. p. 107 [4] Ibid. p. 104. [5] Ibid. p. 130.

and on foot.' [1] It was in the country, at Les Charmettes, that at twenty-four he sought happiness in the last phases of his ill-starred patronage from his adopted 'mother', Madame de Warens. 'Oh mamma, this is the abode of happiness and innocence. If we do not find both here, it will be useless to look for them anywhere else.' [2]

But though Rousseau's joys lay in nature, it was seldom that they lay in the present. 'If I wish to depict the spring it must be winter ; to describe a beautiful landscape I must be surrounded by walls . . . if I were imprisoned in the Bastille, I should draw the picture of Liberty.' [3] In real life Rousseau demanded unconditional liberty, contracted with others with difficulty and with failure, was suspicious of his fellows, embarrassed and unhappy in their presence. In cities he saw vice and squalor, was tempted perhaps, was ill. When he fled his terrors he hid in the country —in reality away from men, or with the simplest of men only about him. And always in the country came this real peace *from out of his fancy*. And always in the country he was well. 'When you see me at the point of death, carry me under the shade of an oak. I shall get well again.' [4] And so this unhappy man came to people an ideal peasant world. In it, freed from the horrors of social life as he had found it, men could behave as he felt he could have behaved, naturally at last. They could associate in friendliness, and contract together to forgo individual liberty for the sake of the larger liberty of co-operative life. Was not this natural ? It must be natural, because it seemed so good a picture. The truth probably was that it *seemed* natural and real, like the spring in winter, or liberty in the Bastille, *because it was absent*. But surely, he felt, it could be !

There must of course have been profound psychological reasons for Rousseau's unhappiness, and the sense of unreality in the present which made his fancy depict and people the absent and the ideal in the way it did. In such a case the modern psychologist would expect to find unconscious conflicts between *ideals* and *impulses* based on some conceptions (often misconceptions) arising early in childhood. Rousseau had indeed the anxiety, the sense of frustration, the protests against underlying feelings of guilt common in one suffering in such a way. The feeling of such men so often is that if they are 'themselves' they will be 'evil'. (See Chapter IV, Case A., p. 130.) Yet be themselves they must ! The fundamental problem of such characters is how to be free to be oneself (and perhaps as aggressive a self as Hobbes depicted in his state of nature), and yet at the same time be loved (with Locke and Hooker) 'as much as possible may be'. In psychoanalysis such anxieties are traced backwards into infancy. In adult life as we normally live it the original feeling-

---

[1] *Confessions*, vol. i. p. 147. [2] Ibid. p. 205.
[3] Ibid. p. 156. [4] Ibid. p. 214.

conceptions of infancy are excluded from conscious memory. But *unconscious* associations recall them time and again, and the victim becomes plagued by his consequent 'irrational' tensions and unrealities, compulsions and phobias. Often his whole attitude to his fellow men is distorted thereby. (See Chapter IV, Case C., p. 135.) In compensation, such a man may erect in his mind a picture of what paternal, brotherly and connubial love *should* be. That fantasy will contrast very sharply with what the subject believes real life actually to be. He will *act* upon his conception of reality ; but he may build his theory either upon the ' reality ' or upon the ' Ideal '. Both Hobbes and Rousseau believed that men are ' actually wicked '. But Hobbes built his social theory on that basic assumption, while Rousseau builds his on what man could be if those clouds of wrong feeling were lifted. ' If only *others* were different ', he seems to say, ' *I* would not be like this ! If only *conditions* were right, I could enter the here and now, reassured and friendly. And spring would be spring, liberty liberty. And *this* is how we would live ! '

Rousseau's intuition told him the fault was not wholly in his star. He probed himself deeply, watched and indeed exposed his ' real ' self with all the honesty his determination could muster. But seeing no clue to its evil manifestations, he concluded that they were the outcome of external influences. The passionate longing for simplicity, easy human friendships and love, which lay beneath his uneasy, distrustful, and tragic actual encounters with life must surely be the reality, awaiting favourable conditions only to flower, in himself and in all men, in brotherly love. Those favourable conditions he felt to be the primitive. ' Savage man, when he has dined is at peace with all nature, and the friend of all his fellow creatures. If a dispute arises. . . . it all ends in a few blows ; the victor eats, and the vanquished seeks provision somewhere else, and all is at peace.' (Cp. Case C., p. 141.) Contrasted with this are ' the secret pretensions of the heart of civilized man—first necessaries, then superfluities . . . delicacies . . . immense wealth . . . subjects . . . slaves. . . . The less natural and pressing his wants the more headstrong are his passions. . . . The hero ends by cutting every throat till he finds himself, at last, sole master of the world "(' Origin of Inequality ', aet. 42.) [1] Here most clearly is the influence of the fantasy that all man's kindly nature (except those occasional few harmless blows !) is in the savage, all his evil nature in civilization. The separation is as crude as in a dream. It is the *state* of man, his condition of life, which determines whether he is good or bad. Rousseau's is a viewpoint which stretches to the farthest the effects of human environment. He shows the savage and the man of culture— two halves of Man appearing under opposing conditions of life. But he realized that both halves were present in each man, as he

[1] *Social Contract*, p. 241.

had found them in himself. And so he must search for the ideal conditions to bring out the good in each man, as in himself.

We have noticed how for Rousseau the good thing tended to be the absent thing. Certainly it was so with the ideal social life. It had to be far away from that of the eighteenth-century Europe as he knew it. It must be fundamentally different, because his actual feelings for his fellows were fundamentally inharmonious. Deeply he felt the lack and the need of the love of his fellow men, and he hated Hobbes for his neglect of the existence of such an element in the life of society. In practice, love failed to manifest itself. He behaved himself in ways that often seemed to justify Hobbes, while of others he laments : ' That men are *actually* wicked, a sad and continual experience of them proves beyond doubt '.[1] Under the influence of such conceptions he remained distrustful, yet longing to trust, hating yet longing to love, anxious to surrender his own ' liberty ', yet forced to assert and to fight for it. Others, he felt, were the same. The fault must lie at the root of that particular society in which he dwelt ; for ' I think I have shewn that man is *naturally* good '.[1] The idea of the ' general will ' seemed to solve his problem for him. For here in eighteenth-century Europe the general will had never been invoked, no real ' social contract ' had been made between men. They had not been able to show the brotherly love and the mutual trust which deposited individual liberty, and took up in return the greater ' moral liberty ' of being freely accepted, loved and loving in the society of one's fellows, and of being ruled by them without feeling that one had lost one's freedom.

Such a change in men's hearts once accomplished, the society built upon it would be one after Rousseau's own heart. For to be able to enter a society trustingly, with all fear for the security of one's individuality lost, would be half the battle won. And to a society enshrining our own best self could safely be entrusted the task of continuing our own self-discipline for us ! It could understand our vagaries, pardon or chastise our faults according to our own highest will. We would have nothing to fear from others or from ourselves. It would indeed be a fraternal society.

And then, once we were fundamentally united with other men as brothers, *let the government be strong !* For the passionate man to secure control over his passions without sacrificing his liberty may indeed be called ' moral freedom ! ' Rousseau's passions were strong, and they alarmed him. ' I forget all feelings of respect, fear, and decency ; I am cynical, impudent, and violent. . . . No feelings of shame keep me back . . . the universe is nothing to me. But it is over in a moment, and the following moment plunges me in annihilation. . . .'[2] Is it surprising then

[1] *Social Contract*, p. 239.   [2] *Confessions*, vol. i.

that, directly he can devise a formula which will satisfy him that *true* liberty is not being lost, Rousseau should give his ideal state a strong sovereign ? Though it must of course behave like a government, it is really the general will of the people. Individual obedience to it is obligatory. It cannot go against the real interests of the individual, because these require the preservation of the society for which it stands. This reason for strong government is the same as Hobbes'. But Hobbes' sovereign government *must* be strong, so precariously erected is it out of men's evanescent appreciation of the identity of their individual and corporate needs. The representatives of Rousseau's sovereign people *can afford to be* strong ; they can hardly do wrong. Of the three philosophers we have considered, it is only Locke who can advocate a government with powers of interference strictly limited to the real preservation of the lives, liberties, and estates of its sovereign people. Locke had noted a steady preponderance of actual mutual benevolence and beneficence among the members of a community, and had presumed to generalize his finding. For Rousseau such a finding was temperamentally impossible.

We have found that what Rousseau *imagines* to happen within his ideal state corresponds at each step with what he *wishes* could be done emotionally with himself. The sequence is as follows : *First*, that upon his surrender of his anxious and self-determining individualism he shall be assured of liberty to be ' himself ' ; *Second*, that the ' true ' self which then emerges shall be acceptable to others and fundamentally at one with them ; *Third*, that, thus having given up individual ' sovereignty ' without surrendering emotional ' liberty ' he shall be strongly handled and disciplined, and if necessary made to suffer, *provided that the new security of a self-surrendered life is maintained*.[1] Psychologically speaking, Rousseau's ' general will ' and the ' sovereign ' that derives from it are a ' *rationalization* ' of a deeply felt personal need. They represent the emphasis which must be placed upon the assurance of emotional ' freedom ' before the mind of Rousseau could contemplate a desired surrender of itself to the domination of others, in the hope of that trust which should be mutual, and that security which should be general.

The ' general will ' is our *idealized social selves* ; what is left after eliminating all that is individual, un-co-operative and un-friendly in each of us. To form a ' sovereign ' from this fantasy of a pooled sociability of man was to lead to much trouble. In the first place it had to be an entity ; in the second that entity

[1] Types of infantile fantasy (of passive enjoyment and voluptuous suffering) are discussed in the section on psychological theory (Chapter III), and illustrations are given among the case notes in Chapter IV. Such fantasies commonly underlie such emotional conflicts between ' freedom ' and ' surrender ' as appear to form the emotional background of Rousseau's social theory.

was an immense power to conjure with. For it represented the socially ' best ' of all the members of the society. It was to become more difficult to dethrone than any other tyrant. Unlike earlier compacts between subject and ruler, unlike even the necessary strong monarch of Hobbes, there were no rights of the individual against this personification of his own best self. ' Whoever refuses to obey the general will shall be compelled to do so by the whole body ',[1] said Rousseau. Translated into terms understood by people who manipulate political power this meant state tyranny. In Rousseau's name they so acted. And so convenient a regression from earlier and simpler notions of the rights of men was this, that philosophers, for whom the splitting of a man's mind into two was a matter of simple division, readily came forward to uphold and elaborate a theory which has had repercussions ever since. We do not all share the delight in being chastised by the object of our affections which the eight-year-old Rousseau showed as he suffered under the hands of Mademoiselle Lambercier—a chastisement ' which disposed of my tastes, my desires, my passions, and my own self for the remainder of my life and that in a manner exactly contrary to that which should have been the natural result '.[2] But Rousseau has indeed proved right in saying that, as a result of his theory, ' all have to fight for their country, but no one ever has to fight for himself ' ![3]

But if we claim that the faults of Rousseau's political theories are largely attributable to his emotional life, we must admit that much of the attraction which those theories have had for generations of idealists, and most of the real virtue of his writings, spring from his passionate desire for the good of his fellow men which he knew to depend upon good human relationships. He passionately upbraided Hobbes for forgetting the ' motives of compassion, a disposition suitable to creatures so weak and subject to so many evils as we are ', and Mandeville for failing to see that ' from this quality alone flow all our social virtues '.[4] Rousseau himself is never cold : in his writings he is at a white heat of fury nearly all the time. And his final messages to those in search of social virtue are to watch simple folk and to turn to nature for strength. ' It is the mob and the market women who hinder gentle folks from cutting each other's throats.'[5] ' Retire to the woods to hear the voice of heaven ! ' Among his detestations were ' all the horrible prejudices which class among the virtues the honour of shedding human blood . . . till men massacre their fellow creatures by thousands without knowing why '.[6] It would be wronging Rousseau greatly to assume that he would himself have approved some of those whose minds caught his

---

[1] *Social Contract*, p. 18.
[3] *Social Contract*, p. 30.
[5] Ibid. p. 199.
[2] *Confessions*, vol. i. p. 11.
[4] Ibid. p. 196.
[6] Ibid. p. 222.

germ of the 'greater liberty we prescribe to ourselves', those philosophers who have tried to rivet upon us the chains of our 'general will' in the form of a much demanding State which to some of us often appears to contain such a very small portion of our individual wills. Rather would he be in the field again, filled with 'indignation, rage, despair', and hurling epithets at the head of the monster to whom in a hopeful but misguided moment he had surrendered so much of his 'natural' liberty. One can well imagine Rousseau being tempted to tear up his Contract!

II

HUMAN GOVERNMENT AS VIEWED THROUGH THE AGES

I. PHILOSOPHICAL DEVELOPMENTS FROM ROUSSEAU

'Idealism', and a reaction.—We have taken the opinions of three different philosophers upon man's 'human nature', and the way in which social life should be organized upon it. Although Hobbes, Locke, and Rousseau were nearly contemporary with each other, local and temporary affairs—the disorder of the English Civil War, the pacification of the Glorious Revolution, and the artificiality of pre-Revolutionary French court society—each in its turn influenced the views which one of these philosophers formed of the nature and needs of mankind. Their different status and training—the first two sheltered and privileged tutors of the rich, the third an orphaned and bemused but aspiring vagabond—also influenced outlook in a way that is perhaps more obvious in Rousseau than in the two Englishmen. It is in Rousseau too that we have most easily found the effects of deep emotional influences upon the intellectual processes by which a philosopher 'rationalizes' his views of his fellows and the motives of their social life.

Such theories as those of Hobbes, Locke, and Rousseau represent widespread and perennial currents of feeling and thought, outcrops of which can be found in hundreds of writings of philosophers from the times of Moses and Plato to the present day. These three philosophers have all been widely quoted in our own time, though not all by the same people. Hobbes, wrestling with the perennial problem of how to use force for the preservation of peace instead of for the perpetuation of war, tends to be quoted by the practical politician faced to-day with the same problem on the largest scale which this world can provide. Locke, clear-cut, sagacious, and judicial, is favoured by the lawyers ; while Rousseau's flaming passion and metaphysical abstractions have made his resounding epigrams and paradoxes the inspiration at once of the social idealist and of a philosophical school which has taken the same title.

Apart from its almost immediate effects upon practical politics, American and French, there occurred a rapid philosophical development of Rousseau's doctrine of the ' sovereign people ' ruling through the operation of the ' general will '. So that before the Napoleonic Wars were over *Burke* was speaking in England of the mystical unit of the ' state ' as ' the individual writ large ', in Germany *Kant* had adopted and developed Rousseau's view of man voluntarily abandoning his ' wild lawless freedom, to find his entire freedom again undiminished in a lawful dependence ', and *Fichte* had gone further, arguing that, as man gains by social organization, and the present organization is the State, therefore : ' It is only in the combination of the State that man attains a definite position in the series of things '. Two thousand years earlier Plato had announced that 'All one's family and all one's wealth belong to the city ', and another ' idealist ', Bosanquet, was later to comment that Fichte was ' too near to Plato '.[1] Meanwhile *Hegel* set out to counteract this ' mistaking of the mechanism of the spirit '. His conclusion was that the state is ' the divine idea as it exists on earth[2]. . . . It has the highest right against the individual whose highest duty is to be a member of it.'[3]

Hegel's theory of the state is grounded on his theory of the *freedom of the will*. Like Rousseau, Hegel starts with a demand for freedom. Like Rousseau, he rejects such a simple definition of freedom as ' absence of constraint '. It must be something more ' positive '. Even in his definition he is thinking ahead to the use he will make of this ' freedom ' when he has it. Rousseau's first ideal act of freedom was to make a formal surrender of it on the assurance of faith that he would get back from society a larger ' moral liberty ' and the feeling of being made part of something both larger and better than himself, i.e. the ' general will '. Hegel merges himself in the larger whole of society in much the same way. But to Rousseau's fiction of giving up liberty without losing it Hegel adds another—that the will is only free when it ' wills itself to obey the State ', by bringing itself into line with ' the universal will of which particular wills are only incidents or phases '.[4] Despite an immense amount of additional reasoning, Hegel's position is essentially the same as Rousseau's, excepting that an actual ' State ' has replaced the idealized ' general will '. So that now *the individual will can only*

[1] Bosanquet, *Philosophical Theory of the State*, p. 246.
[2] Hegel, *Philosophy of History*, p. 41.
[3] *Philosophie des Rechts*, p. 306.
[4] Hobhouse, *Metaphysical Theory of the State*, p. 68. (Allen & Unwin. 1918.)

*be ' free ' if it accepts a certain principle of conduct, the ' ethical use
and wont ' of society,* i.e. *the State.*

When we think of the fundamental problems which at once
arise from the total submission of the individual will to such an
authority, and consider the actual conflicts which occur, for
instance, between political allegiance and religious teaching and
the injustices and the oppressions of the state against which our
consciences so often revolt, we cannot better the comment of
Hobhouse upon this conclusion of Hegel's : ' If we think of the
state as an organization of persons like ourselves, in obeying it
against our will we are simply under the constraint of others . . .
if as impersonal or superpersonal or, as Hegel calls it, divine, we
are obeying an impersonal or divine authority. Even if we are
free in yielding to it, that would seem to be the last act of our
freedom.' [1] But since ' freedom ' does in common parlance
mean absence of constraint and not something more ' positive ',
one cannot help searching for a substitute for Hegel's use of this
term in this connexion. And as we read of Rousseau's and
Hegel's discovery of the good life of the individual in submission
to a deified society, we are tempted to offer ' happiness ' or
' satisfaction ' as being nearer to their real meaning than ' freedom '. Happiness in self-sacrifice ; happiness in conformity, in
restraint ; a greater satisfaction in exchange for that of freedom.
All that makes sense. Freedom in constraint does not. While
freedom cannot properly be found in submission, satisfaction
undoubtedly can ; and it is often so sought by men. We
shall mention later some of the postulates on this subject
which the psychologist finds in the ' unconscious ' minds of
men.[2]

Hegel's arguments were illuminated and developed by
Bosanquet. Man, says Bosanquet, is sometimes ignorant not only
of what is good for him, but also of what he wants. Consequently,
' it may be right to restrain a man for reasons affecting himself
alone from doing what at the moment he proposes to do. . . .
We must show how the actual man of flesh and blood demands
to be governed ; and how a government which puts real force
upon him is essential, as he is aware, to his becoming what he has
it in him to become '. [3] Here Bosanquet appreciated Rousseau's
unconscious motivation. *Men may want to be bullied.* ' The
ordinary individual is at bottom different from what he seems,
is actually determined in all sorts of ways, consciously and unconsciously, by demands and ideas which go far beyond what
he would admit to determine him.' [4] The trouble, of course, is to
find a means of coercing man into his ' best self '. It is the

---

[1] Hobhouse, *Metaphysical Theory of the State,* p. 40.
[2] See Chapters III and IV.
[3] Bosanquet, *Philosophical Theory of the State,* p. 78.
[4] Ibid. p. 125.

problem of the educationalist. The assumption that a clumsy nineteenth- or twentieth-century government was capable of the delicate task of collective education and individual tuition which is required to make of each citizen the ' best he has it in him to become ' was due to the fallacy of confusing the arbitrary ' State ' with an ideal human society, and thus of regarding the legislative or executive government of that state as a suitable means of compulsion of its members. But underlying all this is the mystical ' general will ', without which idea surely nobody would have come to conceive either of state or of society as being above its members in importance. For Bosanquet, the mystical union between members of a community is such that ' the negative relation of the self to other selves begins to dissolve away before the conception of a common self, and the negative relation of the self to law and government begins to disappear in the idea of a law which expresses our real will as opposed to our trivial and rebellious moods. The whole notion of man as one among others tends to break down, and we begin to see something in the one which actually identifies him with the others and at the same time tends to make him what he admits he ought to be '. [1]

Bosanquet developed further his distinction between a man's ' actual will ', which is what he thinks he wants, and his ' real will ', which is what will really satisfy him. To-day we can welcome such a distinction as a means of emphasizing the importance of desires which are deeply set in the personality, but which, because they are normally unconscious, are not admitted to their rightful place of recognition among the conditions which make up our happiness or our misery. Desire for power, for instance, regarded by Hobbes as so universal a quality in man, we often fail to admit to in ourselves, because of its conflict with the ideals we set before us, or because we believe it to run counter to some other desire which consciously we cherish more. In our study of Rousseau we have described how fundamental human desires are frequently distorted and repressed because of a false conception (or ' fantasy ') of the consequences to which their indulgence would lead. Types of repressed ' real ' will we may study later. But we welcome in Bosanquet a theoretical recognition—as in Rousseau a practical demonstration—that *our happiness may be determined by factors of which our conscious ' actual ' wills are ignorant.*

Unfortunately, Bosanquet seems to go very far with Rousseau and Hegel in equating our ' real ' selves with our ' good ' selves, and thence with a common self, which becomes the higher will of society. But our psychological studies will show us that social man (including man legislating) acts under the influence of a will which includes both conscious and unconscious desires ; and also that the division between ' actual ' conscious will and ' real '

[1] Bosanquet, loc. cit. p. 96.

desire does not in the least run parallel with a division between selfish and co-operative impulses. Bosanquet raises an interesting point, however, when he says that the ' real ' will could be discovered by correcting the actual will of a given moment in the light of (*a*) what we want at all other moments and (*b*) what others want.[1] This could mean that if we all knew each other's conscious and unconscious desires, and our own, we would be much better informed than we now are, and would in consequence will differently in present situations than we now do. That is very true. But it is equally true that at the present time neither state can discover nor any law enforce upon us these ' real ' wills of which our psychological studies are only gradually making us dimly aware. We shall have to consider how far the ' real ' will of an individual, revealed to him by knowledge of his own unconscious desires, would be likely to coincide with the socially beneficent and co-operative ' real will ' which Hegel's worship of the state led him to imagine.

For this ' idealist ' school of philosophers, from Rousseau to Bosanquet, the ' real ' will is nevertheless equated with what I would call the ' *socially ideal will*'—' in harmony with itself and others '. When, however, we examine the returns for his ' free ' devotion to which the individual is entitled from the state, and the powers which the state should exercise over its members, we find that, while Hegel echoed or surpassed the authoritarian views of Rousseau, Bosanquet departs from the original doctrine that the state can hardly go wrong. Hegel's doctrine was that both in peace and war the state should consider its own well-being and not that of its citizens ; and he showed his contempt for the masses, their intellects and interests. We must not ask but tell them what they think, he says, and, quoting Goethe, ' They can fight. But their judgment is miserable.'[2] Bosanquet, on the other hand, makes large claims upon his state and seems to alter its character radically from that of the Hegelian tyrant. First he enlarges Hegel's state by definition until it virtually coincides with society as we know it ; for it embraces ' the entire hierarchy of institutions by which life is determined, from the family to the trade, and from the trade to the church and the university. It is the structure which gives life and meaning to the political whole.'[3] Also he greatly limits its functions from those given to it by Hegel. Force remains inherent in it, not only in the ' restraint of disorderly persons, but in the form of instruction and authoritative suggestion to the ordinary law-abiding citizen '. But the aim should be to make the use of force minimal. The function of the state is to ' *remove obstacles . . . to hinder hindrances* ' to the best life.

The place of society in getting the best out of the individual

---

[1] Hobhouse, loc. cit. p. 44.   [2] Ibid. p. 98.
[3] Bosanquet, loc. cit. p. 150.

was also considered by *T. H. Green*. With Green came a broadening of the ' general will ' itself, ' that impalpable congeries of the hopes and fears of a people bound together by common interests and sympathy . . . the will and reason of men as determined by social relations, as interested in each other, as acting for common ends '.[1]   Green fully recognized the fallibility of the state, many requirements of which have ' largely arisen out of force directed by selfish motives '.   For him the ethical basis of the state is a common good which at the same time is the good of each individual citizen.   It rests on a mutual recognition of rights, rights being for each the conditions under which he can live the best life.   Each man has the task of attempting to realize his own perfection as an integral part of the common good. ' *The state is a body of persons recognized by each other as having rights and possessing certain institutions for the maintenance of those rights.*' [2]   This view now resembles and develops that of Locke. Green holds that ' the right of the individual to have certain powers secured to him by society, and the counter-claim of society to exercise certain powers over the individual, alike rest on the fact that *these powers are necessary to the fulfilment of man's vocation . . . the work of developing the perfect character in himself and others* '.[3]

Hobhouse in his analysis of the *Metaphysical theory of the state* (1918) set out to counter the arguments of the Hegelian school, point by point.   He himself was grounded on the position that ' the far-sighted man of to-day is he who holds to the unity of human nature and the common interest of mankind, and places them above all causes of quarrel '.[4]   But Hobhouse held that the way to value all mankind is to value each individual as such. To Bosanquet's ' Individuality lies in a unique contribution to the universal ', he opposed, ' There is something in me I do *not* share with you. . . . Human individuality is and remains something ultimate '.[5]   In the course of his arguments upon ' freedom ' and ' the will ' he recognized the multiple divisions of the will of an individual man, making the points that one part of our will may enslave another part, and that we may be ' slaves to our principles as well as to our impulses '.[6]   Aware perhaps of those works of Freud which were already published when he wrote, he made the important comment that if our deeper wills are invoked they may be found to clash with those of others more instead of less than do our normal conscious wills.   With continued realism he went on to argue that corporate life based on some sort of common will acquires in practice ' only too probably a collective selfishness '.[7]   For Hobhouse, our existing social

[1] Green, *Principles of Political Obligation*, p. 404.   (Vol. ii. of ' Works ', 1911.)
[2] Ibid. p. 443.   [3] Ibid. p. 347.
[4] Hobhouse, loc. cit. p. 114.   [5] Ibid. p. 52.
[6] Ibid. p. 35.   [7] Ibid. p. 49.

orders show 'elements of radical good and radical evil blended.
. . . Society is the outcome of millions and millions of wills
through the generations. In these millions and millions of wills
there is a social element working. There are elements of idealism,
sparks of justice, uniting threads of human kindness, and there
are also selfishness and vanity and pride and hardness, corporate
and collective as well as individual, and these elements acting
upon one another make up the piebald pattern of human society '.[1]
The state is only one of the many possible ways of grouping and
organizing society. Conflicts between state and church Hobhouse
saw as conflicts between groups, ' one association of fallible human
beings against another '. And ' it is not possible to say *a priori*
that either the state is right or the church is right '. But, as the
state is concerned with social preservation ' those responsible for
the state, and all citizens as owing allegiance to the state, are
bound to act in accordance with their final judgment, fallible as
it may be, of what is necessary to social preservation '. But
equally, ' the Churchman . . . if he can find no way of escaping
from the spiritual duty incumbent upon him, seems bound to
take the risks, moral as well as legal, of disobedience '.[2] For
' if men do anything else than what is right in their own eyes,
there is no moral law at all '.[3]

In the field of international politics the conflict between
Bosanquet and Hobhouse took an interesting turn. Bosanquet
has been opposed to the centralization of force in setting up a
League of Nations when the then war should be over. His
grounds apparently were that nothing larger than the state
could be trusted with the use of force. For the state alone had a
' general will' to guide it! And, although he could imagine the
gradual formation of a general will ' in areas larger than the
territories of a nation ', its realization would be ' a problem for
the future '. Hobhouse retorted that degree not kind separated
the will to a larger unit than the nation from existing national
loyalties, and that the use of force as machinery would implement
that will as many group wills had been so implemented in the
past. Again, while Bosanquet had found it difficult to see how a
state can commit theft or murder, Hobhouse opposed as murder
all wars between states which do not satisfy an ' impartial
tribunal '.[4] For him, ' Life can be made good ; ' but only if
we recognize ' the unity of mankind ' and ' cut the tap roots
of those egoisms of state and nation, class and sex, colour and
race, which engender the massive miseries of the world '.[5]
' The higher ethics and the deeper religion do not come to destroy
the simplest rights and duties of neighbour to neighbour but to
fulfil and extend them '.[6]

Thus, after two hundred years, Rousseau's ideal of social life as

[1] Hobhouse, loc. cit. p. 86.   [2] Ibid. p. 90.   [3] Ibid. p. 92.
[4] Ibid. p. 109.   [5] Ibid. p. 117.   [6] Ibid. p. 135.

it should be is still brought up against the reality of social life as
it is. There are individuals, fighting lone battles or enjoying
lonely freedom, grouping in a thousand societies which express
a thousand interests, mundane and spiritual ; groups of territorial
or racial significance exciting loyalties and exhibiting powers, but
' never strong enough to be always the master '. And at each
stage, from the individual to the largest grouping, these men
and women exhibit an inevitable mixture of qualities good and
evil, both as individuals and as groups. That is the picture which
Hobhouse saw where Rousseau had seen an existing ' evil '
which could only be remedied by such a revolution in man's
nature as would throw up an all trusting and all loving ' good '
—a revolution which his imagination had so vivified that the
murderers of thirty years later had believed themselves to be
in the act of its realization.

Throughout this battle over ' idealism ' in political philosophy
we can see two types of mind attempting to explain the social
world in which they found themselves and also attempting to
make it better. One type, the ' idealist ', believes in the submission
of the individual to something larger than himself—' society ',
the ' state ', some special form of state, the idea of the object
varies but it is always a human unit of power and authority.
His opponent reiterates claims to the integrity, value, uniqueness
of the individual, and rejects the ineptitude of any conglomerate
authority which attempts wholly to direct or absorb him.

Though from their several writings some of us might sometimes hardly credit it, it is one and the same world that these
two types of mind look out upon ! And it is the real world !
How comes it then that they see it so differently from each other,
and again that both see it so differently from the ordinary
' practical ' man ? The latter accepts (1) himself and (2) ' the
government ' (or if he be a civil servant the division may be
into the Department and the Public), and he both accepts and
insists upon certain distinctions between the two spheres as
being both requisite and inevitable. The differing analyses are
due of course to the differing minds of the observers. And those
differences of mind are due (1) to profoundly differing *conceptions* of certain essential relationships among mankind, and
(2) to differing *desires* of personal relationship to others. As one
man finds the climax of the day when he springs from his bed in
the morning, and another finds it when he curls up in his bed
at night, so one man's mind is permeated with a zest for his own
integrity, while another desires to identify himself with great and
cosmic forces. While one fears strength and violence unless
he first be safe within the fortress, another will fight to
the death to preserve his solitary domination over himself.
Such men not only value the world differently : they *see it*
differently.

Such personal idiosyncrasies and the emotional and intellectual patterns into which they are woven from our infancy up are largely unconscious in their operation. We shall find that modern psychology can state with some confidence that philosophies which centre upon personal ' surrender ' to attain larger ' liberty ', the abandonment of a lonely ' worst ' self for an acceptable ' best ' self, or the search for social conditions in which ' unlimited ' force can legitimately be invoked, derive from profound ' type ' fantasies of the philosophic minds concerned, and that the philosophers who see and group human social life in this particular way would readily exhibit a definite and peculiar arrangement of concepts and desires if their infant memories were at the disposal of a competent psychoanalyst. The furious individualist would in his turn present a different and again a characteristic pattern of early thought and feeling.

But we shall be wise not to attempt to exclude or to deride opinion merely because it is grounded in emotion. That fact may sometimes be the very source of its value as an interpretation to man of his experiences in terms which he can accept and utilize. In the latter parts of this book our study will be directed to the control of himself through which alone man can live a social life of security and satisfaction. As we continue our review of the outstanding social and legal philosophies of history, we shall bear in mind that they must needs possess roots which derive more from the emotional life of the viewer than from the subject viewed : but we must also be attentive to the diversity of wisdom which these past writers give us. Our task is to attempt to separate that wisdom from certain misinterpretations of fact which it will require all our modern knowledge not only of society but of man himself to reconstrue successfully to-day.

We shall now examine some theories of the functions of law in social life. For our final study is to be the psychological requirements of a stable—that is, of a well-governed—human society.

II. SOME CLASSICAL OPINIONS ON LAW AND SOCIETY

Legal theory about human nature goes back of course to Greece and Rome. From *Aristotle*, thinking of good relationships between people, rather than Plato's good life in itself, come the first recorded notions of a political and legal science, to study and to regulate the social life of man, ' the perfect development and activity of whose powers require the association of his fellows '. Hegel seems to be foreshadowed, in that the ' state ' is the highest form of human association. It is, however, not the modern national state of Hegel, but a union of villages in an association of suitable size and character to achieve a ' complete life '. Even in such a sound society, Aristotle held that although

man is capable of living a good life, the individual man cannot
be trusted to do so. Laws have to be laid down beforehand,
because, left to the moment, man's actions are always liable to
contain ' something of the brute '. But in addition to laws laid
down in a code beforehand, justice can be executed in a given
new situation. Aristotle separated the ' legal ' right acquired
under the former process from ' natural ' rights which man
acquired merely by being a man and a citizen. This second
process of doing justice according to general ideas of what is fair
and right—later to be described as decisions *in ' Equity '*—
Aristotle regarded as a necessary corrective to rigid or inappro-
priate laws. Equally the instabilities of man's animal nature
require that spontaneous justice should be replaced where possible
by the counter-corrective of definite laws. Thus each type of
law corrects the other ; and in this way *the rule of law becomes
better than the rule of any man*. Aristotle had in mind a social
order at once ' ideal ' and ' natural ', towards which the laws
should be shaped. At the flowering period of Greece it was
believed that such a society lay ahead. Ever since then there
have been philosophers who held that a golden age lay behind
them.

The Romans were more strictly practical than the Greeks, and
proceeded to build up systems of law which gave a great measure
of social order to the whole world as they knew it. They drew
upon Greek theory in the process, and indeed their own theorists
Polybius and Cicero were apparently only just in time to explain
the *pax Romana* before it vanished.[1] The Roman practice was
to use both of Aristotle's types of law, though of these Cicero
held the ' law of nature ' supreme and enactments that con-
travened it to have no force at all. The same courts gave decisions
by natural justice—*ex aequo et bono*—as administered civil
written law, and thus ' Equity ' became a recognized means of
checking and supplementing the statute law, just as have become
our Common Law judgments in England. ' Equity ' decisions
were later incorporated into the body of the civil code,[2] again as
in England. But although the idea of a natural justice persisted
in the conception of ' Equity ' which the law of Rome trans-
mitted to that of England, the Romans came to give a peculiar
and narrow meaning to the term ' natural law '. Sir HenryMaine
says : ' The Roman jurisconsults of the Antonine era laid down
that " *omnes homines natura aequales sunt* ", but in their eyes this
was a strictly juridical axiom. They intended to affirm that
under the *hypothetical* Law of Nature . . . the arbitrary distinctions which the Roman Civil Law maintained between classes of
persons ceased to have a legal existence.' [3] In fact the Roman

---

[1] Dunning, *History of Political Theories*, vol. i. p. 101. (Macmillan. 1919.)
[2] Maine, *Ancient Law*, p. 39. (Dent: Everyman, No. 734.)
[3] Ibid. p. 54.

lawyers had adopted the hypothesis of a ' law of nature ' as a convenient doctrine under which they could administer justice to peoples of the Empire who were not citizens. The civil code, by then elaborate, could not be applied to such people ; nor was it possible to learn and apply all their own laws, especially in disputes running across the divisions between different cultures. So it became convenient to assume that there were certain funda- mental principles of law to which all men would give assent as being ' natural ', and which could consequently be applied to anyone anywhere. These principles the jurisconsult singled out by careful observation of existing institutions and believed them roughly to exhibit ' the vestiges of that reign of nature whose reality he faintly affirmed '.[1]

The Romans thus passed on to us three types of law—-(1) the codified Civil Law, on which Europe has drawn very heavily ; (2) the principle of decisions ' in Equity ', which enabled Roman law to adjust itself to changing circumstances without incurring a sudden breach with the past, and which later developed into both an important branch and an important conception of English law ; (3) ' Natural Law ', as a list of elementary principles of justice which could be relied upon to prove acceptable to human nature anywhere. Maine considered that the Greeks had used the ' equity ' principle to the detriment of code law and so allowed their law to develop too rapidly. ' The Greek intellect, unable to confine itself within the strait-waistcoat of a legal formula . . . never hesitated to relax rules of written law whenever they stood in the way of an ideally perfect decision on the facts of particular cases ',[2] and in consequence could only bequeath to posterity ideas of right and wrong which happened to be prevalent at the time. He held too that French law of the eighteenth century suffered from the opposite fault of too great a rigidity and con- servatism, so that French lawyers, coming to believe its vices ineradicable, turned away from any attempt to introduce the cleansing influences of Roman Equity, and contented themselves with philosophizing about the nebulous ' Natural Law ' which ' overleapt all provincial and municipal boundaries, disregarded all distinctions between noble and burgess, between burgess and peasant . . . but committed its devotees to no specific improvement '.[3] To idealize an ineffective law is a dangerous practice.

But other minds than those of jurists trained in Roman or quasi-Roman traditions have been at work upon the formula ' in nature all men are equal '. We have seen that to the Roman lawyer it meant ' for purposes of administering our " Natural Law " all men are to be considered equal '. As a jurist Maine took this as a starting point. And when he found that in the fourteenth century King Louis Hutin had enfranched his serfs

[1] Maine, *Ancient Law*, p. 52.   [2] Ibid. p. 44.   [3] Ibid. p. 50.

with the words : ' According to natural law everybody *ought* to
be born free ', he concluded that a legal proposition had become
political, and added : ' There cannot, I conceive, be any question
that to the assumption of a Law Natural we owe the doctrine of
the fundamental equality of human beings '.[1] Might it not be
suggested with at least equal plausibility that it is to the conception of the fundamental equality of human beings that we owe
the doctrines of a Law Natural? However that may be, in the
middle of the eighteenth century affairs were again taken out of
legal hands, and with Rousseau, the emphasis passed from the
hypothetical ' law of nature ' to its underlying ' state of nature '
and the doctrine ' passed suddenly from the forum to the
street '.[2]

Maine did not like the conception of the ' state of nature ' in
legal philosophy. Whatever it meant to the Romans, Hobbes,
Locke, Rousseau and all the classical writers except Montesquieu
and Bentham based theories upon this ' non-historic, unverifiable,
condition of the race '. As such a conception Maine regarded it
as the chief enemy of the objective and historical basis of legal
theory which he himself sought. Nowadays we must ask ourselves why so many men have been fascinated by the idea of a
' state of nature '. Man has both a nature and a history. As
evidence of his history the ' state of nature ' may be worth little.
But the long persistence of this idea and the many things built
upon it are very valuable evidences about man's nature itself.
If you are studying how laws arose your interest will be in man's
history. But if you are legislating for him now what matters is
his nature. Each will of course have been affected by the other.
So we must study both. As for the French Revolution, the laws
of which Maine instances to the discredit of the doctrine of
' natural justice ', it is not surprising that in a time of the revolt
of a people against oppressive laws and customs, assertions of
the rights of man should be accompanied by denunciations of
a system of law which seemed only to serve the tyrant. The
antithesis between law and justice should never have been allowed
to develop in men's minds. In fact, the French Revolution
initiated a period in which almost the only law that existed was
administered *ex aequo et bono*, though alas by the hands of
partisan judges. It is thus not surprising that Maine found in it
' disdain of positive law, impatience of experience and the preference of *a priori* to all other reasoning. . . . The appeals to the
Law and State of Nature became thicker as the times grew
darker.' The revolutionaries had accepted an antithesis which
seemed to be forced upon them. And, anxious to revolutionize,
they used these terms, honestly or dishonestly, as catchwords.
In their pursuit of *justice* as they saw it they found existing *law*
an enemy.

[1] Maine, *Ancient Law*, p. 54.   [2] Ibid. p. 51.

Medieval and Renaissance writers produced many opinions
and much study of the control of human conduct by law. On
the whole the need of effective regulative law was recognized, the
debated questions being how it came about that human nature
was so imperfect, upon whom the control of the necessary force
was to devolve, and with what reservations. The first question
was answered by the Church from St. Augustine and St. Thomas
Aquinas until the Reformation in terms of the theological doctrine
of ' Original Sin ' in an historical ' Fall of Adam '. The second
was generally answered in some such words as those of *Dante*,
that ' the indispensable prerequisite of man's perfect existence is
general peace, and that is attainable only by a unified government
under a single head '. In times of stress and anarchy men will
pay a high price for peace.

A unique writer upon government and one who addressed
his advice to the ruler alone was *Machiavelli*[1] (1469–1527). His
was an era of strong kings and princes and the dawning nationalities of England, France, Italy, Spain, and Germany. Italy had
condensed her many city-state governments into five states, to
the practical politics of one of which—Florence—Machiavelli
himself was closely attached. But the Renaissance had dawned
as well as nationality. And, unlike his theological predecessors,
Machiavelli returned to the Aristotelian method of contemporary
observation and deduction, free at least from religious bias. He
was well versed in Roman and Greek literature. He valued
history as a guide to human nature, holding men to be essentially
alike in all ages and places. He formally separated politics (which
studies how people *do* behave) from ethics (which concerns itself
with how they *should* behave), and unblushingly set out the
practical advantages of violence, cruelty, and bad faith judiciously
employed by powerful governors. ' Let the Prince look to the
maintenance of the state ; the means will always be deemed
honorable and receive general approbation.' Machiavelli anticipated Hobbes in regarding men as primarily selfish and activated
always by impulses in which the so-called social virtues have no
part. A narrow self-interest affords him a sufficient explanation
of all political phenomena. Men are, generally speaking,
' ungrateful, fickle, deceitful, cowardly, and avaricious '. Men
have endless desires, and the craving for additional satisfactions
of them is the mainspring of all human action. ' Men more
readily forget the death of a father than the loss of a patrimony.'
This is extremely like Hobbes, but the stricture is harsher.
Machiavelli makes an interesting division of society, by which
it is the upper classes that want authority, while the masses as
such only desire peace and order. Republics keep better faith
than princes. But the peaceful desires of the masses give the
strong monarch his chance. Let him aim at being feared, not

[1] Machiavelli, *The Prince*. (1513.)

loved, for fear holds, while love does not. Then let him play upon the individual selfishness and the collective laziness and love of power of his subjects, by all means which knowledge and power suggest. He notes that the successful among rulers, from Moses downwards, have taken pains to have at hand armed force when persuasion failed. The unsuccessful, such as Savonarola and the Old Testament prophets, lacked this force. To force must always be added craft. Machiavelli is the one classical social philosopher who advises rulers that the most should be made of traditionally ' evil ' qualities in themselves and their peoples. His ideal (for all philosophers have their ideals) is strong conscience-free personal government which is justified by its successful ordering of an expanding and conquering community. In order to justify conquest as a sign of excellence, Machiavelli invented a theory that Aryan peoples were superior to Semitic.

With the coming of the Reformation, political doctrines emanated both from Protestant and Catholic leaders. *Luther* himself, chiefly concerned with theological controversy, was politically speaking content with the text of Christ : ' Render unto Caesar the things that are Caesar's ; and unto God the things that are God's ', and he emphasized a need for humble submission to princes. His colleague *Melanchthon* held that correct human relationships were determined by commands of God and also by ' right reasoning '. He called upon rulers to extirpate false worship and heresy—i.e. wrong reasoning. *Calvin*, the law-giver of the Reformed Church, had more to say. In the first place, a ruler as such is divinely endowed with power, however base a man he may have been before he was invested with public authority. The worst king is to be held in equal reverence with the best by the subject, who should do his duty, and leave to God the punishment of kings who do not do theirs. Public officials are in a different category. They are placed in office on purpose to curb the power of kings. Toleration was not yet preached : both Luther and the Calvinists agreed that the government must exterminate heretics. As a whole the Reformers were prepared to attack states upon religious grounds, and to solicit state assistance in the same interests. We may call these interests ' sectarian ' to-day, when religious strife within the Christian community is mercifully a matter of history. But they appeared very high interests indeed to our ancestors, at a time when religious truth, liberty and authority took that vital place in the mind of man which, however it is dominated to-day, is beginning to examine authority and liberty anew, and has been forced by dire necessity to search for truth political.

In great contrast with the Protestant divines was *Jean Bodin*,[1] a Renaissance scholar in close touch with the court life of France.

[1] Bodin, *Six books concerning the State.* (1576.)

Bodin lived in the hard time of those wars of religion which followed the Reformation. Like Machiavelli and Hobbes in similar circumstances he found his solution in strong national states. But while agreeing with Machiavelli that the state is usually formed and extended in violence and conquest, through inter-tribal warfare and enslavement of the vanquished, Bodin does not leave it there and advise his ruler that he may fall in with the ways of evil so long as he is strong. On the contrary, he wishes the state transformed into a power for good. For him the state is ethically bound to conform to the tripartite law of God, Nature, and the Nations, to formulate that law and to enforce it. The sovereign ruler of the state is thus under the rule of God, in Calvin's sense that God will enforce this rule or an appropriate punishment upon a faulty king. The king is thus under an obligation to seek out and observe the laws of God in nature. The ' law of nature ' here is not the law common to all peoples of the Romans, but a moral law, an obligation, as it was for King Louis Hutin. The sovereign cannot derogate from this law, and, although its provisions do not seem to be very closely defined, a definite standard of morality is required from him, e.g. he may not break his oath. Thus constituted, and thus behaving, the king rightly wields supreme power over his subjects, unrestrained by further laws.

Unlike Rousseau and Hegel, Bodin does not confound the state with society. The state is an organ of power necessary to give peace to men, a mechanism of defence, policing and law-making. The sovereign of a state rules over ' an aggregation of families and their common possessions ', and should rule ' by sovereign power and by reason '. But the human societies thus necessarily disciplined arose by slow development under the influence of man's instincts. Originally a ' violent plundering crew ', a divinely implanted social instinct makes friendship a link between men across the family boundary. Upon this impulse the state must operate to attain the end of human happiness. What is required is that the sway of reason, which is on the side of the social instinct, should predominate over that of appetite. This is attained by the subjection of the members of every society to the commands of one another. Thus, where Hobbes sees a society of evil men threatening good men and each other, Locke ostracizes the evil man from a good society and punishes him, and Rousseau turns the evil men into good men by the magic of an altered viewpoint, Bodin sees *in each man a conflict between two instincts*, one of violence and the other of co-operation, one inherent and the other a divine endowment. And where Hobbes and Rousseau recognize in the transfer of men's powers of mutual destruction to a sovereign ruler (or to a sovereign people) the form at once of society and of the state, Bodin sees men form their society by suppressing the violence of personal appetite through *a combination of self-control and mutual control* of each other, all in the interests of that human happiness which can only be found in co-operative social life. They are both impelled, and enabled, to do this by a social instinct which, with the aid of reason, can sufficiently overcome personal greed and passion. The monarchic state was a useful and perhaps an essential agency in securing this life of happiness, in the societies which Bodin had before him. Whatever the baseness of its origins it should, he held, be retained to this end. Here is a recognition of the state as a machinery—however powerful needs and occasions may make it—which is subordinate to the main interests of society, namely the happiness of its members.

The views of Catholic theologians immediately after the Reformation are well seen in the writings of *Suarez*.[1] He was one of a group of Spanish jurists who put forward views of political society to meet the needs of the times. As with Bodin there was in their view a natural moral law implanted in the human soul by which it distinguishes right from wrong. To follow the light by right action then is the command of God, and is defined by them as ' law proper '. But human laws too are necessary, because man is a social being and his ' natural ' social life requires regulation. Suarez does not agree with Augustine and Gregory in considering human government as being due to sin, although sin may require special coercions of men. He vests supreme power in the community—i.e. he makes Bodin's ' society ' control its ' state '. The people are the source of the law. And by nature they are free and equal. But, being so, they make an inalienable contract with their king which binds them to subjection ! We can see that both Bodin, with his society of men controlling each other, and Suarez, whose men have both conscience and agreed laws to rule them, are describing a community as they would wish it to be rather than any existing community. But neither of them could imagine the new national life without the strong monarch. Bodin adopts him regretfully, fully aware that he may be bad, for ' the virtuous leader ', he says, ' is a myth of the golden age '. And Suarez can only justify him by inventing the fiction that a free society has sold themselves willingly and perpetually into his subjection. The fact that both writers go on to praise and justify absolute monarchy, should serve to remind us that the strong monarchs of Europe in the period which we in England call Tudor, with their large, powerful and ordered national states, represented the greatest and most beneficial advance of orderly government which had occurred since the break up of the Roman Empire. It is only natural that the philosophers and jurists who had the highest ideals for human society and its progress should then welcome as an expanding and integrating unit of order and hoped-for peace, the very

[1] Suarez, *Treatise on Law and God the Legislator*. (1613.)

nationalities and nationalisms which hedge and hamper us with their crippling claims to-day.

In England, where a body of law had been built up in practice, with the minimum of theoretical speculation, and in general following the Roman tradition, the Tudors, who were successful monarchs, had given place to the Stuarts, who were not, before theories limiting or replacing the personal sovereign came to the fore. Then practice closely followed theory, where it did not actually precede it. Common-law jurists claimed for Englishmen ' inalienable rights of life, liberty, and property '. The Independents claimed ' freedom of worship and freedom of speech '. Finally, for *Milton* : ' Kings and magistrates are but the agents of the people.' . . . To avoid the discord and violence that sprang from Adam's transgression, cities and commonwealths were founded by agreement with one another, and kings and magistrates were chosen 'as deputies and commissioners, to execute . . . that justice which else every man by the bond of nature and of covenant must have executed for himself and for one another '.[1] Here is an assumption that men, through a lack of adequate self-control which they inherited from Adam, needed the help of each other in the organization of order and government in their societies. They must elect their own kings and magistrates. And then, to guard against the perverse tendencies of persons thus entrusted with authority, laws are devised ' either framed or consented to by all ', to limit the action of governors. For Milton, power over government remains in the people as a natural birthright. This is the doctrine of Locke written when Locke was a schoolboy. But there is this important addition. The departure from the ideal social state in which men could have lived (and could perhaps again live) in the harmony of mutual respect and justice to each other, was due to ' Adam's transgression ', i.e. an initial yielding to appetite, not against reason, as with Bodin, but against *conscience*. ' Adam's seed ' were thereafter cursed with a personal appetite which frustrated and nullified any social life in which self-discipline could have dispensed with external restraints. *Man was thus forced to set up means of controlling himself through others.* He set about a collective organization of a kind of pooled self-control, through magistrates and kings as agents. This is Milton's origin of all organized social, civil, and state life.

III. THE STATE AND ' SOVEREIGNTY '

1. *Early theories of International Law.*—The rise and enlargements of the national states of Europe under strong monarchs had extended the sphere of peace and order within those states. During the seventeenth century, divisions, both civil and religious,

---

[1] Milton, *Tenure of Kings and Magistrates* (1649), quoted by Dunning, loc. cit.,vol. ii. p. 242.

occurred within them, often with tragic consequences. But still they survived, consolidated, grew, developed colonies overseas. The religious division of Europe, apart from the terrible thirty years' war in Germany, tended, although often by virtue of internal persecutions, to bring itself into line with national boundaries. These strong new states, for the most part still monarchies, faced each other, with little or no legal theory to guide or explain their *mutual* relations. The absolute monarchs of an earlier time had lived with each other very much as men ' in nature ', trying to conquer each other if they were enemies, fêting each other if they were friends. But now, behind the monarchs, however imposing their persons or power, there stood, in theory, Bodin's ' society ' of Frenchmen, subject to the commands of each other, even although ruled by a sovereign state, Suarez's ' supreme community ' of Spaniards, although still bound to an elected ruler, and finally Milton's Englishmen, demanding life, liberty, and property, and the power to subdue princes till they became mere agents of their will. Plenty of laws now governed the relations between man and man within each of these states. People had ' rights ' and ' obligations ', must keep ' contracts ', could be punished for misdeeds. They were ruled over by kings still claiming divine right, or absolute authority, or delegated authority; or else by parliaments claiming to execute the people's will. Once the civil wars were over there was increasing order and prosperity within the states. The same governments represented peoples abroad. Wars broke out. They were usually popular at the beginning, often less so towards the end. Were they necessary? Men and lesser princes had in the past fought very unnecessarily and to the public woe until they were kept in order by law. What laws were to govern the relations between the greater princes and between the nations ?

Gentilis, a refugee to England from religious persecution in Italy, published *De jure belli* in 1598. In it he made an analysis of the existing laws of war and peace and suggested improvements, one of which was that controversial theology should be excluded from doctrines of international law : ' Let the theologians hold their peace in work that belongs to others than they.' Stimulated by this work, *Grotius*, a Dutch barrister who had previously written on the ' Freedom of the Seas ' and on the Law of Prize, set himself first of all to show that there *was* a law in time of war, and then to study the whole question of international law in the light of its failure to limit warfare. In *De jure belli ac pacis* (1625) he gives his reason for writing. ' *I saw prevailing throughout the Christian world a licence in making war of which even barbarous nations should be ashamed, and when once arms were taken up no reverence left for divine or human law, exactly as if a single edict had released a madness driving men to all kinds of crime.*' Under such conditions what restraining law

actually existed between sovereign nations ? Or rather, what laws
could be laid down ?

Grotius had a clear field. His contemporary observation led
him to aim, like Gentilis, to eliminate the cross currents of theological controversy—to find common law between Protestant and
Catholic. Naturally enough he looked for this in the ancient
' law of nature '—a conception of natural justice such as the
Romans had. We have seen that the Romans applied this law as
law which would be found to be acceptable between man and
man among the nations external to Rome itself. Grotius took the
different view of most of his predecessors since the Reformation
(such as Bodin, Suarez, and Melanchthon) that the law of nature
is a *moral* law—not custom but precept, not what men do ' in
nature ', but what they ought to do. ' The law of Nature is a
dictate of right reason, which points out that an act, according as
it is or is not in conformity with rational nature, has in it a quality
of moral baseness or moral necessity, and that, in consequence,
such an act is either forbidden or enjoined by God, the author of
Nature.' [1] This means that nations may reasonably be asked to
behave according to certain moral principles which all of them
can recognize and ought to accept. The moral impulse comes
from God, i.e. it is inherent in man's nature, though it requires
to be brought out in some way. A sense of justice, he says, is
' part of the true social nature of man '.

These moral standards for the conduct of international
relations are in direct antithesis with the immoral precepts of
Machiavelli, and they did form common ground between Protes-
tants and Catholics. For Grotius himself they were principles
' so certain that no one can deny them without doing violence to
his own nature '. They are in fact the same imperative of the
normal social conscience of man which requires a minimal moral
conduct from him in his dealings individually with his fellows.
For, unlike Hobbes, Grotius held that if self-interest were the
criterion of right and wrong, human society would be impossible.

Grotius, citing Aristotle, next divided law into : (1) this moral
instinct or ' natural law ', and (2) ' voluntary ' laws based on
man's will. He speaks variously of ' political society ' as being
derived from nature and from contract, and Dunning [2] suggests
that he intended something like Bodin's separation of human
' society ', with its origin in man's God-implanted social instinct,
from the formal and ' voluntary ' organization of ' states '. It is
then these latter which are grounded by Grotius on contract
and by Bodin on force. But as Dunning points out, Grotius'
' fixed and eternal laws of the nature of man embody merely his
own personal subjective ideal ' of what man naturally is. Indeed

[1] Grotius, *De jure belli ac pacis*, vol. ii. p. 38. (1625.) Published by the
Carnegie Endowment for International Peace.
[2] Dunning, loc. cit. vol. ii. p. 180.

we may say equally of Bodin, Suarez, and Grotius that, as Maine
put it : ' the greatest difficulty is always to discover . . . whether
they lay down that which is, or that which . . . ought to be '.[1]

Grotius was well aware, however, that societies required
means of enforcement of law. ' We have need of obligation.
For counsels and instructions of every sort which enjoin what is
honourable indeed but do not impose an obligation do not come
under the term statute or law.' The difficulty was that when it
came to international law Grotius could find no existing ' obligation ' other than the moral code ; although in one place, quoted
by Lauterpacht,[2] he speaks of the advantage and the need of
conferences in which ' steps may be taken to *compel* parties to
accept peace on fair terms '. But although a right should often
be given up in order to avoid war, and though everything should
be done to distinguish just from unjust wars and to limit the
occurrence and duration of wars, Grotius cannot find that war
in itself is in conflict with the law of nature.

In a further search for orderly interstate relations Grotius
defined the sovereign of the state, who shall make war and peace
in its name, as : ' He who has the moral faculty of governing
and . . . whose acts are not subject to the rights of any other '.[3]
His reference to international conference and the desirability of
compulsion of parties to a dispute seems to have been lost or
passed over by his followers. What they noted were : (1) his
apparent failure to find any grounding of international law,
except his adapted moral law for nations in a state of nature,
(2) his ' legalization ' of war, and (3) his apparent assumption
that, since the moral ' law of nature ' could hardly offer legal
redress, rulers of states were rightly above all sanctions and
limitations except those of God, *at once in their internal and in
their external relations*. Thus was international law launched with
indifferent auspiciousness on its course of ' legislating ' without
power or authority to enforce, to be treated with deferential
mockery by governments, and to become the laughing-stock of
such peoples who are probing enough to learn of its existence in
the clamour and chaos of an anarchic world. So that among the
nations of to-day we have indeed ' need of obligation '.

The reason Grotius gives for his writings shows that he was
sincerely concerned to limit the horrors of warfare. His adjura-
tions to the human nature of rulers are of such a different moral
order from those of Machiavelli because he placed a higher value

---

[1] Maine, loc. cit. p. 57.
[2] Lauterpacht, *The Function of Law in the International Community*, p. 7.
(Clarendon Press. 1933.)
[3] Grotius favoured absolute monarchies, allowing peoples to ' choose '
their governor provided they chose in that particular way. There their elective
functions ended. And the only legitimate revolt was against commands
conflicting with the laws of God or nature. Grotius thus offers no contribution
to clear thought in the relationships between people and government.

on the social conscience of normal man, whether ruler or ruled, than did the Italian cynic. He admits the evil in human nature, and notes that warfare brings it to the surface. It is interesting that, where Hobbes and Rousseau think of evil men, Grotius' unit is still the nation. 'Not without reason do I speak of peoples " more advanced in civilization ". Some nations have become savage and inhuman.' He ended his work with pragmatic ' admonitions on behalf of good faith and peace ', such as : ' In war he who is not much the stronger ought to refrain from exacting penalties ', and ' In war, peace should always be kept in view '.

a. *The theory of ' sovereignty ' in International Law.*—We have seen that for Grotius, the ' founder ' of International Law, the nation-states of Europe were to be regarded as entirely separate communities each represented by a ruler (preferably monarchic) who was, at least for legal and administrative purposes, sovereign and supreme within his dominions, and sovereign and independent in his relations with his fellow monarchs and their kingdoms. Relations between state and state, or monarch and monarch, were governed by moral laws alone. Despite Grotius' attempt to stereotype them, such moral laws must needs have the variable content given them by their various interpreters. In fact, the relationship was closely analagous to that between man and man in the ' state of nature ' which so many writers have thought to precede the first dawnings of orderly community life. But were international relations to be regarded as the ' state of nature ' as conceived by Locke, from which joint agreement can be won to protect life, liberty, and estates, and the whole ruled by majority decisions ; or rather as Hobbes' ' state of nature ', in which men start as enemies and only through stern law and force can be welded to a commonwealth ? Certainly Locke was legislating for a national community, and never contemplated a society which was not strictly limited. Hobbes, on the other hand, writing only a generation after Grotius, pointed to the relationship between sovereign princes as a very good example of his ' state of nature ', which was synonymous with war. (' For war consisteth not only in actual fighting, but in the known disposition thereto, during all the time there is no assurance to the contrary.') Hobbes and Grotius were thus in close agreement about the state of international affairs and the horrors of war. But while Hobbes offered the same solution to princes in a world community as to individuals within a state—namely that they must abnegate their sovereignty if they were to attain order—Grotius accepted national sovereignty as inevitable, and so must needs fall back upon the moral law, God's light from within, and thus upon a self-control which, if it were adequate, would seem to render law-making a regulative, polite, and essentially superfluous convention. His ambition was thus frustrated. For it is clearly impossible to lay down from *without* what the conscience of a man or a ruler shall tell him from *within*. Machiavelli's crafty and ruthless prince could make as good a claim to be obeying his reading of the law of nature as Grotius' idealized ruler with his inherent desire for justice. We may attempt to lay down from without what a recent writer [1] has called a ' minimum of altruism ' in the conduct of individuals or governments. But we are probably still far enough from being able to tell a man, not only to obey his conscience, but also what his conscience says.

The fundamental fault of International Law, that as such it carried no means of enforcement external to the parties whom it was supposed to bind, being thus exposed by Grotius and Hobbes in the seventeenth century, it might be thought that lawyers would strive to remedy such a fatal defect, or that they would at least warn laymen, both ruler and public, that these new rules were not law as they knew it and would not function as law. The eighteenth century might not have been interested. But the public of the nineteenth and early twentieth centuries ought surely to have been told repeatedly that, while the whole stability and efficiency of law as they knew it at home was based upon the power of the community or its rulers to secure that unwilling parties either observed it or were punished, no such power and no sign of a machinery which could evolve such power existed anywhere in the international community. It was not until the first Covenant of the League of Nations had been launched, amid the hopes and fears of the whole world, that, in a book at once authoritative and accessible to ordinary English readers, a British Lord Chancellor told us that : ' *Treaties form the contract law of states and it is in dealing with their enforcement and duration that international law most conspicuously fails. In the absence of a supreme authority capable of developing a system of law and enforcing its decrees, all rules are of the nature of suggestions for the guidance of conduct. And while nations are so careful . . . to reserve their right of action on questions concerning their " honour and vital interest " . . . these rules must remain . . . pious aspirations* '. [2]

In the meantime attention concentrated on the very ' sovereignty ' which made nations unable to create an enforceable international law, not with a view to weakening but to strengthening it. Lauterpacht, who himself defines the function of law as being ' to regulate the conduct of men by reference to rules whose formal—as distinguished from their historical—source of validity lies, in the last resort, in a precept imposed from outside ', describes this attention as being ' the work of international lawyers anxious to give legal expression to the State's claim to be independent of law '. [3] It is difficult to know how that claim persisted into the modern world. It presumably arose when

[1] C. K. Allen, *Legal Duties*, p. 220.   (Clarendon Press. 1931.)
[2] F. E. Smith, *International Law*, p. 141.   (5th edition, Dent. 1918.)
[3] Lauterpacht, loc. cit. pp. 2 and 6.

strong rulers felt that, in addition to ruling their subjects by divine right, they could face ' the four corners of the world in arms '. Since strong monarchs rapidly became limited in strength internally, and often replaced by parliaments in all claims or exercises of sovereignty, there must have been a relative fostering of the doctrine of irresponsibility in external as opposed to internal national affairs. The truth probably is that rulers, faced with claims such as those of the common lawyers, the Independents, and Milton, were glad to resort to limitation of their sovereign authority internally, so that nothing worse should come to them, while their ministers frequently adopted the façade of complete subjection to the public will. But in relation to external affairs there was no pressure to limit sovereign independence except threats of war. And such threats usually found the defiance of peoples behind their governors, especially if these were also their ' elected representatives '. There remains the attitude of the lawyers and jurists. And having neither legal system, nor institution of international justice to which they could be loyal, nor even a theory which could inspire their imaginations, they set themselves ' to supply a legal cloak for the traditional claim of the sovereign State to remain the ultimate judge of disputed legal rights in its controversies with other States ' (Lauterpacht). They proceeded as follows.

A Swiss diplomatist, *Vattel*,[1] found that, as by ' natural law ' states, like individuals, were equal and free, each state was the sole judge of its own actions. Vattel here follows Pufendorf's [2] ' naturalist ' view of a binding ' natural law ' inherited from a good ' state of nature ' as opposed to Hobbes' evil and inequitable ' state of nature ' from which it is in man's power and self-interest to escape. Vattel's state is ' sovereign ' (i.e. above all law) by this higher ' necessary ' law, as distinct from any self-limitation imposed by ' voluntary ' laws. It was inherently unlikely that the latter would bind a state very far against its own interests. By declaring states ' equal and free ' Vattel had intended to champion liberty ; but actually he ' cut the frail moorings which bound international law to any sound principle of obligation ' (Brierly).[3] We see the result foreshadowed in his own advice to states. It is their duty, he says, to seek peace by compromise, mediation, arbitration, conference, or congress ' where interests that are not essential or are of small consequence are involved '. But ' when one should seek to rob it of an essential right, of a right without which it cannot hope to maintain its existence ', the nation should ' exhaust its resources, and nobly shed the last drop of its blood '. It is thus advised to withdraw its ' vital interests ' from the scope of all law and jurisdiction.

[1] Vattel, *Le droit des gens.* (1758.)
[2] Pufendorf, *De jure naturae et gentium.* (1672.)
[3] Brierly, *The Law of Nations*, p. 33. (2nd edition. Clarendon Press. 1936.)

5

During the next half-century, the ' law ' and the ' state ' of
' nature ' came more and more into favour as a theoretical basis
of social order. We have seen how Rousseau's ' general will '
closed the valuable separation which Bodin had made between
the *society of peoples* and their *government by the state*. So that,
when we come to *Austin*,[1] who has received great credit and great
criticism for his studies of ' sovereignty ', we find that all law,
internal and external to the nation, has become the creation of the
state. Austin's original enquiry was into the fundamental nature
of a political society. He grounded it in force, a doctrine with
which we are now familiar. That force is apparent in its laws.
And their force is derived from their ' sanction ', the compulsion
that can be put behind them. It is often debated whether law
is truly law if it cannot be enforced. Austin's general answer is
in the negative ; ' positive ' law requires a sanction. The force
behind the law he defined as the ' *sovereign* '. But he believed
there to be *a* source of law, and *a* power which gave it all and
received none of it—a person or body, exercising ' absolute, unlimited, indivisible, uncontrollable, inalienable power over all
the members of the society of which it is the organ '. [2] This
' sovereign ' source of all authority Austin found in the state.
Manning [3] reminds us that Austin concluded that his sovereign
power in the state depended on the law-abiding nature of the
majority of the citizens. As with Locke, it is a case at bottom
of a · sound majority controlling a recalcitrant minority.
But instead of a group of individuals ruling for their own
good with the aid of a machinery of government, control is
achieved through this majestic repository of ' sovereignty ', the
state.[4]

[1] Austin, *Province of Jurisprudence Determined*. (1832.)
[2] Jenks, E., *Sources of the Law*. (The Law Journal. 1924.)
[3] Manning, C. A. W., in *Modern Theories of Law*. Section on ' Austin ',
p. 180. (Oxford U.P. 1933.)
[4] The intricacy of the controversy over Austin is one into which as a layman I am not competent to enter. His contributions do not appear to have
aroused much interest and controversy during his lifetime. They would
appear to have undergone a period of neglect, until they were ' rediscovered '
by Maine. There seems reason to believe that Austin as he is now generally
interpreted is in some respects more the Austin of Maine and what T. H.
Green called ' the Austinians ' than the Austin of *The Province of Jurisprudence*.
Maine gave it as Austin's view that ' There is, in every independent community—that is in every community not in the habit of obedience to a superior
above itself—some single person or some combination of persons which has
the power of compelling the other members of the community to do exactly
as it pleases.' Dewey (*Political Science Quarterly*, ix. p. 31. 1894) and
Manning (loc. cit. p. 183. 1933) have protested that ' no such conception
of sovereignty as consisting in absolute force is to be found anywhere in Austin ',
and Manning notes (p. 195) as Austin's conception of law that it is ' a declared
wish, the disregard of which is *in principle* liable to be visited with sanctions '.
But to an outside observer of jurisprudence to-day Austin stands for the
extreme rigidity of the doctrine of state sovereignty. It is in this light that he
has been praised or blamed by most writers on the subject during the past
half century.

As Brierly says, philosophers and lawyers had come to speak of sovereignty ' almost as if it were a substance '. And where Locke's community need have found no particular theoretical barrier to realistic relationships with others, if they kept in mind his own dicta on the object of all government and the value of toleration, Austin's legal following, with what pleasure or pain it is hard to say, felt themselves forced to represent what was a comparatively harmless fiction in *internal* administration as a figure incapable of accommodation to the ' vital interests ' of other ' sovereigns ', humbled by the very thought of external limitation, a god like figure representing the inflexible will and might of the British state, facing, alas, across the sea to similar fancies of similar brains in other lands, and notably to the ' divine ' idea of the Prussian state of Hegel, so incapable of external limitation that, if the shadow of limitation appeared in reality, it must be regarded as ' auto-limitation '. For, in the logic of the nineteenth century, self-limitation is no limitation. Thus was preserved, not a necessary or desirable ' fiction ' which assisted in useful legal adaptations, but the ' honour ' of the fantastic representative of an infantile pride in the immaculate which the human adult is so ready to express in his collective life. As *individuals* we usually have to abdicate our ' absolute sovereignty ' comparatively fully by the second or third year of life. But individually we retain, and collectively we luxuriate in expressing, traces of those early forms of thought which represent us as free and independent in *all* our actions.

This doctrine of ' sovereignty ' still persists. Specialists in international law increasingly protest that their task is a difficult one, though they seldom say that it is hopeless. The ' laws of nature ' have been ransacked again and again in search of a principle of political obligation by which states could be held to the ' laws ' which from time to time, and increasedly since 1919, have been drafted for them. The governments concerned are cautious about pledging themselves to arbitration in general terms : indeed thay are more ready to renounce war outright, because such renunciations always carry with them an explicit or implied reservation excluding ' vital interest ' or ' defence '. Reluctance to sign binding agreements is at least a recognition that a moral public opinion, either within the state (including of course its government), or in the world outside, may make itself felt, and embarrass an executive anxious at some later date to break its pledge. So far, so good. And if societies had become more used to regarding their governments (with Bodin) as inevitable repositories of the force necessary to the keeping of law, but as in no way identified with the essence of the social community which they serve (and certainly not as custodians of public morals), if societies could watch their governments as a municipal mayor might watch his police officers about their duty, we might expect

public opinion to act far more than it does as a check and a
' sanction ' upon governmental peccability in its external relationships. But such checks would never suffice, and that for a
number of reasons. Intellectually, both governments and peoples
too readily become tainted with the doctrine, as demoralizing for
groups as it is for individuals, that in certain ' higher ' interests
promises can be abandoned, and contracts broken. Emotionally,
the very essence of loyalty makes people identify themselves with
their governments in critical times, rather than criticize them.
We shall later find profound psychological confirmation for the
legal maxim that a man cannot be a fair judge in his own cause.
Governments and peoples are alike in this. If human nature
could find an adequate principle of social obligation arising within
itself, we could aim, and expect, to abolish the rule of law within
our several communities, rather than to extend it to function
between them. But historical records show us that comparative
order and social stability have been achieved with the aid of law,
but never without it. And it is Austin, so anxious to trace
authority to its lair, who gives us on his way the clear statement
that *laws function because they have behind them the force of*
EXTERNAL *compulsion*.

IV. THE STATE AND THE INDIVIDUAL : MODERN THEORIES OF THE FUNCTION OF LAW

In the century since Austin there has been a great deal of
discussion as to the origins and functions of law in the social
systems of man. The question of interest to us is *how* the relationships between men in society are regulated—the *function*
of law. With this is included the nature and the operation of
the *obligation to obey* the law. And here, as Brierly says, the
problem is the same whether it be for international or domestic
law. ' The answer must be sought outside the law and it is
for legal philosophy to provide it.' [1] The origins of law are of
interest where they demonstrate its needs and functions. It is
the functional rather than the historical origins that concern us.

There is a common general definition of law as ' *rules for the
guidance of conduct* '. Such a definition lacks completeness and
begs a question. Those who argue that ineffective laws are no
laws, add that the rules of law must be *enforceable*. Others,
wishing to include ' moral laws ' among the realities of law, and
mindful too that in fact many ' laws ' are not obeyed, contend
against this addition. Compromises have been attempted, such
as defining true laws as carrying a ' sanction ' alternative of
obedience or punishment, or by saying that laws are habitually
obeyed. It is certainly desirable that the one word ' law ' should
cease to be used to cover such different meanings as (1) things

[1] Brierly, loc. cit. p. 45.

which happen invariably or inevitably—as ' scientific laws ' ;
(2) ideals which are seldom or never achieved, or which ought
to be achieved—as ' moral laws ' ; (3) regulations laid down by
an effective authority which either will or can either enforce them
or punish their breach—as the ' law of the land ' ; (4) rules for
conduct under certain conditions, issued without discoverable
means of their effective support in execution, such as the rules
of a debating society under an ineffective chairman or, alas,
' international law ' as at present constituted.   If the word ' law ',
meaning juridical law, had implied to the average man a precept
only, as distinct from the actual regulation of conduct, it could
no more have become the terror of evil doers and the protector
of society against violence, injustice, and fraud, than have the
churches.   The call to good and the deterrence of evil may work
in the same general direction, but they operate through different
agencies, frequently affect different people, and always play upon
different elements of the human psyche.   The *effective regulation
of conduct* is the ' law ' which men desire and respect and recognize
by the term.   Let this remain our meaning of the term ' law ',
here.

We have seen the sources of law distributed by the Romans
between ' nature ' and ' reason ' ;   on the one hand the simple
notions of justice and right which would be recognized by men
of all nations because they were ideas natural to mankind, on
the other the elaborate codes which an elaborate society could
build up for itself.   We have seen too how the Reformation
writers emphasized the Law of God, tending to separate it from
that of nature, and how for instance Milton regarded the whole
regulation of a man's social life by law as being due originally
to a punishment of God, though ultimately it had been incorporated in the requirements of man's nature.   We have seen how
the different views of man's nature, typified by Hobbes, Locke,
and Rousseau, led to various views as to the government and
laws which he needs.   We have seen his laws given him from
above by divine Providence through kings (before the Reformation), his inherent powers delegated by him to strong external
forces for the control of his violence (Hobbes), directly organized
by a society of reasonable men for its own advantage (Milton
and Locke).   We have seen the ' state ' arise as a necessary
mechanism of law and force, become separated from essential
society with its mutual subjection of its members to the commands of each other (Bodin), then brought under its control
again, so that it is the human soul of social man that becomes
the repository and guardian of God's law proper (Suarez).
We have seen the state and people unified as a source of law
(Rousseau) ;   then the state raised again above the people by
virtue of its symbolism of sovereign power (Austin) and finally
released from its subjection even to the laws of God and the moral

precepts of nature (Hegel). This provoked in its turn a reaction towards demands for individual liberty and a society regarded as consisting essentially of individuals (Hobhouse).

Each of these various expositions is partly due to the peculiarities of the contemporary scene as viewed by the author, and partly due to his own temperament. So that each new conception, whatever its date of origin, gives us the attitude towards society of a certain man, and often of a certain type of man. We may see how contemporary so many of these varied opinions really are by the schools of thought, both secular and religious, which survive in our own time and derive frankly and often with little essential modification from views of society which have been expressed over and over again for one or two thousand years. With such a variety of theories finding their advocates among philosophers throughout the ages, it is natural that we should find a similar variety of views of the function of law among lawyers and legal philosophers of our own time. There follows a very brief exposition of some of those which have carried most weight.

(1) *The function of law is to maintain the state.*—There has been repeated support both for Austin's view of the state as the origin of law, and for Hegel's view of the support of the state as constituting the chief function of law. *Jellinek* taught that legal rules were primarily to uphold the political system, and *Ehrlich* that the object of law is the organization of the state (Vinogradoff).[1] The meaning of such views depends a great deal upon the conception of the ' state ' which lies behind them.

(2) *The function of law is to enrich the community.*—*Jenks,*[2] opposing Austin's ' pernicious theory ', describes the state as the few score or few hundred individuals who have got hold of the machinery of central government. On the other hand he finds the source of law to be the ' largely unconscious efforts of the community to realize its material and spiritual ideals '. Like Hobhouse, Jenks regards the state as a particular instance of a community among the many others which society forms, and its laws as particular instances of the rules which any organizing community must make. ' The state as we know it will ultimately cease to exist. The alternative to anarchy is not the state but law.' And the law of the future will aim to achieve ' not authority but harmony ', asking not ' What is written ', but ' What will work ? '

(3) *Law as the minimum interference to protect the interests of the individual.*—This was the view of Locke. It found an endorsement in *Bentham*, with his statement that law was a matter of ' expediency' in securing what *Priestley* had described as 'the

---

[1] Vinogradoff, *Historical Jurisprudence*, p. 143. (Oxford University Press. 1920.)
[2] Jenks, E., loc. cit.

greatest happiness for the greatest number', and his opening up of what Allen calls 'the master-problem of whether law exists for the sake of enlarging or for the sake of restricting the liberty of man'.[1] Among recent writers *Saleilles* regards society as composed of individuals protecting themselves by 'measures of expediency' which lead to renunciations and self-sacrifices (Vinogradoff). A not dissimilar view is that of *Lundstedt*, that rules of law arise from the 'sheer necessity' for order, security, and self-preservation of individuals in society (Allen).

(4) *Law consists solely of duties.*—The protagonist of this ('positivist') school of legal theory is *Duguit*,[2] inspired by a dictum of Comte, that one should always substitute 'duties' for 'rights', the better to subordinate personality to sociability. Duguit puts forward the view that to encourage men to think of their 'rights' is to encourage an anti-social tendency, to emphasize individuality. So we are told that : 'Every man has duties towards all, but nobody has any right, properly so-called'. The positivist school derives law from society rather than from the state. Individual liberty exists in order to develop 'social solidarity'. The aim of political power is to realize 'the right'. The similarity to Rousseau is striking. If something could occur within us all which would call forth a perennial stream of altruism, nobody need bother about his competitive life in the world. We cannot feel this emotion of unlimited generosity or unselfishness, even for a moment, as long as we doubt others—doubt, that is, their respect for the 'liberty' of our individuality. Rousseau reassures himself by the double stratagem of feeling that his own best will is included in the general will to the control of which he is about to submit, and of visualizing the larger 'liberty' which generous and harmonious relations with others seem to offer. Duguit asks us to feel our freedom as something which is a gift to us, and which it is our duty to sacrifice to 'social solidarity', receiving as compensation the satisfaction of our social instincts. The laws of society are made to implement this process. This doctrine, like that of Rousseau, is a call to social idealism and the joys of devotion of one's fellows. Is there no danger of 'social solidarity' developing an intolerance to the manifestations of individualism, similar to that which emanated from the 'general will' ?

Duguit has had a following and an opposition. To *Laski*[3] the doctrine came as 'the dawn of a new Renaissance'. It meant that 'the state is only entitled to use force to fulfil its obligation to assure to each and all the means to contribute all it is in them to give to the fullest realization of social solidarity'. Who is to

---

[1] Allen, C. K., loc. cit. p. 156.
[2] Duguit, *Law in the Modern State*. (Allen & Unwin. 1921.)
[3] Laski, H. J., in *Modern Theories of Law*. Section on 'Duguit.' (Oxford University Press. 1933.)

decide what this ' all ' is to be, the giver or the solid society ? Are we not still rather too near to Rousseau ? For if it is the society— and it may be a long time before all men habitually put their duties before their rights !—then one wonders what this ' social solidarity ' is. It is clearly an idea that some minds take to. And the writer is reminded of a remark of Laski's in another connexion : ' It was natural for a humane factory owner to believe that good conduct consists in maintaining the prosperity of the manufacturing classes '.[1] Are Duguit and Laski in fact saying, first, that men ought to obey their consciences, and second, that those consciences ought to lead them towards self-realization through social service ? If so, these are precepts from the conscience of one man applied to others as a law. That may be very necessary. But the process should be recognized, lest all unsuspecting we should one day be told of ' social solidarity ', as we were of the ' general will ', that he who does not obey its dictates should be executed, or that no one can deny its claims ' without doing violence to his own nature '. For here we are also very near to Grotius, so near as to reproduce his ' law of nature ' conceived as a social instinct.

Laski, at least, does not intend this result. For he is especially concerned for the ' preservation of individuality ' : ' A man has, above all, to be true to himself. . . . Once he humbles himself, against his inner promptings, before the demands of authority the way to acquiescence is easy '.[2] It is more difficult sometimes to avoid trying to force other people to be true to *our* inner promptings. When is another man to be stopped from being true to himself ? Directly he ceases to contribute to *our* notion of social solidarity ? In reviewing Duguit's theory Laski pleads for a revival of a theory of ' natural law ' as the basis of constructive theories to replace those grounded on ' sovereignty '.[3] I believe it to be the duty of the social psychologist to try to provide such a theory.

(5) *Law regulates both duties and rights.*—A protest against the ' positivist ' system of a moral code with doubtful rewards of virtue is made by *Allen* : ' The principle of social solidarity is no more an objective law than was the Law of Nature ', and ' There is no self-sufficient sanctity in mere plurality for its own sake '.[4] He regards as unreasonable the claim that : ' Man's only right is to do his duty '. *Pollock* [5] quoted by Allen holds that in law ' Duty and Right are not more divisible than action and reaction in mechanics '. This suggests that the relationship of man to society is not very adequately described by its primary

---

[1] Laski, *Authority in the Modern State*, p. 38. (Yale University Press. 1919.)
[2] Ibid. p. 58.   [3] Laski, loc. cit. (1933.)
[4] Allen, C. K., loc. cit. p. 158 et seq.
[5] Pollock : *A First Book of Jurisprudence*, p. 73. (3rd edition. Macmillan. 1911.)

division into duties and rights, obligations and rewards. Is it not rather *human conduct* which the law is designed to regulate in order to secure certain ends (1) for the individual, and (2) for the society in which he lives ?

There are other views of the function of law, and many modifications of the five described above. There is the doctrine that the state is primarily an aggregate of institutions whose interests fall to be controlled by law ; there are theories based on the view of Kant that individuals should only obey rules set up in accordance with their own consciences. These instances must suffice. We leave jurisprudential and philosophical theories of law, as we left philosophical conceptions of the state, with the twin convictions, that a reconciling principle is absent from all this diversity and contradiction, and that the very diversities and contradictions are themselves products of the individual variations of the human mind in properties and reactions which are in part at least determinable. It should become a task for social psychology to correlate each main theory as far as may be with a type of mind ; so that each theory may have a corrective applied to it, towards the end of achieving a truth which shall be the more complete for being composite.

In the meantime, let us examine our present knowledge of the motives and mechanisms of the human mind, to see if we may not already learn more about the qualities which have to be controlled by laws than these legal and philosophical theories can tell us. In doing so we may also gain some light as to how we have come by some at least of these theories. Let us turn now to modern psychology to find out what it can teach us about human nature that the student of society ought to know.

III

PSYCHOLOGICAL THEORIES OF HUMAN NATURE

I. PRINCIPLES OF PSYCHOANALYSIS

IT would probably not be difficult to find as many contradictory theories of human nature among the psychologists of the last hundred years as among the philosophers and lawyers. But this survey will be restricted to the last generation or so. That is the period during which the subject has increased its claims to be called a science, through the technique of discovering motives of conduct which are normally hidden from consciousness, the ' free-association ' technique of Freud. Freud himself has contributed more than anyone else to the records of the ' repressed ' contents of the mind of man, the primitive, infantile, and often grossly distorted pictures of the realities of life which lurk in tne background of our adult minds. These ' other selves ' observe through our eyes, hear through our ears, and contribute so largely to the way in which we respond to the impressions of our senses, that our logical, ' reasonable ' selves are often either overruled entirely, or have a hard task to explain our conduct to our own satisfaction. Has it not long been a platitude that we can seldom account for it adequately, *in toto*, to the satisfaction of anyone else ?

That man is not a rational being, that he is constantly engaged in inventing his intellectual processes to make a ' reasonable ' justification to himself of conceptions given to him as facts by his emotions, no one who has manipulated the technique of Freud for a moment holds in doubt. Observing philosophers who do doubt this are only being reasonably cautious in a matter which it is impossible for them to sift. Any who would *deny* it should first make themselves familiar with the Freudian technique of psychoanalysis and see for themselves. Otherwise they will go on with their systems which assume that philosophic man is capable of cold thought uninfluenced by unconscious passion, until in due course the analytical psychologist lays before them a key to the windings of their own mental processes derived from psychoanalyses of similar types. Then they will probably be very angry.

The above remarks do not mean that the philosopher will be replaced by the psychologist. He will certainly not be replaced by the psychoanalyst, who is a manipulator of a technique of limited scope and requiring limited mental powers. Psychoanalysis no more threatens a truly philosophic mind than the sun need fear the rivalry of an electrician. But there are dark places and dark times, even dark deeds to be unravelled from the human mind. And the illumination of the night may have done more to bring order to our modern cities than all the works of daylight. It is in this spirit, of introducing for consideration certain findings of a new technique, that we shall present the results of psychoanalysis in assaying human nature.

Freud discovered a very great deal about the human mind. He himself lived to correct a number of his earlier misapprehensions and misemphases ; and he founded a school which has already enlarged his work and corrected many more of his views in the light of greater knowledge. Thousands of laymen and doctors flocked to take up the new opportunities of alleviating human suffering which psychoanalysis offered. And among them healthy schisms occurred. The two dissenting schools of Jung and Adler, modifying and abbreviating Freud's technique, stressed different findings from those of their master, each bringing contributions of his own into theory, and each discovering matter allied to his own temperament in practice, matter mystical and religious in the case of Jung, pragmatic in the case of Adler. By many modern analysts a high degree of synthesis of these three main schools has been achieved, and the same analyst will now treat cases, according to their type and requirements, along ' Freudian ', ' Jungian ', or ' Adlerian ' lines.

Material.—We say ' treat cases '. For, with the rarest of exceptions, the only people whose minds are in practice explored by systematic psychoanalysis are : (1) patients suffering from a disabling neurosis, treated by doctors ; (2) doctors or educationalists, mostly the former, under training as specialists in the subject ; and (3) a certain very limited number of wealthy dilettanti who can persuade medical or lay analysts to explore their minds in this way. It may safely be assumed that a high proportion of these last are in fact neurotics liable at any time to develop more or less disabling symptoms. The limitation of the number and type of persons submitted to this peculiar form of investigation must be mentioned as one of the limiting factors when general conclusions about human character are being drawn from the results of psychoanalysis. Other limiting factors must also be explained.

Let us take a patient, say a man who fears that he may suddenly go blind, or who is in an agony of mind whenever he travels, as he daily must, in an Underground train. He will consult his doctor, and fail to be ' argued out of ' his trouble or to get any permanent satisfaction from assurances about his physical health. He may find his way to one of the big clinics for ' psychotherapy ' —often after an unfruitful visit to a ' neurologist ' on the way ; for these ' nerve specialists ' are not trained to treat the particular condition of ' nerves ' from which such patients suffer. He commences treatment. And there follows from one to several hourly sessions per week, lasting perhaps for twelve months, and often running into one or two hundred hours or more of ' treatment '. Of what does this lengthy ' treatment ' consist ?

Complexes.—In the early days of research, Freud and his colleagues were largely ' exploring ' the minds of their subjects. But they had certain guiding hypotheses from the first. The chief was that the symptoms from which their patients suffered (e.g. loss of voice in a clergyman, or a paralysed right arm in a soldier) were connected with an important function in their lives to which an emotional stress was attached. (Needless to say a competent medical examination can soon disprove the presence of an ' organic ' disease—cancer, say—in the clergyman's throat, or a ' stroke ' in the case of the soldier.) The symptom itself was the chief guide. Freud persisted hour after hour in making his patients talk about their symptom, and ideas connected with it in their minds. Thus it was that he evolved the technique of ' free-association '. For he found that, if known associations of the symptom were thought of (say the pulpit and the firing-trench in our two examples) and then the mind were allowed to wander freely, and its first next thought recorded—be it a father, a mouse-trap, or a playing field of boyhood, whatever its apparent irrelevancy—the chances were that a link in a strictly relevant chain of *unconscious* mental association had been found. By employing this discovery that *unconsciously directed associations of the mind were determined by significant emotions*, Freud next found that he could trace his symptoms to a *misconception in the patient's mind*. For there are various logics of the unconscious mind, which stretch from the type of reasoning we accept in consciousness as adults backwards into our past lives, to the sort of reasoning we performed in childhood and even in infancy. To an ordinary adult a wasp may be a clumsy yellow insect with a sting a little worse than that of a mosquito, best to be left alone unless it gets into the jam. To five-year-old child A it may be a very jolly sort of butterfly, until it suddenly betrays confidence in a never-to-be-forgotten way when grasped firmly in the hand. But in five-year-old child B, it may excite an incomprehensible terror, because in earlier infancy its arrival had been accompanied by a panic in his mother, which had awakened a terror in himself. And in after life, while the ' ordinary ' man will go on with his breakfast, A will rise determinedly with : ' Better kill that wasp ! ' while poor B, otherwise ' ordinary ' enough, will need every ounce of his self-control to avoid grasping his serviette and retiring into a corner while the hunt is in progress, panic-stricken, he knows not why. The misconception is that the part of B's unconscious mind which is ruling his emotions does not see a wasp at all but a nameless terror of infancy. Under treatment, if he sought it, ' free-association ' would lead him back to his original misconception that some evil of cosmic force was encased in these nightmare insects. And, perhaps because the human mind is reassured by acceptable explanations, the reassurance brought by the discovery might in itself cure him of his particular over-emphasis, or ' insect-phobia '.

Repression.—It should be noted that the exciting or painful incidents which thus over-emphasize, or ' over-determine ', certain significances for us are usually forgotten. They tend to be forgotten in a particularly significant way, ' *repressed* ' because of their painful nature and also because of their frequent disharmony with the later judgments of which we approve and on which we have come to act. There is always a logic of sorts about these earlier associations, though it often clashes with normal adult reasoning. ' There is that thing that makes Mother look frightened and wave her arms about. That Mother should look confident and reassuring is a vital necessity to me. Therefore that is a very terrible and menacing thing,' is the infantile unconscious logic of the men with the insect-phobia. Consciously he reasons : ' There is one of those wretched wasps again. No-

body minds them but me.   They are relatively harmless, and this
one will never settle on me.   As the commercial representative
of Messrs. Smith, and a well-known cricketer, indeed as Mr. B.
himself, I cannot allow myself to leave the table '.   The panic of
the child is in conflict with the ethical standards of the man, the
desires of the child for security with the desire of the man for
respect.   Adult and conscious reasoning is on the side of the man.
Infantile and unconscious reasoning, from infantile conceptions
and values, presses upon him, and tries to take charge of his
actions.   If it succeeds, we find a neurotic symptom.

Conflict.—The element of *conflict* is always discoverable in
the mind of a neurotic.   But the possible conflicts are very
various.   There may, as in the case just imagined, be a conflict
between a self-preservative impulse deriving from an infantile
setting and the requirements of adult decorum.   There may also
be quarrels between adult desires and an adult sense of right and
wrong, between infantile desires and infantile standards of right
and wrong, between two different desires which, without any
ethical problem arising, merely appear incompatible, desires of
the pattern expressed by the phrase ' to have your cake and eat it '.
Many, though not all, of these apparent incompatibilities will
appear to the ' adult ' and ' impartial ' mind of the analyst as
depending on misconceptions in the mind of the patient.   Some
are indeed very gross errors—for instance when a child thinks,
' If I am like Father at all, which I want to be, I shall be like
Mother thinks Father is, which is horrible '. (See Case A., Chap. IV,
p. 131.)   Such a type of argument is often found in the mind of
the child within a grown man.   The putting of an end to the
shadows of such conflicts developed out of stressful family life
may bring infinite relief to adults who have never been able to
' be themselves ' for fear of an illusionary nemesis.

Treatment by psychoanalysis consists in removing misconceptions which have produced conflicts.   The subject, at least
if he has not informed himself by reading of the common types
of repression which are revealed by this technique, will often
be greatly surprised at some of his ' thoughts ' and ' desires ' of
which he was previously unaware.   Some problems arising from
' tilting at windmills ' may be readily exposed and resolved as the
' windmill ' becomes apparent and is accepted as such.   In the
long analyses required by patients whose whole lives have been
built upon early misconceptions (e.g. Case C., Chap. IV, p. 135)
alternative aims of life and conduct are often brought to the fore,
and the subject has to choose between *real* incompatibles—a
selfish unloved life or a co-operative and disciplined one, a
sensual life or a dedicated one.   These are old choices seen in
new light, and the judgments are made with a knowledge which
most healthy men do not need, and may indeed be better without,
but which has become vitally important to a man whose judgments

have hitherto been warped by some passion or prejudice which he could neither combat nor comprehend.

Transference and projection.—In struggles to find new standards, or to weigh up old ones, it is inevitable that the personalities of patient and analyst should react upon each other. In his pioneer efforts to establish an objective science of the mental and emotional life, Freud set himself prescribed conducts intended to avoid the patient becoming ' suggestible ', i.e. influenced by the thoughts and feelings of his doctor. That proved impossible, because the influence is great and inevitable. Indeed even if the doctor sits day after day in utter quiet, out of sight, at the head of the patient's couch, the latter will *endow* him with a personality, in default of one emerging. It will probably be compiled out of three elements : (1) something of the doctor which is actual and detectable ; (2) a ' *transference* ' of properties real or imagined from one of the chief actors in the drama of the patient's life ; (3) a ' *projection* ' on to the doctor of some of the patient's own feelings. The latter will then set himself to get some responses from his doctor. And sooner or later he will succeed !

Validities.—It must be admitted that *the influence of the analyst upon the patient is always considerable, and may be decisive.* How then can we attach due weight to the emotional drives which appear in the patient under these conditions of emotional and intellectual exchange with his doctor, particularly, one may add, in view of the fact that the leaders of the main schools of practice —themselves the authors of much of the chief literature on the subject—have all been men of very marked and forceful character ?

The answer lies in *the common nature of the reactions shown* by patients. But it must be put in this way : Hundreds of doctors have analysed tens of thousands of patients during the last twenty years. The hypothetical cases cited as illustrations in the foregoing pages—a fear of blindness, an inability to travel by Underground, a paralysed voice or arm, a fear of insects—give but a faint idea of the variety of symptoms presented by these patients. Among ninety-two cases of neurosis seen by me at a London hospital in 1938 I had to classify forty-two different categories in my notes ! It is in fact a medical truism that there is no organic disease of the body which cannot be simulated in its symptoms by a neurosis, no function of the body which cannot be seized and modified or paralysed by our uncontrollable emotions. Yet if Freud's technique of ' free-association ' be conscientiously applied to all these sufferers by all these doctors, the underlying mental reactions of the patients show less and less diversity as they are freed of their incidental factors (the pulpit for the clergyman, the firing-trench for the soldier, the London ' Underground ', the failure of the electric light) and come to show the common human patterns of boyhood's fears, childhood's arrogance or the infant's need of love. These *are* after all the common heritage of clergyman, soldier, and commercial traveller alike. But then it will be found that each of these patients carries with him certain elementary type reactions from the life of childhood and infancy —reactions to games, to feeding, to toilet, etc.—which are based essentially on the simplest of all formulae, the attempt at *satisfaction of the self in the light at once of the primitive sensations and of the primitive logic of infancy*.

At this level of the mind you will find psychoanalysts of different schools all accepting certain simple classifications. A child is an ' oral ' type giving prominence in his emotional life to the satisfactions which come through the mouth ; or he shows predominant ' aggressiveness ' or ' anxiety '. When it comes to deeper analytical findings, so *few* are the types of case, that it is difficult to find titles diverse enough for their classification. And one eminent analyst once remarked to the writer that ' really they are all alike '.

But emotional reactions of emotionally dependent patients under strictly artificial and comparatively rigid conditions of analysis might well be similar either because of the artificiality of the setting, or because of the similar fundamental training of the analysts. The fact is that it is only after months of work that these common properties emerge. They then show qualities which are the most natural ' logical ' antecedents of their diverse surface manifestations, each patient proceeding to his ' oral ' (or other), ' aggressive ' (or other) infantile setting by a different path. And they are in fact *not* all alike, but show a most interesting diversity—namely one of degree, a varied proportioning of qualities, which tip the balance decisively in the formation of character. X, whether it be as an adult, or an infant, or in the dissection of survivals of infancy which psychoanalysis attempts, will always *tend* to grasp the nettle of life firmly, while Y will always *tend* to draw back. And however far we press our analysis, we do not seem to be within reach of a technique which will fully separate the inherent from the environmental factors in determining these fundamental trends of character.

Thus it will be throughout the analysis. Whoever the analyst, Mr. Brown will show his characteristic self. First he will show the diversity and peculiarities of his conceptions and misconceptions of things and people upon which he acts. This is his adult attitude, and it is determined by the three mental processes of : (1) ' unfettered ' adult logic; (2) the prostitution of adult logic to serve unconscious motives and mechanisms (' *rationalization* '); and (3) the unfettered influence of his unconscious and archaic inheritance itself, of his ' instincts '. Next he will discover his underlying ' *complexes* ', repressed conflicts born of infantile desires considered by infantile logic in the way we have indicated. The dramatis personae will be himself and the people who mattered most in his infancy. He will usually proceed to confuse the analyst with one of these, and it will not necessarily be a favoured one. And then, if the analysis needs to be a ' deep ' one, there will emerge the thoughts and feelings which seem quite foreign to us as adults, but which Freud has persuaded us are present and significant (by the method we suggest to the critical philosopher, that of personal experience). At this stage the analyst or the analytical student, whatever his creed or temperament, will have to report the arrival of the analysis upon a plane common to others. The ' oral ', or ' anal ' or ' genital ' interests have to be tabulated, as surely as the medical student, be he never so inclined to homeopathy, will have to report to his professor that so much digitalis has slowed the heart-rate of his patient by so many beats per minute.

The above paragraphs do not mean that psychoanalytical findings are to be accepted as ultimate validities, as the collection of ' fundamental ' human desires which some people seem to consider them. They are nothing of the sort. The human mind usually grows up. And when a man thinks he prefers smoking a pipe to sucking a baby's comforter, or climbing a mountain to straddling his father's knee, there is no reason to suppose that he is making a mistake. That there may be a discoverable emotional link between the pipe and comforter, or between the mountain and the knee, does not give pre-eminence to the interest which it is the more difficult to unearth. It is when an infantile interest has had to be suppressed that it is liable to clamour its way into adulthood. It is the man whose infant mind said : ' Mother takes the comforter away : it must be wicked ', who will be the more likely to regard a pipe as a temptation, and non-smoking as a test of character. It is the repressed and forgotten and un-assimilated infantile desires that bring strange pressures to bear on healthy adult life, as unassimilated social minorities with grievances neglected by the majority produce disproportionate political sores. But let the man who has forgotten the comforter, or for that matter its prototype, be cautious in claiming that he knows why he smokes.

Divergencies of technique.—It must now be confessed that different schools of psychoanalysts *do* find their patient's treatments taking different courses. This is to be expected. Differences in technique always yield different practical results, though inference may resolve the differences. And there are, of course, many differences in technique between the schools, particularly between those which mark the widest points of the aforementioned schisms. A strict ' Freudian ' sits behind his patient, and tries more or less to efface his own presence. A ' Jungian ' confronts his patient across a table as a friend and leader whose help should be sought by frankness. Listening to his patient's dreams, the first is on the look-out for symbols of primitive sexuality, the second for mystical signs and religious needs. An ' Adlerian ' will note the development and frustrations and compensations of his patient's ' drive for power ', a follower of Suttie his evidences of ' need for love '. I have said that many modern analysts trained by exponents of all these schools, become eclectic exponents of none, and looking for a balance between these excerpts of unconscious human motivation, try to incorporate the vastly insufficient collective wisdom of all the schools, and allow the needs and characters of their patients to determine the type of analysis they will get. But each analyst should admit what is certainly a fact, that he has his own bias of interest, determined by the bias of his training in a subject which started with a definite, indeed a truculent, dogmatism from which neither the original nor the dissenting schools can yet be said to have fully freed themselves. His bias is probably determined not less by the type of his own unconscious mind, whether in his training this has been ' analysed ' or not.

The bias of the analyst will determine to some degree the responses of his patient throughout the analysis. For the patient is talking to a personality (partly appraised, partly imagined). And at every stage of the treatment he is to some degree studying his appearance before the personality of his doctor, with his growing knowledge of a ' self ' that often appears new and dangerous to its owner. Further, even the technique of free-association is in practice frequently modified by the analyst. No device for excluding him is used. In the search for means for shortening the exhausting length of most analyses, the analyst both consciously and instinctively draws upon his knowledge (and upon his bias) to direct overtly or covertly the course of his patient's responses. A patient's associations may often be made fertile or the reverse by the tone of voice in which his doctor accepts them. Probably most experienced analysts are guilty of a scientific weakness of method here. And most can justify it by results. For a skilled ' cast ' may save weeks or months of delay, and the very similarity of cases makes skilled anticipation at once a possibility and an aim in treatment. All this naturally militates against the scientific validity of psychoanalytical material.

Fact and inference.—It is now time to mention a cardinal duty of the psychologist who wishes to make a contribution to the study of human nature with the aid of this technique of psychoanalysis. This is *the rigid separation of observed fact from inference.* Despite the bias given him by his training and by his own character, the modern analyst will still make an immense number of repeated observations which make common experience with all his colleagues. There are first the reactions characteristic of the various main types of neurosis—such as the ' hysteric ', the ' obsessional ', the ' phobic '. And there are also reactions characteristic of common ' human nature ', in that they are found in all who will submit themselves to the technique required for their manifestations. These are facts, though there is much more to be said about them. To be kept quite apart from observable facts, if any claim to scientific validity is to be made for discoveries about human nature derived from psychoanalysis, is the whole wide realm of inference.

Having said so much in the hope of making plain the object and method of psychoanalysis, and the properties of the human mind which it employs, we will now go on to consider the actual theories of human nature which have been put forward by psychologists who have drawn upon the material yielded by psychoanalysis. The psychological theories which will chiefly concern us all claim origin from the material of ' deep ' analysis —that is from the fullest possible explorations of unconscious motivation by the technique of Freud. First, and most important, are the views of Freud himself. His conclusions are very definite. We shall then consider other observers who, with Freud's technique fully open to them, came to conclusions not less definite but very different from those of the master.

II. THE FINDINGS OF FREUD IN NEUROSIS

I have said that in examining psychological data it is as necessary as in every other scientific investigation to make a strict separation between findings and inference, between fact and theory. Theoretical speculations often have to be made early in a scientific investigation, in order to direct that investigation. Their function and their provisional nature must always be recognized. And, unless they are proved to be true, they must never be allowed to masquerade subsequently as facts. In the following review of the findings of Freud, upon which he formulated his theory of human nature, it will be convenient to give the deductions which he made from his discoveries with the discoveries themselves. The two will, however, be separated by recording the *findings* in ordinary type and Freud's *inferences* in italics.

1. *Early hysterical cases of Freud.*—When Freud and Breuer,[1] his early associate, started tracing neurotic symptoms to the faulty conceptions of the mind which underlay them, they worked with patients suffering from hysteria. Both the very childlike manifestations which as laymen we recognize as frank hysteria, and the more subtle forms of ' sabotage ' of dignity and self-control—for instance the voiceless clergyman and the paralysed soldier of our earlier examples—come from repressed and conflicting emotions within the unconscious mind. All hysterical manifestations are associated with scarcely veiled anxieties. Among the most dramatic, they are also the most superficially

[1] Freud and Breuer, *Collected Papers of Freud*, vol. i. p. 24. (1892.)

disguised of all neurotic conflicts. It is the almost visible and almost voluntary departure of the mind from adult independence and rectitude towards infantile demonstrations of temper and pathos which so often tempts the onlooker to apply to the frank ' hysteric '. such rehabilitating measures as the old-fashioned cold water douche. Applying their new technique of free-association, Freud and Breuer found that hysterical patients soon passed from the immediate setting of their symptoms to emotional upsets of childhood, and that sooner or later an account was given of some early event connected with ' sexual ' emotion, although often the neurotic symptom itself had no sexual association near the surface of the mind. What Freud had discovered was that, by his new technique of mental association, a limited number of neurotics of a certain special type gave accounts of some exciting event of a sexual nature in their childhood or infancy. *Freud drew and published the conclusion that ' no neurosis is possible with a normal* vita sexualis ', and *gave it as his opinion that all hysterical patients had suffered an actual sexual assault in childhood.*[1] Later he confessed that his conclusions were based on ' a not very plentiful material containing a disproportionately large number of cases in whose infantile history seduction by adults or other older children played a part. I overestimated the frequency of these occurrences, which are otherwise quite authentic, and all the more so since I was not at that time able to discriminate between the deceptive memories of hysterics concerning their childhood and the memory-traces of actual happenings '.[2]

This was Freud's first excursion both into the collection and the evaluation of unconscious processes. Neither the difficulty of the subject, nor the newness of the technique, nor Freud's subsequent engagingly frank withdrawal, can alter the important fact that he had made two very significant blunders. First, he had allowed the assaults which *some* of his few hysterical patients were led by his method to *imagine* they had suffered in childhood to deceive him into thinking they had actually happened. This is the minor fault. But every dentist is trained to protect himself against the sexual imagination of hysterical patients under gas ; and a reasonably critical attitude would have protected Freud at least to the extent of a caveat about the validity of his patient's claims. But the much more serious fault in a ' scientific ' worker was that Freud allowed himself to apply to a finding of such obviously limited scope a deduction so full of unwarranted assumptions. A *few* patients with *one* type of neurosis *describe long past* disturbances of their sexual life. The conclusion is that *no* neurosis is compatible with a (*present*) healthy sex life !

Freud's first conclusion was doubted : his second was laughed to scorn throughout Europe. His first conclusion was wrong, and was soon discovered to be wrong by himself. But his second

[1] Freud, *Collected Papers*, vol i. p. 272. (1905.)　　　[2] Ibid. p. 276.

was the forerunner of his greatest enlightenments : it has lived
to be accepted as true for a vast field of the major neuroses, and
many of his followers hold it as strictly and universally true
to-day ! As for the early sexual event, it was its unguessed origin
in the *imagination* of the patient which made his major conclusion
so nearly correct. And it was Freud's own sympathetic imagination which enabled him to make it.

We find, then, at the outset, that Freud is highly untrust-
worthy as a strictly scientific worker. His conclusions far outstrip
his facts. Scientifically, this particular conclusion should at most
have been a provisional hypothesis, awaiting years of experimental
support. It was converted into an affirmation, *not by scientific
reasoning, but by intuition.*

2. *Early ' obsessional ' cases of Freud.*—In addition to hysterics,
there is another great group of neurotic patients, the ' obsessional '.
These include all those who are forced by ' conscience ', or by
they know not what, to live in a certain (distorted) way or to
perform certain (peculiar) actions as a means of securing peace
of mind. Freud next turned his attention to this group of individuals. Their problem is often a more general one than that
of most hysterics. Hysterics are often enough concerned with
a problem of conscience—for instance the fearful soldier whose
honour demands that he shall stay in the line until his unconscious
desires for safety prove to his satisfaction that his arm is paralysed
and cannot hold a rifle. But with them the problem tends to be
a special one. It is so much so with a soldier suffering from
' shell-shock ' that, if he could have lived his life freed from the
claims of society that he should risk his life in the stress of modern
battle, he would probably never have shown any abnormality, if
' abnormal ' such a reaction can be called. It is likely to be less
so with a voiceless clergyman ; for how comes it that his ' unconscious ' mind has attacked him in his chosen vocation ? But in
the performer of obsessional acts, of ' washing ' or other rituals,
or the avoider of certain situations, such as the ' claustrophobe '
or ' agoraphobe ', or in the more general ' obsessional character ',
with its meticulous devotion to accuracy, its unhappy over-
scrupulousness and its never-satisfied conscientiousness, we find
deeper conflicts of desire and guilt, deeper misconceptions of the
mind which extend down to fundamental relationships with
others, and often back to very near the beginnings of life.

From the first, Freud made monumental and unique contributions to knowledge in this unexplored field of research. Again, it
was not long before he found an imagined situation, borrowed
from early concepts of infancy, to which the patient was responding as if it were real. But, finding signs of obsessive sexuality
in a number of these cases, and himself still under the influence
of his early conclusion about hysterics, Freud essayed the conclusion that *in both types there had been an actual abnormal sexual*

experience in early life—he suggested between the ages of two and five—in which the obsessional patient had played an active part, where his counterpart, the hysteric, had suffered a passive rôle.[1] Considering how very few of these long and difficult cases Freud can have analysed at all fully at that time, and remembering how both obsessional and hysterical groups shade off to merge with vast numbers of ordinary folk, the conclusion was again a very bold one. He later came to realize what an extreme over-simplification of a whole character-type he had made. His own modifications of his theory have been so much further modified since, that a doctor commencing an analysis of a neurotic patient to-day will look forward to great varieties of possibilities of infantile notions concerning all the recollectable sensations of the body (including those of ' infantile sexuality ' which Freud intuitively foresaw and seized), and in those recollections there will be an arrangement of ' active ' and ' passive ' traits of great technical interest, but no such antithesis between the child mind of the hysteric and the obsessional as Freud's active imagination painted.

3. *Sexuality and aggressiveness in psychoanalysis.*—Freud continued to put forward firmly and repeatedly his theory of the sexual origin of the neuroses —e.g. : ' Detailed investigations during the last few years have led me to the conviction that factors arising in sexual life represent the nearest and practically the most momentous causes of every single case of nervous illness.' [2] The cold reception given to this view by his medical colleagues made manifest in him a sense of mission in the face of inevitable persecution. ' I belonged ', he said, ' to those who have disturbed the sleep of the world. . . . To stir up contradiction and arouse bitterness is the inevitable fate of psychoanalysis. . . .'[3] But my confidence in my own judgment was by no means slight.'[4] He was temporarily deeply shaken, however, by his error in mistaking for real the imagined assaults suffered by hysterics in their recollections of childhood. ' I persevered only because I had no choice and could not then begin again at anything else.' But ' at last there came the reflection that one must not despair at being deceived in expectations, but revise them.'[5] Thereafter his pertinacity appears to have been unfailing. He courageously sacrificed his reputation,[6] and temporarily his medical practice, to his theory, and pursued it with the utmost vigour, ' in spite of all difficulties '.[7] First he described the phenomenon of ' transference ', by which the patient's mind transfers some of its earlier emotions, good or bad and often most fluctuating and varied, from their former objects (e.g. mother, father, nurse, husband, wife) to the analyst. But this transference, in Freud's experience, was either of a sexual nature

---

[1] Freud, *Collected Papers,* vol. i. p. 149. (1896.)
[2] Ibid. p. 220. (1898).   [3] Ibid. p. 288.   [4] Ibid. p. 304.
[5] Ibid. p. 299.   [6] Ibid. p. 221.   [7] Ibid. p. 296.

or else a reactive hostility against sexual affinity. And '*the fact of this transference appearing, although neither desired nor induced by physician or patient, in every neurotic who comes up for treatment, in its crude sexual, affectionate or hostile form, has always seemed to me the most irrefragable proof that the source of the propelling forces of neuroses lies in the sexual life*'.[1]

There is no need to stress unduly Freud's interest in sexual matters, his sexual curiosity. It is very strong, and without it he would never have given us in one lifetime almost every conceivable ramification of sexual feeling in the unconscious life of man. His own view was that a thirst for knowledge was inseparable from sexual curiosity, and that sexual precocity and intellectual precocity went together. It is, however, necessary to note how the apparent disproportion of this interest in Freud did bias both his findings and his interpretations. It may also be thought by many to have biased his judgment of ' normal ' behaviour. Two quotations will suffice : '*Fidelity, especially that degree of it required in marriage, is only maintained in the face of continual temptation. Anyone who denies this uses unconscious mechanisms as a protection.*'[2] And, of a girl of fourteen who was disgusted by an unexpected and sudden kiss from a married man, he writes : '*I should unhesitatingly consider a person hysterical in whom an occasion for sexual excitement elicited feelings that were preponderantly or exclusively unpleasurable. Genital sensation would unquestionably have been felt by a healthy girl in such circumstances.*'[3] Let the reader judge these remarks for him- and herself. And he may take it that if he had been fully psychoanalysed the chances are that his judgments would still be much the same.

Freud soon extended from the neurotic to the normal man his theory that physical sexuality is an instinct at almost all times overriding all others, whether its operation is overt or repressed by unconscious conflict. '*In normal character-formation either no repression occurs or it easily attains its aim, which is to replace the repressed impulses by reaction-formations and sublimations.*'[4] He traced the complexity given to ' sexual ' manifestations by erotic sensations from organs not those of generation, but associated with those organs by anatomical contiguity or else linked with them by common sensory nerve-tracts or by associations of ideas in the mind. By him we were forced to recognize that ' erotic ' elements enter into sensations of early infancy, and that not only the misconceptions of hysterical and obsessional neurotics but also those causing sexual perversions are traceable to strange confusions and interplay of sensation in very early life. During his analysis of the minds of sufferers from these various derangements Freud continued his attempt not only to

[1] Freud, *Collected Papers*, vol. i. p. 293.   [2] Ibid. vol. ii. p. 233.
[3] Ibid. vol. iii. p. 37.   [4] Ibid. vol. ii. p. 126.

describe type mechanisms for the distortions with which he was dealing, but also to discover thes ignificant sensations and the early logics common to normal mental development.

It was a gigantic task. Freud made the most of every clue. It is impossible to do justice to his skill in tracing the ramifications of hatred as well as of sexuality in the unconscious mind. He discovered the infantile furies of that emotion, the infantile logics of its various discharges, its seeming dangers, and the consequent need of the repression from which it might emerge in later life to produce a symptom or to modify a character. He found, for instance, that the hyper-conscientiousness of his obsessional patients led back to a fear of punishment for (repressed) aggressive designs against others. Sometimes such people had combined their primitive aggressive impulses to smash and annihilate with sexual fantasies (' sadism '), and sometimes they imagined themselves being the victims of some such combination of suffering and sexuality (' masochism '). Such qualities Freud found to be repulsive to the other ' self ' which he artificially separated from the ego, the ' super-ego ' or conscience. He drew wide inferences about the mechanism and significance of his findings in these sufferers. Again, many of these inferences were extended to ' normal ' men. Sometimes Freud met with conspicuous success, as when he forced on an unwilling world the broad generalizations of his ' Oedipus Complex ' as an all but universal landmark in the development of the sex-life of the individual, or when he insisted on the importance of the ' auto-erotism ' of infancy ' which such astonishing trouble had been taken to overlook '.[1] But in all cases where his intuition was true for limited types of individual but his findings were generalized to cover all humanity, or where what was required was an evaluation of degree (as where a sexual-aggressive mechanism is off-set by totally different desires and needs of the human psyche), Freud tended to mislead.

From his studies of the hyper-conscientiousness of obsessional patients, Freud's active imagination led him to formulate the following conclusions. First, *he gave primacy to the ' positive '* (' *sadistic* ') *impulses, and imagined the passive (' masochistic ') ones as resulting from a thwarting of the former* based upon the argument : ' I can't hurt others, so I'll be hurt myself '. Next he concluded that *except in special circumstances constitution and not environment determines the type (obsessional, hysterical, etc.) of a neurosis.* He separated the ' self ' (' ego ') of the individual from the stream of his desires (' libido '). And, because a façade of conscious virtue was drawn over the unconscious aggressiveness of the obsessional patient, he again inferred that *aggressiveness takes the primary place*, and that *hate is the precursor of love*. Finally, because of certain similarities between the excessive conscientiousness and virtue of some obsessional characters and the con-

[1] Freud, *Collected Papers*, vol. i. p. 301.

sciences of ' normal ' men, Freud hazarded that his colleague
Stekel was right in saying that *hate not love is the primary state of
feeling between human beings*.[1]

4. *The ' primacy ' of aggressiveness and sexuality—case material.*
—We must now describe the importance given by Freud to
sexuality and aggressiveness in normal character formation, the
sources of his evidence, and his methods of inference.

There is a famous essay of Freud's entitled '*A child is being
beaten* '.[2] In it Freud recounts the mental associations of patients
who suffer from this persistent fantasy of a child suffering a
beating. The fantasy becomes conscious in obsessional patients
who are ready to deal in their psychoanalysis with events in
their childhood which drew out either aggressive and sadistic
impulses or suffering and masochistic desires in them. Such
cases show a now well-recognized yield of ' obsessional ' interests
—great curiosity, precocious and perverse desires, aggressive
' sadisms ' against the mother, passive ' masochisms ' from the
father, are all recoverable from the fantasy life of their childhood.
But Freud laid down an *order* of the development of the child's
ideas about being beaten ; an inflexible order such as that which
he attached to the Oedipus Complex. First, the fantasy starts
' not later than the fifth or sixth year '. Next, the first object of
the imagined beating is ' the child which the patient hates, a rival
brother or sister '. This enables the patient to argue : ' My
father doesn't love my brother or sister : he loves only me '.
According to Freud, the next ' phase ' is a reaction of guilt, the
child saying to itself : ' He *doesn't* love you. And it's *you* he's
beating ! ' By this means original ' sadism ' is converted into
' masochism ', and ' so far as I know ', adds Freud, ' *a sense of
guilt is invariably the factor that transforms sadism into masochism* '.[3]
A little later he writes : ' *There seems to be a confirmation of the
view that masochism is not the manifestation of a primary instinct
but originates from sadism, which has been turned round and directed
to the self. . . . Guilt is the cause of the transference : it takes as
much objection to sadism as to incest* '.[4]

As far as I know neither Freud nor any subsequent writer
has produced any *evidence* of a primacy of sadism over masochism, either in time of development or in infantile logic. As for
the former, an historical temporal order for the development of
infantile fantasy cannot be achieved, except for the broad and
tentative divisions of infantile history which have been made
from the study of large numbers of cases. Even so, the inextric-
able combinations of personal heredity and particular environment blur the edges of the divisions which have so far been made.
But the admitted association of masochism with excretory interests might suggest to an analyst who followed a widely held view

[1] Freud, *Collected Papers*, vol. ii. p. 131. (1913.)
[2] Ibid. p. 172. [3] Ibid. p. 184. [4] Ibid. p. 189.

of Freud himself that it was likely to have origins *earlier* than those of the ' phallic ' sexuality which associates technically with the sadism of these cases. In the matter of *logical* (as against temporal) order, a case of the writer's has points of interest to set against this sequence of Freud's. First, the patient, as an only child, was able to contradict Freud's assertion that the first object of jealousy *is* a brother or sister apparently receiving preference from the patient's father. A paraphrase of my own patient's derivations of her beating fantasy appears in the record of case notes (Case B, Chap. IV, p. 132). In her case, the excitement, which was partly pleasure, partly pain, came from the fact that she imagined *herself* being beaten by a loved father. And, when the beating became too painful, she imagined that she reacted by refusing to suffer further, and by turning in fury from the passive to the active rôle. This, combined with certain facts' of anatomical and psychological association which heighten the value of the part of the body beaten (the buttocks), appeared to be the essence of this particular complex in this particular patient. For her, the order of Freud was reversed, her masochism took pride of place and her sadism was reactionary.

This one case is a commentary on Freud's tendency to wide generalizations about mechanisms, and also upon the dogmatism about order in which he was so unjustified. But aggressive reactions are so various and deep in such cases as these that it seems to me to be quite impossible to say that there is *not* in them an abnormal tendency to react to life in an aggressive way from the very first. They are also voluptuous and egotistical : they desire to drain the cup of physical pleasure to the dregs. But when pleasure becomes associated with pain, then either an attempt at fusion, or an angry reprisal, takes shape in the patient's mind. Whether to ' suffer in silence ' or ' take arms ' remains (for primacy of reaction) an open question.

As for the sense of guilt which these patients suffer, there can be little doubt that Freud is right in attributing it to an awareness or an apprehension at once of hostile and voluptuous personal desires and of their futility and dangerousness. This guilt-sense certainly goes very deeply into their characters, which have been built up amidst the constant demand for two incompatible things—the gratification of every competitive and aggressive and voluptuous desire on the one hand, and on the other that love and care shall pour in from the outside world in an unceasing and reassuring stream. The demands of the self are so insistent, and require such discipline, that we may say of the large sense of guilt which these sufferers have, that they very badly need it. Though it may at times become intolerable, it is this sense of guilt which keeps them ' straight ', which replaces the ' give and take ' in the lives of more happily endowed people. For it must be remembered that throughout the whole of this all too technical discussion, we have been dealing with abnormal people, people whose very stress is at the point of how to reconcile incompatible urges of great power, those of desire and love, of gain and security. Freud himself started by admitting the abnormal nature of his material : ' We must remember that we are dealing with children in whom the sadistic component was able *for constitutional reasons* to develop prematurely and in isolation '.[1] Whatever the reasons, these characters certainly have an abnormal problem of adjustment to society throughout their whole lives. The demands of self are more insistent, intolerance with thwarting is greater, friendliness is harder to achieve for them than for others ; mistrust is present from early days. (See e.g. Case C., Chapter IV, p. 135.) All this is not necessarily ' constitutional '. But it does render such characters a valuable study for the social psychologist.

What no extant study of obsessional neurosis does is to justify any of the following :

(1) An assumed order of historical primacy of sadism over masochism.

(2) An assumed primacy of importance of sadism over masochism.

(3) The assumption that mechanisms actually or supposedly present in these obsessional cases—and where present especially necessary to a solution of their problems—may be inferred *ex hypothesi* as part of the normal development of normal character— But all these things Freud did ! We will now study the evidences by which he sought to establish his theory of human nature in its social relationship, and to the arguments he used. This time, however, we will place *evidence* cited from case material in italics so that it may be clearly separated from discussion and theory.

III. FREUD'S THEORY OF HUMAN NATURE—CASE MATERIAL (IN ITALICS) AND DISCUSSION

1. *The general attitude of man to life.*—' The sovereign tendency of the unconscious is to fulfil the pleasure principle '.[2] So wrote Freud in 1911. The mind of man seeks its own gratification, and where it cannot attain this by appreciating reality it will turn to dream and fantasy. The conscious mind is disturbed by the moral considerations introduced by conscience. But ' conscience is only a dread of the community. And when the community has no rebuke to make there is an end of all suppression of the baser passions, and men perpetrate deeds of cruelty, fraud, treachery, and barbarity so incompatible with their civilization that one would have held them to be impossible ' (' Thoughts on War and Death ', 1915).[3] Thus the only limitations

---

[1] Freud, *Collected Papers*, vol. ii. p. 184.   [2] Ibid. vol. iv. p. 14.
[3] Ibid. p. 288.

set to man's search for personal pleasure are set by his dread of the community, of his fellows. Apart from that his life would be one of thoughtless optimism. ' In the unconscious, every one of us is convinced of his own immortality.' And ' the first and most portentous prohibition : " Thou shalt not kill ", was merely a reaction against an underlying gratification of hatred in the death of others '.[1]

A little later Freud began to doubt whether conscience alone sufficed to explain the ' renunciation of manifold possibilities of pleasure and the temporary endurance of pain on the long and circuitous road to pleasure '.[2] We have already seen how he was disturbed by the problem of the desire to suffer pain, and the curious fusions of pleasure and pain which occur in masochism. In *Beyond the Pleasure Principle* he tried to establish a goal of unconscious human effort lying beyond the motives of self gratification which he found so prominently displayed in the ' unconscious ' minds of his patients.

Here Freud had very little clinical material to go upon. But he felt intuitively that gratification of the senses did not suffice as a complete description of human endeavour. Freud was still considering the individual in isolation, so to speak—in fact the reactions elicited by the two processes of psychoanalysis and intro-spection—and not man's behaviour when in a group or society, to which he turned a year or two subsequently. He already regarded pleasure as a ' relief of tension ' ;[3] and it seems a natural turn of his mind which brought it into line with the Buddhist principle of ' nirvana '—that man's search is for relief from pain rather than for positive pleasure, and that behind the ' pleasure-principle ' there lies in every man the desire for the final peace of death.

Now, as an intuitive feeling, or as an idea, there is nothing remarkable about this conception. ' Besides being a cardinal doctrine of one of the great religious philosophies of the world, it finds its way into the literature of all cultures, and is often implied in the serious speech of old and young alike, though perhaps it is as often denied. It is clearly one among the deeper feelings of the human mind : or at least it is a frequent attitude to life of certain minds. It is quite possibly an attitude often held repressed in the unconscious mind, in contradiction to Freud's earlier assertion, quoted above, about the universal unconscious affirmation of immortality. Such a repression is not disproved by the fact that most analysts have found it remarkably difficult to elicit this sentiment as repressed material on a par with such repressions as voluptuousness, aggressiveness, or a fearful search for love. But in *Beyond the Pleasure Principle* Freud gives the impression that he has been forced to this second and ultimate aim of man's unconscious mind by the reactions of his patients

[1] Freud, *Collected Papers*, vol. iv. p. 305.
[2] Freud, *Beyond the Pleasure Principle*, p. 5. (1920.)   [3] Ibid. pp. 2, 3.

in deep psychoanalysis. Or perhaps it is fairer to put it that Freud is liable to be misunderstood as to the authority with which he affirms that the ' goal of life is death ', because he is assumed by the layman to be drawing upon sources of knowledge, at once beyond and more reliable than those accessible to our conscious reasoning. That is not so. Even the most strict school of his followers are divided in their adherence to this point of his doctrine ; and this division must in all probability depend less on their patients than on themselves. Furthermore, on this matter Freud's own factual support for his theory is of an order totally different from his repeatable and repeated findings in the sexual neuroses. We will endeavour to repeat it faithfully, though in summary.

Freud cites five pieces of evidence in support of the ' deathwish ' which underlies the ' pleasure-principle ' :

(1) *Patients suffering from what is called a ' traumatic neurosis ', that is to say one the symptoms of which have been precipitated by an injury, are found not infrequently to dream about their accidents.*[1] This fact of common experience should meet with no sort of theoretical difficulty in explanation. Traumatic neurosis is usually predominantly an ' anxiety state ' ; and dreams which are at once the product and the recapitulation of states of anxiety are common enough in practice, though they are in conflict with Freud's personal theory that dreams always express the fulfilment of a wish. Freud retains his theory in the face of these facts, and thus concludes that ' the expedient is left us ' of supposing the dream function peculiarly dislocated in these cases, or else that these patients did in some way desire to relive their accident ! He favours the second alternative—the dreams are masochistic, and the patients must *desire* to relive their unhappy experience.[1]

(2) *The behaviour of a little boy of eighteen months, not intellectually forward but of ' a good reputation for behaving properly. He did not disturb his parents at night ; he scrupulously obeyed orders about not touching various objects and not going into certain rooms '. He showed the ' remarkable cultural development ' first of being willing to let his mother leave him without creating a disturbance, and second of hiding his toys for the (' delayed ') pleasure of their rediscovery.* This complacent child subsequently showed no regret when his mother died, but Freud regarded his behaviour as a striking example of ' willingness to suffer pain on the circuitous route to pleasure '.[2]

(3) *Children often react to alarming or unpleasant experiences by replaying them in games.*[3]

(4) *On the stage, tragedy is played to the enjoyment of the audience*—another fact alleged to support man's delight in ' reliving ' unpleasant experiences.[4]

[1] Freud, *Beyond the Pleasure Principle*, p. 10.
[2] Ibid. p. 11.   [3] Ibid. p. 15.   [4] Ibid. p. 16.

(5) *In psychoanalysis, patients often have to be forced against their wills to repeat, as if current, an experience which has been repressed because it was painful.* He holds that this is because a part of the mind which dislikes the experience, the ' coherent ego ', represses a ' deeper ' desire to relive it.[1]

That is the material. Only two of the evidences, the first and the last, are drawn from psychoanalysis. The first is widely taken to-day at its face value, as a limited refutation of Freud's theory of dreams. The last is in reality a point in refutation of this particular claim that the ' self ' *desires* to repeat its misfortunes. As such it has the wealth of the endless findings of Freud, and all other analysts, in support of the pleasure principle behind it. Freud only solves his self-made difficulty by the invention of a new, deeper, and more elusive level of the mind, in conflict with that which appears so abundantly both in real life and in analysis. The weight of the remaining three evidences can be judged as well by the layman as by the psychologist.

We now turn to the superimposed theory. Freud set himself the task of finding, not evidence, but arguments for man's under-lying desire to die. On the strength of the five points I have quoted, he postulated a fundamental desire of the human mind to repeat previous experiences—a ' *repetition-compulsion* ', which, by hypothesis, is ' more primitive than the pleasure-principle which it displaces '.[2] He then devised a mechanistic theory of mental functioning which required diagrams of a ' spatial ' analogy, and the metaphor of painful discharges ' breaking through ', being ' bound ' and ' discharged ' by special means which allow the pleasure impulses to remain ' free '.[3] He himself characterized this portion of his work as ' speculation, often far-fetched . . . the exploitation of an idea to see where it will lead '.[4] There follows an excursion to consider the nature of ' instinct ', the function of which he defines as ' impelling towards the re-instatement of an earlier condition ',[5] a definition which seems to mistake method for object, as strikingly as if such a definition was allotted, say, to fishing. The ' repetition-compulsion ' thus becomes a fundamental ' instinct '. ' It would be counter to the conservative nature of instinct,' writes Freud, ' if the goal of life were a state never yet reached. It must rather be an ancient starting-point, which the living being left long ago, and to which it harks back by all the circuitous paths of development '. ' The goal of all life is death. The inanimate was there before the animate.'[6]

This argument may state a truth. But it bears so clearly the evidences of being itself the fulfilment of a wish, and the grounds for each step of it are so slender and so selected, that as an argu-ment it merits little consideration. With ' Golden Age ' philo-

[1] Freud, *Beyond the Pleasure Principle*, p. 18.   [2] Ibid. p. 25.
[3] Ibid. p. 42.   [4] Ibid. p. 26.   [5] Ibid. p. 46.   [6] Ibid. p. 47.

sophy we are familiar, as with the notion of eternal circles of life.
But the present balance of biological knowledge opposes the view
of instincts and developments as being essentially unprogressive.
And while psychological evidence may be adduced in support of
a ' death-wish '—or at least of an acquiescence in extinction,
which is not the same thing—there is no present justification of
which I am aware (and Freud certainly gives none) for elevating
that particular adaptation of the mind into prominence over the
' pleasure-principle ' or the desires of life and love.

Freud next made an antithesis between the instinct of the
' ego ' towards death, and the sexual impulse passing on from
man to man through reproduction towards eternal life. To
complete the picture, he sought evidence of ' repetition-
compulsion ' in the sexual instinct itself.[1] He could only find it
in a legend of the Veda, and in a drunken story which Plato
attributes to Aristophanes in the *Symposium*, that of man and
woman originally being one, and for ever attempting reunion.[2]
In posing his question he had said he did not know how to
answer it.[3] Having at last reached this answer, he adds : ' I do
not know how far I believe this '.[4] But he affirms thus early :
' I do not *believe* (and the verb should be noted) in an inner
impulse towards perfection. . . . The restless striving of a
minority of men towards further perfection is easily explicable
as the result of a repression of instinct upon which what is most
valuable in human culture is built '.[5] In fact, *for Freud, only
impulsions to hatred, erotism, and death are real instincts*. But what
is it that we satisfy with the ' valuable repressions ' which ' build
our culture ', and the ' inturned aggressiveness ' and the ' fear of
society ' which develop our conscience ? Are these less fundamental to man's nature than the repetition-compulsions listed
above ? Freud thought they were. And he passed on to consider
man's attitude to his fellows in society. Freud had made his
intuitive, his feeling judgments on the unconscious aims of man,
and had searched high and low for arguments in their support.
Of those which he found, not one appears to be a legitimate inference from the mass of analytical material available. The
feeling that Freud is probably right will arise in doctors and
laymen whose minds are in sympathy with his in these matters.
At present the *evidence* necessary to put the theory of a ' death-
instinct ' or ' death-wish ' upon a footing of equality with the
surer of Freud's discoveries about unconscious motivation must
be said to be entirely lacking.

2. *The attitude of man to others.*—We must again recall that,
in his analysis of the phenomena of sadism and masochism, Freud
elected to regard aggressiveness and delight in hurting others as
a primary quality, and self-humiliation and delight in suffering

---

[1] Freud, *Beyond the Pleasure Principle*, p. 54.
[2] Ibid. p. 74.   [3] Ibid. p. 55.   [4] Ibid. p. 76.   [5] Ibid. p. 52.

hurt from others as a revulsion of this upon the self under the minatory influence of that conscience which is only ' a dread of society '. In *Beyond the Pleasure Principle* he had affirmed his belief in a desire for death as being more fundamental than a desire for joy. He next attempted to place this ' death-instinct ' behind the original aggressiveness of sadism so that sadism became a projection on to an external object, that is on to someone else,[1] of a man's own desire to die. With no support at all from psycho-analytical findings, Freud surmised : (1) that a man wished himself hurt because his dread of society prevented him wishing others hurt, and (2) that he wished others hurt or dead because of a displacement of an original desire to die himself. It is impossible to avoid this sounding ridiculous. Practical studies of masochism have much enriched knowledge since these theories were first put forward : they are important because it is upon his views of that period that Freud built his whole conception of man in society. The process was as follows :

In *Group Psychology and the Analysis of the Ego* (1921) he considered the behaviour of individuals in crowds. He quoted *Le Bon's* observations [2] on the fickleness, impulsive irritability, and childlike omnipotence and credulity of crowds, and attributed these qualities to a discarding of the repressions with which fear modified the conduct of the isolated individual. He further noted that crowds are at once intolerant and obedient to authority.[3] And, curiously, while he regards the conduct of isolated individuals as ' animated almost solely by personal interests ', with the individual in a crowd he sees chiefly ' abnegation and unselfish idealism '. Unlike *McDougall* [4] in his study of group ' sentiments ', Freud makes no distinction between the impetuous common actions of mobs, and the attitude of individuals to or in a society in which they retain their full individuality. The two conditions are clearly poles apart. Members of a mob surrender to a common impulse of a low intellectual and a variable moral order—such as cheering, or jeering, or charging, or panicking—filled with the feelings of power or danger, joy or grief, which animate those around them, sharing with them this ' herd instinct ' as it was so well studied by Trotter.[5] In contrast with this, the responsible member of a group has to attempt that highest attainment of the individual, a balance between self-interest and social obligation which alone will make for his success in a successful community. Most of our life is not lived in crowds. But a need and a sense of social obligation is constantly present in us, and requires the study of a psychology more broadly based than that of Freud. Many men recognize themselves to be below their best selves

[1] Freud, *Beyond the Pleasure Principle*, p. 70.
[2] Le Bon, *The Crowd*. (1903.)
[3] Freud, *Group Psychology and the Analysis of the Ego*, pp. 9 et seq. (1921.)
[4] McDougall, *Social Psychology*, chaps. v to ix. (1908.)
[5] Trotter, *Instincts of the Herd in Peace and War*. (1916.)

when they are in crowds ; and men with strong senses of social obligation often avoid crowds, perhaps because of their awareness of the reduced control of both their hostile and orgiastic emotions which follows surrender to mob sentiment. Crowd feeling is often that of a group against hostile forces outside it, and counter hostility is pooled as well as the fellow-feeling. A member of a social group as such, has his hostility to canalize or repress on his own. And both greater self-control and higher sacrifice of individual interest are demanded of a man when he discharges his obligations *towards* rather than *with* a community of which he is a member. A man in a crowd identifies his sense of *meum* with that of others, and sinks his sense of *tuum*. A true social instinct requires a constant awareness of *meum* and *tuum*. These distinctions, appreciated and studied by McDougall, are all passed over by Freud. To him, a self-sacrificing *individual* is ' masochistic ', has turned daggers intended for others against himself. But what interests him here is not the individual as such, but the almost hypnotized docility and willingness for sacrifice of members of a sort of idealized mob. The members of an unorganized mob are probably seldom very self-sacrificing ; and this ' mass of men ' imagined by Freud, is more in the nature of a well-trained and devoted army. Indeed he discards Trotter's views of the herd and its instincts because for Freud a herd must have a leader.[1] Why ? To fit his definition of a ' primary group ' which is ' a number of individuals who have substituted one and the same object for their ego-ideal, and have consequently identified themselves with one another in their ego '.[2]

The ' ego-ideal ' (or ' super-ego ') is the conscience, which we have seen Freud derive from a fear of punishment from society for the natural, and to him always self-seeking and aggressive, impulses of the individual. It is the self-hatred which follows the fearful repression of a natural hatred of others. So Freud's individual in a crowd has surrendered at once his conscience, his self-control, and his self-hatred. Then he should no longer be capable of self-sacrifice or masochism ! Yet he is. So Freud thinks of the individual in a crowd as essentially hypnotized. And the hypnotist (or leader) has replaced the ' ego-ideal ', i.e. the conscience.[3] He is left completely without an explanation for the fact that in *hypnotism, though the subject becomes widely* ' *suggestible* ', *the* ' *moral conscience shows independence and resistance to influence* '.[4] This was a finding which should have made him doubt his source of conscience in the external repressions of the ego by the super-ego. For here is a residual ego which is more moral than its master !

Freud continued his study of this highly peculiar ' crowd ' which he had imagined—and continued to regard it as the type

---

[1] *Group Psychology and the Analysis of the Ego*, p. 85.
[2] Ibid. p. 80.　　　　[3] Ibid. p. 78.　　　　[4] Ibid. p. 79.

of all society. Borrowing the finding of psychoanalysis that *the mind of a child may ' identify ' itself with a loved or a hated person* (e.g. *a loved mother or a cruel father*), *imagining itself as that person and acting accordingly*, he argues that since, *ex hypothesi*, men start as individuals hating each other, and since, again *ex hypothesi*, they end as members of a crowd with exhibitions of a self-sacrificing devotion to each other, some such process of ' identification ' has occurred in them ; so that they now emphasize their common love for their father-leader rather than their jealous hatred of each other. This attitude can secure stability only through their ' absolute equality '. Hence it is implemented by the Hobbesian demand that each shall renounce the advantages of freedom and power so that others shall do so too. ' Social justice means that we deny ourselves many things so that others shall have to do without them too. . . . This demand for equality is the root of social conscience.' [1] Freud's mind, here, as subsequently, has so close a resemblance to that of Hobbes that his phrases are almost identical. The difference is that, while Hobbes [2] looks for arguments to the philosophy and religion of his day, Freud turns to psychoanalysis. For evidence he is content with this mechanism of ' identification '. It is true that in psychoanalysis it is not infrequent to find that a veneer of loving (which deceives the patient himself) may cover a great deal of dislike and hatred. This may be a hatred of individuals or it may spread into an attitude to society as a whole. Such an attitude, where widespread in the personality, can always be traced to some cardinal misconceptions of infancy. It is characteristic of the obsessional character (See Chapter IV, Case C). Freud claims, without justification, and in the face of the evidences of analysis of ' normal ' people, that such a mechanism is not only universal but that it lies at the root of society. In this essay on the ' crowd ', which claims to be a study of society, he concludes : ' Social feeling is based upon the conversion of what was first a hostile feeling into a positively toned (loving) identification. . . . So far as we have been able to follow the course of events, this reversal appears to be effected under the influence of a common tender tie with a person outside the group . . . the preliminary condition being that they shall all be loved in the same way by one person, the leader '.[1] For Freud, society has a family basis. But it is not the ' aggregate of families ' of Bodin, but rather one large family created by the identification of a band of jealous ' brothers ' to secure an equal share in the love of a ' leader father '. The father which Freud's imagination painted was a ruthless one. He 'loved no one but himself, or others only as they served his needs '. The sexual element is introduced, and Freud imagines this father-leader of common human fantasy ' forcing ' all his sons into a sort of passive, feminine

[1] *Group Psychology and the Analysis of the Ego*, p. 87.   [2] q.v. p. 13.

attitude to his own dominance.[1] Here he is drawing upon a deep unconscious trait of some obsessional cases (see Case C.) in which a loved father has become viewed in infancy from something akin to the imagined angle of the child's mother. A point of note is that Freud does not give the impression that this view of society is to him a fantasy in the unconscious mind of its members. He seems to suggest that at some archaic epoch these events actually happened, and speaks, e.g. of the actions of this imagined father as if they were real : ' He *forced* his sons into sexual abstinence ', etc. So that it is impossible from reading this monograph to decide whether Freud believed that he was exposing a fantasy of all mankind, which he himself shared the less by having exposed it, or whether he felt he was describing an actual origin of society. In the latter event, it is difficult to note the close similarity between his view and that which can be elucidated as peculiar to patients of ' obsessional character ', and avoid the conclusion that Freud was not abstracting a fantasy from the common mind of man, but *endowing that mind with a fantasy of his own, a type fantasy of a certain type of mind.*

Freud's theory of the origins of society is as schematic as that of Hobbes, and requires certain basic conceptions in Freud similar to those of Hobbes. These are : (1) *That men as individuals naturally hate each other.* Both philosopher and psychologist go back to the domestic hearth in collecting their evidence—Hobbes to the precautions a man takes against the members of his own household, Freud to the nursery, where ' elder children would certainly like to put their successors jealously aside . . . rob them of their privileges. And at school, ' the first demand is for justice, that no one else shall be the favourite . . . *Esprit de corps* was originally envy '.[2] (2) *That society is a mere* modus vivendi, *a product of the very necessity of man's eternal aggressiveness against his fellows,* and its machinery as surely a result of the dire necessity of original human nature, as for Milton and his Roman Catholic predecessors it was the result of the Fall of Adam. The scanty citations from his own analytic experience which support Freud's views in their development up to this point will have been noted. What occurs is merely that Freud uses *excerpts* of the findings and mechanisms of psychoanalysis in support of intuitive views, upon as definite a bias as are the selections which Hobbes makes from the surface manifestations of man. It is in part his additional knowledge of unconscious mechanisms, and in part no doubt a divergence of interest from that of Hobbes, which makes Freud complete his picture in the peculiar way he does.

Freud elaborated the unconscious sexual elements in his grounding of society in a separate essay,[3] drawing his material

---

[1] *Group Psychology and the Analysis of the Ego*, p. 92. [2] Ibid. p. 87.
[3] Freud, *Collected Papers*, vol. ii. p. 232.

this time from cases of sexual perversion. *In several cases of homosexuality, he found that ' during early childhood feelings of jealousy derived from the mother-complex and of very great intensity arose against rivals, usually older brothers. This jealousy led to an exceedingly hostile aggressive attitude to the brothers or sisters concerned. It might culminate in actual death-wishes. But it could not survive the influence of training and its own constant powerlessness. . . . It was repressed, so that the rivals of the earlier period became the first homosexual love-objects. . . .* This represents, too, an exaggeration of the process which, according to my view, leads to the birth of social instinct in the individual. . . . In both processes there is first the presence of jealous and hostile feelings which cannot achieve gratification. Then feelings of personal affection and social identification arise as reaction formations against the repressed aggressive impulses '.[1]

Here it becomes difficult to make our separation between adduced fact and inferential deduction. The last (unitalicized) portion of the above quotation is certainly inferential. Neither Freud nor any other analyst is in a position to state that normal feelings of personal affection and of social ' identification ' *are* reactions against aggressive impulses which cannot be gratified. Freud here recognizes that fact : some of his followers have been less cautious. But elements of inference are also discernible in Freud's quoted reactions of his abnormal, homosexual patients. Jealousy among brothers for the love of a mother may arise and lead to aggressive hostility and projected death wishes. But what, in his case notes, corresponded with his statement that ' It could not survive the influence of training ' ? The answer is ' It was repressed ', forgotten, to emerge in distorted form as an unnatural trait in after life. That means that ' free-association ' led the patient from his symptoms back, first to his ' attraction ' to his brothers, ' behind ' which was then discovered an intense hostility towards them. The hostility had been thwarted ' by its constant powerlessness ', and by the influences brought to bear on him to show love and kindness to his brothers, which probably constituted his ' training '. When these thoughts were recaptured in analysis, the hostility vanished, and either the old affectionate feeling returned or a new feeling of affection took its place. The introduction of the sexual element which distorts normal into abnormal affection is a matter into the intricacies of which Freud does not enter in this connexion. But what he recounts from his analytical notes leads us to infer the retention in the unconscious mind of traces both of hostility and of abnormal ' love ' to brothers in early life. This is the condition of ' ambivalence ' which is a characteristic feature both of obsessional cases and of those of sexual perversion (see e.g. Case A., Chapter IV, p. 130). Thus if we annotate this quotation of Freud's, which

[1] Freud, *Collected Papers*, vol. ii. p. 242.

takes his conclusion into the sexual sphere and beyond that of
Hobbes, we may rewrite it as follows : In certain cases of
homosexuality Freud unearthed—as with the technique which
he has given us it is comparatively easy for us to unearth—
childhood jealousies which appear to be linked with the 'Oedipus'
complex—a phase of infantile erotism of which the mother is the
object and which often occasions jealousy of the father. In these
particular cases Freud noted an intense hostility against rivals—
usually older brothers—which might even culminate in desires
for their death. On the other hand it was easier to find affectionate attitudes towards these brothers, though the affections
were liable (in memory or in fantasy) to develop perverted trends
similar to those for which the patient had claimed treatment.
That is the end of the case note. One reaction may 'underlie'
another. One may be more 'fundamental' than another. One
may 'repress' another. Or alternatively, different associations
(real or analytical) may call up differing responses. My patient,
Mr. A., could be made loving or angry with his father over and
over again in the analytical setting. Freud's conception is that
the aggressiveness is always the fundamental reaction in analysis,
and in real life too. Suttie, to whose opposing views we shall
presently come, regards love as fundamental, and all aggressiveness as resulting from thwarting. The neuro-physiologist, who
knows nothing of these 'layers' of emotional responses or of
'pockets' of pent-up 'libido', would look for the explanation of
varying responses in variations of the form of stimulation applied,
without invoking the question of 'fundamental' responses at all.
It is for the future to evolve improving theories as the facts to be
accounted for become clearer, and are added to. All Freud has
here described is a variability of response between emotional
attraction and hostile raging over the same object, a brother.
And this 'ambivalence' is now known to be very common in
the depths of the minds of the particular type of neurotic with
which he was dealing, as it is also in most cases a very common
phenomenon much nearer to the surface of their minds. It is
primarily not by Freud's *reason* but by his *feeling* that such a
phenomenon with such an interpretation is made a basis of
society. In fact it forms no such basis.[1]

3. *The development of social conscience.*—Freud's theories of
the social relationships of man would have been treated with
much less deference than they were if it were not that he had
previously substantiated a claim to have acquired an access to
motives and mechanisms of the human mind which had been

[1] A year or two later, in another monograph, Freud himself throws a doubt
upon a parallel interpretation of his. 'The ambivalence shown in regard to
parents may even be attributable entirely to bisexuality and not to an identification in consequence of rivalry.' (*Ego and Id*, p. 43. 1923.) But he
never subsequently doubts the edifice which he builds upon the earlier
interpretations.

denied to his predecessors. There is no doubt about the justice of that claim. But by following the development of psycho-analytical practice and theory in his hands we have endeavoured to show the relative importance of sympathetic intuition on the one hand and keenness of intellectual deduction on the other, first in Freud's brilliant but limited discoveries and then in his generalizations and the fabrication of his theory. We have seen how an intuitive sympathy led to his persistence in attacking the surface manifestations of conduct and feeling until they yielded the hidden stores of their painfully repressed origins. We must remember that it is a *painful* experience that leads to repression, and that such experiences may themselves lead to limited or to widespread misconceptions about life and love. Sympathy for such experiences Freud undoubtedly possessed. He had a flair amounting to genius for unravelling hidden stores of repressed hatred and sexuality—the two emotions, which by their excess or abnormality can most easily wreck the social life of man. It was subjects of undue stresses in these fields that provided the vast bulk of neurotic material for Freud's analyses. By his hard-won technique, and his laborious transcriptions of the enigmas and symbolisms in which repressed ideas appear upon the surface of the mind, he surrounded himself with the forces of man's ego-tistical and megalomaniacal cravings, the very cravings which, because of their disharmony with the needs of social life, were repressed from consciousness and action, though because of their strength they were always knocking at the door of the mind. It was with the sympathy of one who *believed* from the start that aggressiveness and hatred preponderated over kindliness and co-operation in this world, that Freud surveyed these newly revealed evidences from the souls of the men and women who came to him because they could not bear the weight of their own aggressive or sexual feelings and the threat which these offered to their major selves.

Jung and Suttie received similar patients. But in Freud something prevented his playing a rôle which would extract their need of love in its more mystical or in its friendlier aspects. He felt that they must suffer a painful cure. And also he felt that, as it was their aggressiveness which was repressed, so it was that which was the fundamental emotion. In what sense funda-mental? Not because stronger than the forces that held it in check! Perhaps deeper merely, because the metaphor of digging comes readily to the mind in psychoanalysis. Yet Freud allows the concept of ' fundamental ' to take its usual meaning of prime or most important. Whence then the counter forces which hold our aggressiveness in check, and, as we shall see, produce effective citizens even of neurotic sufferers ?

The source of repression of our unconscious egotistical desires Freud had found in that conscience which is ' merely the dread of society '—the ' super-ego ' or ' ego-ideal '. Later he tended to make the ' ego-ideal ' mean, not the repressive force which disciplined the selfish egotism of the ' ego ' to meet the realities of the outside world, but rather what the growing child decided in the light of such influences that he wished to be. It is this ideal-of-the-self which makes us refuse to follow the immediate pleasures of life and of the body, and choose instead to live in a way which will win the approval, first of parents, and then of the outside world. Freud tried to make this ' ideal ' an attempt to be *like* the parents, to ' identify ' with each of them in turn. And to do so he admitted to finding in the child a love of *both* parents, though he called it a ' complicating bisexuality ' because it conflicted with his original idea of a universal ' Oedipus ' complex with its love for the parent of the opposite sex and a hatred of the remaining rival. Children, of course, turn naturally and instinctively to their parents for standards of right and wrong, for the elements of social conduct. In *The Ego and the Id* (1923) Freud offers a schematic theory of how these standards are developed in the mind.

In this scheme the ' ego ' is no longer the self as a whole. It has become that part of the mind which comes into contact with the external world, and so is modified by its ' realities '. A remaining deeper mind or ' id ' is full of feeling rather than thought, obeys the ' pleasure-principle ' implicitly, and makes itself felt in consciousness only by the pain caused by its various thwartings. Freud regarded the formation of the ' super-ego ' as a revolt from reality to idealism. The ' ego ' appears to be realistic as long as it is adapting itself to the world exclusive of the parents. Where they are concerned, love forces an unreal situation, and it is an ideal rather than a real parent that the child is both in love with and trying to live up to. The only reason one can see for refusing the same ' realism ' to a child's adaptation to its parents as to its adaptation to the rest of the world is the very stressful Oedipus reaction, of which, however, we now find a modified enunciation which marches far better than its crude original with subsequent analytical experiences. It is ' the *double* identifications with father and mother in varying proportions '. *The modification in the ego thus caused is the ego-ideal or super-ego. Its object is to dominate the ego in terms of ideal parents, and it tends to abolish original Oedipus situations and then to become a general conscience.*[1] It is because of its devotion to fantasy and ' ideal ' conceptions which satisfy the deepest needs of the psyche that the formation of this ' super-ego ' is regarded as placing the realistic ' ego ' in subjection to the deeper feeling ' id '.

In plain language, the terms and the scheme repeat merely that the child owes its standards of conduct, self-control, and general conscience to its emotional devotion to its parents.

[1] Freud, *The Ego and the Id*, p. 44. (1923.)

Conscience is thus derived from a conception of, and love for, idealized parents. It is clear that this is only an early and common *manifestation* of conscience. For though he does not refer to such obvious contingencies as the absence of parents, or their replacement by others in respect of this function, Freud at once allows that individuals may share their ego-ideals with others. He then widens this basis of idealization to gain the point reached in his *Group Psychology*: ' Social feelings rest on the foundation of identifications with others, on the basis of an ego-ideal held in common with them '.[1] There is in this conception the material for a derivation of society straight from the fundamental needs of the human soul, which crystallize in ideas and ideals of strong, simple, and loving relationships with brothers and sisters, and a common turning to parents (transmuted by idealism into the ablest of mentors) for guidance in the attainment of self-control and of acceptable standards of social conduct. Freud does not take such a course. He has now omitted the fearsome ' hypnotic ' leader which his own partiality for a strong ' father-figure ' had formerly insisted upon. But he cannot forego a reference to the rivalry which lurks behind the mutual love of the members of the younger generation. And this reference brings back the whole tide of his conviction that hatred, rivalry, and aggressiveness do lie at the bottom of things, despite any evidences to the contrary. ' Even to-day,' he writes, ' social feelings arise in the individual as a superstructure founded upon impulses of jealousy and rivalry against brothers and sisters. Since the enmity cannot be gratified, there develops an identification with the former rivals '.[2] The kindly feelings must remain derivations of the frustrated aggressive feelings. And thus *the hatred we repress with difficulty remains the mainspring of our corporate life.*

We now have before us Freud's general picture of man in society. Each individual is possessed of the two main groups of instinct, the ' erotic ' desires for conjugation and reproduction, and the personal desires for the ' repetition compulsion ' of death. The death instincts ' are by their nature mute, and the clamour of life proceeds for the most part from Eros '.[3] The deeper self, the id, ' has no unity of will . . . Eros and the death-instinct struggle within it '.[4] The ego perceives the realities of life and attempts, with the aid of the super-ego, to achieve some sort of balance between the conflicting demands within and the realities without. Much of the ' death-instinct ' turns outwards as hostility to others. And, sexuality apart, this is man's primary attitude to his fellows. Both groups of instincts are first developed and first shown in the domestic setting. Infantile sexuality focuses its desires upon a parent ; the projected death-wish turns to meet all the thwartings of impotent jealousies, whether

---

[1] Freud, *The Ego and the Id*, p. 49.
[2] Ibid. p. 50.   [3] Ibid. p. 66.   [4] Ibid. p. 88.

by parent or by brothers and sisters. Then come conscience, with its ideal parents to be loved, and fear, with its demand for suppression of hostility. Under the combined influence of conscience and fear, the hatred of rivals is transformed into 'identification' with them. Any primary altruism is thus avoided by Freud, not because any analytical findings forbid its assumption, but because of the author's inward conviction.

4. *The nature of Society.*—Freud's social theory is rounded off and restated in two later works : *The Future of an Illusion* (1928), and *Civilization and its Discontents* (1929). In *The Future of an Illusion*, Freud takes up the question of the strength of the 'identification' between men in society, brought about, as he held, by a necessary repression of an underlying hostility. Because of this very conception of its origin, he regards society as essentially unstable. The real desires of the individual are against society and against his fellows. 'Every individual is in fact an enemy of culture.'[1] And 'all the institutions and laws of civilization are directed to protect it against the individual '.[1] ' To be able to abandon coercion and suppression of instinct, to reorganize human relationships so that, undisturbed by inner conflict, men might acquire and enjoy the natural resources of the world . . . would be to reach the golden age. . . . It seems more probable that every culture must be built up on coercion and this instinctual renunciation.'[2] He considers civilized society as having been ' imposed upon a resisting majority by a minority which knew how to manipulate the means of coercion '.[3] Furthermore, the masses are both lazy and stupid, and their ingrained laziness will not be removed by kindness but only by leadership prepared to use ' appalling ' force.[4] They are ' unconvincible and unruly ' and have no love for the instinctual renunciation by which alone man can live an adequately self-disciplined life in a civilized community.

Thus we find within society a minority, an *élite*, which attempts the task of living together without the leadership and domination which the masses require. This *élite* suffers from the ' terrible burden ' of the repression of their mutual aggressiveness, a burden from which they seek for relief or compensation, and with which they find reconciliation with difficulty. The price of their progress is ' happiness forfeited through a growing sense of guilt '.[5]

Since man's underlying desire to wreck his fellows, his society, and his civilization is due to a fundamental instinct, uncountered by any equivalent opposite instinct, Freud regards

---

[1] *The Future of an Illusion*, p. 9. (1928.)
[2] Ibid. p. 11.   [3] Ibid. p. 10.
[4] *The Future of an Illusion*, p. 13. Here Freud drops a hint to anyone who would study his personal psychology : ' One cannot deny the grandeur of this project ' !
[5] *Civilization and its Discontents*, p. 123.

civilization as a *fight against nature*. ' One of the few noble
spectacles is of men uniting against nature '.[1]   Man is naturally
at war with every other man.   Through the operation of his
conscience he forms groups and cultures with which he ' identifies ' himself.   ' Culture ' helps man in the fight, and so in the
past has religion.   But the latter should now be discarded in the
interest of truth.   For ' man stands alone as the originator of
his laws and institutions '[2] and the ' illusions ' of religious belief
hamper the freedom of thought with which alone man can control
his instincts (i.e. defeat nature).   And nature rises pitiless, with
earthquake, storm, disease, and death to remind us of our weakness.   She ' does not *ask* us to restrain our instincts ', but ' de-
stroys us, coldly, cruelly, callously.   The *raison d'être* of culture
is to defend us against her.'[1]

The social group offers only a temporary counter to man's
aggressiveness.   For in these groups men unite their aggressiveness against each other, every culture trying ' to despise the
others, and overcome them in conflict '.[3]   *Whatever the unit of
man's organization, be it a nation-state or a world community,
Freud believed that the fundamental aggressiveness in man which
desires the death of others, and in the last analysis of himself, will
threaten and may in the long run break it.*   ' If civilization should
progress to a group embracing humanity, then an intensification
of the sense of guilt . . . will be inextricably bound up with it,
until perhaps it swells to a magnitude which individuals can
hardly support.'[4]   Against this trend to death are arrayed man's
procreative instincts, together with the suppression and repression of aggressiveness which his rulers and his conscience have
won from him.   If these prohibitions were withdrawn, ' one
could choose any woman who took one's fancy, one could kill
one's rival, and seize what one wanted of another's goods '.   To
Freud's ' man ' these are attractive propositions.   ' How splendid ! '
exclaims the author himself, ' What a succession of delights life
would be ! '[5]   ' But what would then remain would be the *state
of nature*, and that is far harder to endure.'[6]

Freud here ranges himself behind the artificial conception of
a ' state of nature ' which we have already traced through the
centuries.   For him it is *the state of chaos which would exist if men
yielded simply to the emotions which Freud elects to call fundamental.*   The fundamentality lies in the mind of the thinker.   But
here Freud is in close general agreement with Hobbes.   Among
the case material of psychoanalysis given in Chapter IV, I have
placed notes of a patient (Case C, p. 135) whose conscious attitude
to the essentials of social relationship closely resembled that of
Hobbes, and whose analysis showed the motives which Freud

---

[1] *Civilization and its Discontents*, p. 26.   [2] Ibid. p. 73.
[3] Ibid. p. 22.   [4] Ibid. p. 121.
[5] *The Future of an Illusion*, p. 25.   [6] Ibid. p. 26.

cites in support of the same viewpoint. But in Mr. ' C ' I was able to trace one case of what we may now call the ' *aggressive-obsessional character* ' to its earliest origins, and to find, in the earliest conceptions which the young child formed of his family life, misconceptions which went a long way towards explaining his adult emotional attitude, and his philosophical opinions. Those misconceptions removed, the behaviour of this patient became more normal, his fears of persecution were occasional and slight, and the Hobbesian and Freudian ' state of nature ', once a constant nightmare, seldom returned to trouble his mind.

5. *Freud's personal attitude towards society.*—In *Civilization and its Discontents* Freud sums up his social theory and describes his personal attitude to his fellows. Views which are echoed in my forthcoming Case C are here italicized for reference. First, ' Man found genital love gave him his greatest gratification '. Consequently he ' *made genital erotism the centre of his life* '. He thus ' became dependent on his love-object and was exposed to suffering thereby '.[1] ' Unbridled gratification of all desires ' is the ' *most alluring guiding principle in life* ', *were it not for the ' penalties '* encountered.[2]

Secondly, ' Human life in communities only becomes possible when a number of men unite together in strength superior to a single individual, and remain united against all single individuals. The strength of this united body is then regarded as right.' And ' this substitution of the power of a united number for the power of a single man is the decisive step towards civilization. The essence is . . . that the members of the community have restricted their possibilities of gratification, which as individuals they would not do. The first requisite of such a society is justice, the assurance that a law once made will not be broken in favour of any individual. This implies nothing about the ethical value of any such law. . . .[3] The rules of the brothers (united against the father) were the first law.'[4]

The individual renunciations required in forming a community, Freud now sees partly as the conscious voluntary renunciation of Hobbes—the product of an obvious necessity, and partly as the unconscious mastery of aggressiveness by the processes we have enumerated : a guilty ' conscience ' over aggressive lust [5] and a consequent ' identification ' with hated rivals—the products of a necessity unconsciously perceived. Thus nothing but external necessity and the conscience are left in support of culture and community—always excepting ' Eros, aiming at binding

---

[1] Freud, *Civilization and its Discontents*, p. 69. (1929.)
[2] Ibid. p. 29.   [3] Ibid. p. 59.   [4] Ibid. p. 68.
[5] Now defined as ' a universal non-erotic instinct of aggressiveness and destruction . . . an innate, independent instinct . . . the most powerful of all obstacles to culture '. Ibid. p. 99.

together individuals, families, tribes, races, nations, into one great unity of humanity '. [1] How Eros manages to perform this function without becoming a Social Instinct, Freud never attempts to explain. At only one point does he allow even the conscience or super-ego to be ' partly ' innate.[2] What is innate for him is the ' primary hostility of men towards one another'.[3] Everything else is externalized. It is ' civilization ' which ' obtains the mastery over the dangerous love of aggression in individuals by enfeebling and disarming it and setting up an institution within their minds to keep watch over it, like a garrison in a conquered city '.[4] This personification of Society has to be introduced in order to avoid the admission of that Social Instinct which is clamouring to be derived from Freud's deepest ' Id ' of the mind, as the child's idealization of human relationships for which Freud's theory otherwise lacks an ' innate ' origin.

For Freud, no socially beneficent impulses can arise from within the soul of man, who is *not* primarily a social being. With this discovery we come suddenly upon Freud's personal judgment of the experiences of his own life which really determined these theoretical views.

' The truth ', writes Freud, ' is that men are not gentle friendly creatures wishing for love, who simply defend themselves if they are attacked, but that a powerful measure of desire for aggression has to be reckoned as part of their instinctual endowment . . . . Their neighbour is not only a possible helper, or sexual object, but also a temptation to them to gratify their aggressiveness upon him, to exploit . . . to use him sexually without his consent, to rob, humiliate, torture, and kill him.' [5] There is no reason to doubt that this strange, woefully distorted, and tragic conception of normal human relationships represents Freud's own opinions independent of his knowledge of psychopathology. Freud comments on the Sermon on the Mount : ' Love your enemies ? Not [quoting Heine] until they are brought to execution ! ' ' Love thy neighbour as thyself ? If he is so like me that I can love myself in him, or so good that I can love my ideal in him— Yes ! Otherwise, I have very little love to spare from myself, and he does *not* love me ! ' Here is ground where Freud was not prepared to, indeed could not, lead. ' If *he* behaved differently, if *he* showed me consideration and did not molest me . . . I should be willing to treat him similarly. . . . As it is, he does not even need to get a real advantage ; if he can but get a little pleasure out of it, he thinks nothing of jeering at me, insulting me, slandering me, showing his power over me.' [6]

[1] Freud, *Civilization and its Discontents*, p. 102. 1929.
[2] Ibid. p. 116.   [3] Ibid. p. 86.
[4] Ibid. p. 105.   [5] Ibid. p. 85.
[6] Ibid. p. 83. The substance of Freud's attitude as described in these paragraphs was repeatedly reiterated by my aggressive-obsessional patient, Mr. ' C.' (Chapter IV. p. 135.)

These partial, prejudiced, and subjective evaluations of human relationships are here more fundamental to our study of Freud than any of those scientific discoveries which they so deeply tinge. It is upon them, for instance, that his famous exchange of letters on war with Albert Einstein was grounded. The reader will remember the language in which he first introduces the hypothesis of a Death Instinct. But now the ' far-fetched speculation and the exploitation of an idea'[1] has become ' the least of speculative efforts by which we are led to conclude that the Destructive Instinct functions in every living being, striving to work its ruin and reduce life to its primal state of inert matter'. Nothing but his own enthusiasm had intervened to convert the wild guess into the established axiom ! He continued his letter : ' It might well be called the " Death Instinct ", whereas the Erotic Instincts vouch for the struggle to live on. The Death Instinct becomes an impulse to destruction when, with the aid of certain organs, it directs its action outwards, against external objects, with beneficial effects. Here is the biological justification of those vile, pernicious propensities [towards warfare] which we are combating. We can but own that they are really more akin to nature than this our stand against them, which, in fact, remains to be accounted for.'[2]

From our survey of his works, we have seen that Freud was unable to account for any stand against violence and aggressiveness from within the individual himself, only because he refused all designation of ' primary ' to other than aggressive and sexual instincts, and because throughout his life and work he consistently met impulses of friendliness, co-operation, social devotion, and (non-sexual) love, only to thrust them aside or to class them as reactions to underlying hostility. Whatever of it be inherent and whatever remains environmental in the origin of Freud's own attitude to his fellows, neither his brilliant mind nor any other has furnished us with the means to ascertain. We can have nothing but sympathy for one who could write late in his life : ' The time comes when every one of us has to abandon the illusory anticipations with which in our youth we regarded our fellow men, and when we come to realize how much hardship and suffering we have been caused by their ill will'.[3] But I do not think that this view would be endorsed by old men generally. As for ' biological justifications ' for war, it is true that, by his twin discoveries that aggressiveness is often severely repressed by conscience and that social approval can cause its welcome release, Freud has offered us an acceptable theory of a number of the lamentable phenomena both of individual and of crowd

---

[1] Cf. *Beyond the Pleasure Principle* (see this Chapter, pp. 80–82).
[2] Internat. Instit. for Intellectual Co-operation. League of Nations. (1933.) Also published as a monograph by the New Commonwealth Society.
[3] Freud, *Civilization and its Discontents*, p. 87.

psychology which manifest themselves in war.[1] To these we shall return. But the doctrine of the *inevitability* of warfare as an outlet for individual sadistic aggressiveness is but our latest example of the illegitimate universalization of certain mechanisms of the mind to which Freud chose to give primacy in his patients because they harmonized with certain of his own thoughts. International warfare will be found to be no more inevitable than rioting when man has taken full account of his means of avoiding it.

Throughout the works of Freud we have found three processes at work in the following order: (1) interest and bias; (2) investigation and discovery; (3) inference. In final summary we may say: (1st) In the light of a certain philosophical attitude to mankind, Freud investigated certain cases of neurosis. (2nd) He discovered that in these (obsessional) neurotics there lay hidden an abnormal hostility to their fellows, and that the mastery of this hostility was attained, with difficulty, by certain tricks of the mind. He and his followers further discovered that traces both of the hostility and of the mechanisms for countering it can be found in people whose minds could be classed as within the limits of normal. (3rd) In the complex tangle of action and reaction which he found in the ' unconscious mind ', Freud intuitively chose to regard the aggressive reactions as being more important, more fundamental, more likely to win in the long run, than those of co-operation and love, not only in his aggressive neurotics, but also in ' normal ' people, and finally in all mankind. He then built up a theoretical conception of society from individual attitudes to family relationships, many of which contained stresses of aggressiveness and sexuality which might reasonably be classed as abnormal, even in a ' deep ' psychoanalysis. In practice, Freud's view of society appears to have been guided by his own conscious and unconscious attitudes to his fellows and his conception of their attitude to him. And on this subject his language marches so closely with that of Hobbes, that we may hazard it that if Hobbes had studied psychoanalysis, his views and findings would broadly have agreed with those of

---

[1] See e.g. E. Glover, *War, Sadism and Pacifism*. (Allen & Unwin. 1933.) This author in the course of a racy and confident exposition of the Freudian doctrine on the subject, well describes some of the possible workings of repressed aggressiveness in war. . . . ' An ordinary person, not actively warlike but not actively peace-loving, is fired by some ideal, e.g. love of his country. Suppose further that he is exhorted by the representatives of social law and order to rise in defence of his fatherland, or pursue a crusade, or take part in a " war to end war ", the chances are that his inhibitory mechanism will give way under the strain of social sanction, and the full sweep of his aggression will once more turn outwards. But not on this occasion towards his old enemies of nursery times ; he will now assure us that much as he hates war, he must gird up his loins and go forth to fight the Afghans or Basutos or Chinese or Dutch or English or French or Germans—or whatever appointed object is indicated to him in the first place by the Secretary of State for Foreign Affairs of his own country.'

Freud. They are those, in fact, of the aggressive-obsessional character, whose influence upon society we shall presently study.[1]

Note.—Since writing this section I have read the work of an American writer, *New Ways in Psychoanalysis*, by Horney. 1939. The author's critical approach to Freud's work closely resembles the one I have adopted here, and which I believe to be a just one. That Freud's observations are pioneer though often inadequate and highly selective, while his deductions are distorted by his own pre-occupation with sex and destructiveness are clearly set out. The author proceeds to a far wider survey of the present position of psychoanalysis than I have attempted. Her work is directed first to replacing the doctrine that ' hatred is at the bottom of all relations of affection between human beings ' by continued observations of man's real motivations, and second to diverting the aim of treatment from the ' liberation ' of aggressiveness to the relief of anxiety. This work marks a notable stage in the re-examination at once of findings, of interpretations, and of the aim of treatment, which is needed if the peculiar bias which has been given to this new science by the personalities of its founder and of some of its early exponents is to be corrected.

IV. PSYCHOLOGICAL THEORIES OF HUMAN NATURE WHICH CONTRAST WITH THAT OF FREUD

In contrast of character with Freud stands Ian Suttie. He was trained in the Freudian school, manipulated the same technique of psychoanalysis, dealt with the same classes of patient, with their wide variety of surface manifestations, and elicited the same underlying reactions, exposing conflicts of desires, aggressive and sexual. But when he came to weigh up the fundamental needs of his patients and, like Freud, to extend them by inference to humanity in general, his conclusions are very different from those of the pioneer.

In the first place, Suttie [2] rejects any hypothetical ' state of nature ', that non-historical imagined state, into which man would relapse if this or that quality, which he has always manifested, were removed from him. Historically, any ' state ' of man other than as a social being is an unnatural state, and in the long history which present biology and anthropology give to society there is little room for any exclusive conception of the natural, and none at all for any conception of an isolated natural man. Cavedweller, tree-dweller, medieval tyrant and serf, modern agricultural labourer, factory-hand or soldier—none has an exclusive claim to the term ' natural ', and from none, as such, can the designation be withheld. A concept of ' natural ' as covering *all* that happens in nature may offer difficulties : the limitation of the term to *certain* things that happen offers more. In common usage a natural man, like a natural plant, is using his instincts and faculties in the general way of his species and in one which does not obviously distort or limit him. A ' state of nature ' *before* society, and a ' state of nature ' *against* which all man's social achievements have been won, are both inventions, figments, one might almost guess, of an unnatural imagination.

[1] Chapter VII, Section II, p. 218.
[2] Suttie, *Origins of Love and Hate*. (Kegan Paul. 1935.)

Suttie's starting-point is a human being adapted to its functions. The child is born with a mind, not primitive, but adapted to infancy. For instance, the newly-born infant has no stereoscopic vision, and no locomotory ideas of space. To it people do not come and go, they appear and disappear, are indistinct, speak in tone and pitch only. Its wishes and angers are at first undirected to individuals. It recognizes the self and the not-self by discovery. The latter is powerful for good and ill, and arouses both anger and love. Suttie brings forward the biological and individual rôle of the nourishing and protecting mother, and the sociological reactions which may result from her place in the life of the child, as opposed to those of Freud's threatening father. ' Social animals differ from solitary animals in that they nurture their young. The social disposition seems to be a modified continuance of the infant's need for the nurtural parent's presence. . . . The child has one dominant instinct, to retain the mother.' There is thus no primary instinct for destruction ; ' Anger in an infant does not express aggression—does not lead to self-help, but expresses the cry : " Help me ! "—which is a protest against neglect and is not aimed at destruction. . . . Hatred. . . . is just a standing reproach to the hated person, a demand for love. . . .'[1] Love of others comes into being with the recognition of their existence. Hate results from the anxiety of separation. Love is social rather than sexual in its biological function. It is derived from a self-preservative instinct and not from a genital appetite.[2] The desires to love, give, be good, receive and co-operate are at first undistinguished desires for well-being. But when the infant discovers that its gifts and demands are treated apparently whimsically by others, then comes the crisis of anxiety, and how it reacts then may determine its character, or its neurosis or psychosis. For then love turns to anxiety, and then, if frustration is severe, to guilt or hate. In the presence of such hate, love is (1) retained for the mother if possible, or (2) devoted to a mythical mother who does not behave so whimsically, or (3) transferred to a substituted nurse or father.[3] It is the refusal of the mother to give which leads to anxiety, hate, ' aggression ', or the ' quest for power '.[4] Thus, for Suttie, both the primary instinct of Freud, and the fundamental urge of Adler become secondary reactions resulting from thwarting of desires and demands for love.

This love quest is regarded by Suttie as being a deeply-rooted trait throughout life. ' We seek to influence, impress, or please other people, in order to demonstrate to ourselves that we are loved.'[5] Where Freud argues that ' the wisest possible human policy can do no better than find socially harmless targets for man's unavoidable hatred ', and Adler feels that the baby must

---

[1] Suttie, *Origins of Love and Hate*, pp. 15, 23–30. [2] Ibid. p. 36.
[3] Ibid. p. 43. [4] Ibid. p. 50. [5] Ibid. p. 49.

be ' forced into co-operation from its earliest possible moment ',
Suttie thinks ' the germ of goodness and of love is in the individual
from the beginning ',[1] and only traditional faults of upbringing
substitute a ' guilt-anxiety ' morality (which says in effect,
' What am I doing wrong that I'm not loved ? ') for natural
goodness. But of course thwarting, real and imagined, inevitably
occurs, and, just as Rousseau's society has parted irrevocably with
the ideal ' state of nature ', so Suttie's man has had to face and
deal somehow with the inescapable thwartings of his infantile
love.

Suttie's reaction from Freudian hatred is as sharp as was
Rousseau's from the court life of eighteenth-century France. He
lists man's emotions in terms of love, as : Hate is love denied,
anxiety is love threatened, despair is love rejected, grief is love
lost, pity is love sympathetic. And for him all go back to the
loving mother of infancy, as for Freud everything went back to
the Oedipus Complex and the feared father. For the adult, the
' whole social environment ' replaces the mother.[2] And for the
infant ' the bodily self acquires a value over and above its capacity
for yielding sensory satisfaction, in so far as it is the object of
the mother's interest '.[3] Thus infantile ' narcissism ', which for
Freud was an early self-love later to be ' projected ' as object-
love, becomes for Suttie an ' off-shoot ' of the child's love of its
mother.

As for culture, ' We need not hesitate to proceed with our
hypothesis, that in all his social activities—Art, Science, and
Religion included—man is seeking a restoration of, or substitute
for, that love for Mother which was lost in infancy '.[4] For Suttie,
the germ of society is a band of brothers and sisters gathered
under a mother, as opposed to Freud's brothers banded in
hostility to a father.[5] He attempts to trace the varying importance
of women in different cultures—nomadic, agricultural, city—
suggesting a tendency for them to attain relative social prominence
in the second of these, rather than in the physical stresses and
physical and mental specializations of the first and third respectively. In religion, he allocates cults of Mother-earth to the
one phase of development and of the ' Sky-Father ' to the others.
He judges the better cultures to be the matriarchal. But in general,
' Love, not selfish appetite, is the mainspring of social life '. A
chief emotional task of man has been ' the harmonization of his
love-needs with his appetite-needs to the maximal satisfaction of
both '.[6]

Enough has here been quoted to show that *Suttie takes as a
primary relationship between individuals in society the loving-
kindness of a recognized mutual dependence, which derives emotionally
from the attitude of the infant to the nourishing mother.* Here we

---

[1] Suttie, loc. cit. pp. 51–52.   [2] Ibid. p. 16.   [3] Ibid. p. 37.
[4] Ibid. p. 71.   [5] Ibid. 117.   [6] Ibid. p. 125.

must pause to note the striking fact that such views of fundamental human relationships can be derived from the manipulation of the actual technique of ' free-association ' from neurotic symptoms with which Freud arrived at his precisely opposite conclusions. Jung had modified the technique, and found a chief concern of adult men and women to be for religious assurance. Adler shortened the Freudian technique, and brought out of his patients reactions indicative of their drive for power. But Suttie practised the full technique, to which he was trained for many years, taking the emotional drives of his patients by ' free-association ' back to infancy. And there (as probably at every stage of the analyses) his patients' reactions were different from those of Freud's, *because the personalities, the mental adherences, and the faiths of the two analysts diverged.* Freud's theory in part allows for this. As I have explained in the introductory remarks on psychoanalysis, the ' transference ' [1] of each case would be to a differently conceived person who would be replacing a different member of the caste on the stage of the patient's recollected infancy, or at least a different aspect of the chosen character. It is a questing adult that comes for treatment. The psychoanalyst exposes a frightened child, and in the process himself becomes a fantastic parental figure. Infants are not free from doubts about the nature of their parents : often they are ridden by them. The personality of an analyst may thus confirm the best, or the worst, of previous doubts, or have some intermediate effect. Some psychoanalysts certainly have greater powers of passivity and receptivity and self-effacement than others. It is possible for a psychoanalyst to have his views of human nature modified by the reactions of his patients : cumulatively, that probably always happens to some—and often to a considerable—degree. But the unconscious influence of the views of the analyst upon his patient is inevitably a considerable one. And, however ' scientific ' they attempt to be, men who hold deep convictions with tenacity will tend to find in the personalities that come before them, so malleable and responsive as they are, confirmation of their views.

To Suttie the treatment afforded by psychotherapy is not the removal of inhibitions which fear has placed upon the expression of ' innate anti-social egotistical and sensual desires ', but ' the overcoming of barriers to loving and feeling oneself loved '. [2] To him, sexual love itself is the old infantile need, ' utilizing genital appetite as a means as it were of restoring the lost sense of union with the mother '.[3] For him, the mother's disapproval and not the father's anger is the main obstacle to the Oedipus wishes. And so on, until it becomes abundantly clear that Suttie is giving us his view of life, picking and choosing

[1] See pp. 66–69.　　　[2] Suttie, loc. cit. p. 53.　　　[3] Ibid. p. 72.

phenomena as 'important' or 'unimportant', and viewing all from his very definite angle of interest, just as Freud did from his.

J. A. Hadfield [1] seems to take a broader view of the origins and nature of our mental processes, and to this he adapts his technique of psychoanalysis. It is that real divergences of conduct from the normal will find their explanations, or at least *an* explanation, in certain particular combinations of experience and fantasy—infantile misconceptions as I have called them—and that the discovery of these 'nuclear complexes' should be a sufficient goal of psychotherapy, provided any striking divisions of aim of the personality as a whole which have become manifest in connexion with the symptoms are also analysed and corrected. He leaves the deeper and more subtle conceptions of life, which are the basis of normal character, untouched both in the practice and in the theory of his treatment. In their common qualities they remain the basis of 'human nature' and in their divergences the origins of the variations of characters from type. He takes his patients through the stages of infancy to wherever their particular misconceptions have occurred. In one case it will be a 'fetish'—an excited over-valuation of an incidental accompaniment of an old love-scene, a shoe perhaps or a red cheek—which dominates and disturbs the feeling-life wherever it chances to occur, and has to be sought wherever it is lacking. In another, a sexual perversion has occurred, or perhaps a division of sexual interest into objects revered and objects sensuously desired. Whatever the chief symptom, it will be carried back by the free-association technique until a particular and apparently adequate misconception (usually of childhood or infancy) is reached, and the reason for the false valuation, or for the division within an interest which should be single, can be pointed out. There the main analysis stops. It was particular to that case. Naturally, there are underlying type reactions of the mental group into which the patient falls. And again there are the reactions which underlie those and which are common to all humanity. It is characteristic of these deeper and more general reactions that they show more vaguely in analysis of the parts of the character where stresses have been less than in those connected with the symptoms. Hadfield considers that the general needs, demands, and frustrations of normal infancy can be found by a searching analysis of normal men and women. But he does not attempt to fasten upon the normal mind a string of complexes derived from analyses of abnormal sufferers. If aggressiveness is a problem in the patient's life, its repressions can usually be analysed, and 'Freudian' mechanisms will be discovered to underlie them. If the anxieties of Suttie's 'lost-mother' type are present, a bitterness over unsatisfied breast-feeding may appear as the

[1] Hadfield, *Psychology and Morals*. (Methuen. 1925.)

nucleus of the complex. ' Normal ' people, undergoing a ' training analysis ' as doctors, are analysed through those of their character traits or abnormally strong interests which most nearly approach to neurotic symptoms.

Hadfield has his own views of the general balance of forces, good and bad, in human nature. Partly they are obtained from his analytical experiences, partly they are the judgments of his experiences of everyday life. Both are made in the light of a certain cast of mind largely determined early in his own life. All this he is aware of. And the result is a clear and simple analytical technique, combined with considerable reticence and an absence of dogmatism in estimating ' human nature ' as a whole, though he gives general assent to the views of Suttie rather than to those of Freud : ' Love is protective as well as sexual, and the sense of security is more important to the child than feelings of sensual pleasure '.[1] In general, this author seems frankly to recognize that modern psychoanalysis is dealing in a special way with certain manifestations of the mind, rather than plumbing the depths and spanning the width of man's character as a whole.

IV

THE ACTUAL BEHAVIOUR OF MAN

INTRODUCTION

IT is by collecting and not by selecting that we shall best understand human nature. All men have their enemies and all men have their friends, among ideas as well as among people. Between friendship and loyalty on the one hand, and hostility and distrust on the other, it is as hard a task for any one man to give a picture of the human mind which does justice to its various traits as it is to do justice to the varying types of men in the various races and cultures of humanity. It is in fact more difficult. Whenever we allow ourselves to select human qualities for appraisal we are certain to select with prejudice. It is perhaps well for mankind that so many and so varied selections have been made. For it is by occasional contact with their multiplicity that the ' common man ' so often becomes the best judge of the 'isms and 'ologies of life. He lacks the enthusiasm and the bias which marks the investigating selector, with his inevitable ' axe to grind '. Either he hears, or he feels instinctively, that there is another side to

[1] Hadfield, Preface to Suttie's *Origins of Love and Hate*, p. xv.

the argument which is put to him with such enthusiasm. The normal mind shuns fanaticism, and is inclined to take a grain of salt with each mouthful of any strong doctrine which it is persuaded to sample.

The imparter of doctrine is always a specialist. In that rôle we press upon others ideas to which we believe inadequate importance has been attached by them ; ideas, in fact, to which we attach the undue importance of our special and abnormal interests. And when the attempt is to describe the balance of qualities which make up ' human nature ' as such, we may be sure that to certain qualities of the whole mind we shall turn the blind eye of our own unconscious repressions, while others we shall elect to magnify with an interest akin to that of the ' fetishist ' patient. The psychologist, for example, who, surveying the manifold interests of man's lives and the fine balance of selfishness and consideration for others which runs through them, and who says : ' In all the significant interests of these people I shall find sexuality,' or ' aggressiveness ', or ' love ', or ' power lust ', ' a fear of father and jealousy of brothers ', ' a search for mother ', or ' a link with magic and religion ' is himself a fetishist. If your hearer is malleable you may persuade him. Often he will be almost persuaded ; until the resilient mind springs into its own accustomed shape again. If he shares your fetish, you will indeed be brothers. The ordinary man will shrug his shoulders, at least for a time. But, alas, if enough of the ' clever ' people can be persuaded to accept a doctrine—and ' clever ' people, anxious as they are to control their lives by their intellects, have an inherent weakness for schematic doctrines as such—the ordinary man will come at last to be affected. The common taints of ' education ' and its inalienable associate of false doctrine permeate all society in varying degrees. And, as a general quality of the mind is to swallow doctrines whole (albeit with the grain of salt), we find an unproven hypothesis which is ingenious enough to convince the clever come to be accepted by the majority—albeit with a shrug—until only the small minority whom it utterly stupifies or utterly bores, and those who are fortified against it by a contrary doctrine, can escape its attenuated ' philosophical implications '. It was thus with the materialistic determinism which followed the Darwinian theory. It has been thus with Freudian psychology.

It is with psychology that we are here concerned. *How can the facts of human nature be collected in a way which will avoid the partial and prejudicial selections which we have had to record ;* selections which have brought the theories of psychologists, with all their vaunted knowledge of the unconscious mind, into mutual disagreements only rivalled in significance by their individual agreements with various of the theories of philosophers and lawyers since the beginnings of civilization ? We shall have to record that at present we have neither a technique for measuring emotions nor any means of comparative evaluation in terms either of personality or of society. Such means may come. All we can do at present is to collect our observations of actual human behaviour upon as wide a field as possible, and then see what deductions about the relationships of the individual to society it seems legitimate to draw. Both our observations and our deductions will be subject to our personal bias. The best reason for accepting them will be if they ultimately appear to the greatest possible body of average men to be reasonable. The test of human nature is the behaviour of men, and in general that is open for all to see if they will. Any theory which asks us to believe that man is far other than he appears when we really examine him, should rightly have a long way to travel before it convinces the generality of men.

The observations which we can make about human nature in the absence of a quantitative technique will be useful to society in so far as they can help us to enrich human life. They may be direct observations of man's behaviour, under ' normal ' conditions or under abnormal conditions where these are relevant. Since psychoanalysis is responsible for most recent theories of human nature, and since it has a technique both for bringing repressed emotional responses to the surface, and, under certain conditions, for modifying character, it is of interest to observe how men of various types behave as a result of psychoanalysis, and in the psychoanalytical setting itself. But a good book of careful observations of the behaviour of men and women under the varying but repeatable conditions of personal, domestic, and community life—such as their reactions to pain, success, failure, family stresses, death, religious faiths, calls on partisanship, and the varying fortunes of war—would be worth a dozen text-books on psychological theory to mankind to-day. We have hardly begun to study ourselves in our various moods and settings (each of which we tend to forget or to falsify as we pass on to the next) with any attempt at documentation. Doctors, lawyers, policemen, the clergy, maternity nurses could all provide valuable statistical material on basic human reactions to important special events if they kept notes appropriate to that end. At our present stage of study a chief function of the social psychologist should be to draw up forms for others to fill in. This method has already yielded valuable information where it has been skilfully applied, as for instance in a recent paper upon the emotional life of middle-class married women.[1]

In the absence of such elementary statistics about behaviour, what useful inferences may we draw (*a*) from general observations of behaviour and (*b*) from the opinions and behaviour of

[1] McCance, Luff & Widdowson, *Journal of Hygiene*. Vol. xxxvii. p. 571. (1937.)

patients under psychoanalytical treatment ?   In the first place, what sort of information is most needed by society at the present time ?   We will assume that the object of a society, be it great or small, is the welfare and interest of its members—the object given to it by Locke.   Its ultimate aim may be sought in providing its members with such things as the 'greater freedom' of Rousseau and the idealist philosophers, or the means to realize the best for themselves or give the best to others of Green and Laski respectively.   But it is only in the speculative theory of its fat years that the world society in which we live touches these points.   And they will never come nearer to becoming realities until we realize that we have not yet solved the more fundamental problem to which Hobbes so urgently addressed himself in the England of the Civil Wars.   I mean that of elementary law and order.   The first concern of a civil society should be to protect the lives and liberties of its members, and to give them justice and peace.   A society that cannot achieve this need not concern itself with the ideal social relationships of its members.   For it is itself in danger of liquidation.

The problem of law and order in the World Society was rightly called 'The Problem of the Twentieth Century'[1] by Lord Davies in a book with that title written during an interval of armed peace in 1930.   An observer writing in 1910, or perhaps even in 1925, might have argued that the problem of world law and order had been solved or was on the way to solution.   At the former date it could be said that internal disturbances within most states had been put an end to by strong and increasingly representative governments ;   at the latter that machinery existed for dealing with international disputes which threatened breaches of the peace.   But no one who had reached years of observation in 1914 and is alive in 1942 can for a moment doubt that we dwell in Hobbes' 'state of war' antecedent to the formation of a stable commonwealth, when the life of man is indeed liable to be 'nasty, brutish, and short'.   *And so it will be first of all from the point of view of this first aim of society, the maintenance of law and order and the securing of life and liberty, that we shall note certain behaviours of mankind (1) in 'real' life, and (2) as revealed in the setting of psychoanalysis.*

I. INSTINCTS IN ACTION

1. *Variations of sociability.*—With exceptions so rare that we may exclude them as quite abnormal, all men and women show both an aptitude and a desire for some sort of community life.   The most elementary community is the family.   How far is family life the prototype of our more complicated communities ?   Freud has rightly traced many of our attitudes to others

[1] Davies, *The Problem of the Twentieth Century.* (Ernest Benn. 1930.)

to our earlier attitudes to parents, or to brothers or sisters, within the close and disciplinary contacts of family life. How far the family relationship as such is an essential factor in normal development can only be ascertained by studying those who (as orphans, only children, fostered or communally educated children) have been shorn of some features of this normal environment. Most of us still have most of it, and we tend to use its personnel as prototypes throughout life, though perhaps in a less specific and more pragmatic way than is credited by those of us who tend only to regard as vital that which has ascertainable roots in childhood. We repeat that children do grow up ; and a cursory glance at the orphans and only children among us does not very strongly support a view that they have always lost absolutely vital and irreplaceable sources of emotional development.

A first impression one gets in watching children certainly is that it is difficult to replace a good father and mother, chiefly because of the love and care and gentle discipline they bring so early into the life of the child and retain so constantly available within it. With bad parents it is easy to substitute a superior source of security and love to which infantile weakness may turn. But it is the good (or at least the adequate and constantly present) parents with whom strong ties are formed and around whom the emotional problems and attitudes of Freudian psychology develop. How far these can be transferred or developed round foster parents in very early life does not seem to have been much studied. Certainly by the age of four or five strong emotional ties with nurses may exist.[1]

Another impression is that children lacking some normal element in their home environment (e.g. only children) attempt to remedy the defects when opportunity serves. Taken to school at five or six they play the elder brother with smaller children and the younger with older, and, unless an ineffaceable diffidence or intolerance has already settled upon them, their relationship with their playmates will cover a large slice of the brotherly or sisterly one which occurs within the family, even though they are still able to exercise their jealous determination never to share their parents.

But what is the normal brotherly relationship within the family ? And what the fatherly, motherly, and sisterly ? Our psychologists have been busy seeing the family turning up all through a man's social life. Is it not rather that a man's social attitude shows itself first in his family ? An individual of strongly marked character will show his or her fundamental and peculiar qualities within the family if it offers the necessary targets. Aggressiveness, brutality, ' toadying ', chivalry, trust, suspiciousness, deceit, pertinacity or its lack—there are few fundamental qualities of adult man which do not cast their shadows before

[1] See Isaacs, *Social development in young children* (infra, p. 114).

them from the nursery. And family life may be less the life we are all reliving with dummy brothers and sisters afterwards than the early opportunity of showing our developing characters as fully as possible in settings where those characters may still be controlled and modified, before we pass on to vindicate them in the wider world.

One striking thing about man's social life is that it is so natural to him that he makes the utmost use of his earliest opportunities to develop his various powers of relationship with others. Another is the corollary that even within the limitations of a family the utmost variability of character type may be found.

It is easier to enumerate variety in human nature than to indicate cardinal qualities. In the *Leviathan* Hobbes has a chapter on the ' passions', of which he defines some seventy varieties. But consider the following simple contrasts : the selfish, egotistical, and unbending with the unselfish, humble, and kind ; the aloof and ' unsociable ' with those who are ' alive ' only in ' society ' ; those who rush to co-operate, with those to whom joint enterprises are so difficult ; the organizers with the organized ; the ' managing ' folk, tactful, understanding, adaptable, intuitive, with those they practise upon ; the suspicious and cautious with the open and unsuspecting. Consider the different groups which different people are ' at home ' in, the variety and powers of exclusion of man's loyalties, and of his phobias. How very many of these various characters may be found within the scope of one large family !

But this variability of conduct between men may be of less significance to society than the variability of behaviour within a single individual. Who can scan such a list as that set out above and declare himself quite out of sympathy and eternally free of any one of those contrasting qualities? Who has not been selfish and unselfish, aloof and sociable, organizer and organized, the tactful negotiator and the dupe, suspicious and unsuspecting? And who has not become ' a different person ' in a different setting ? Who lacks loyalties ? And who irrational antipathies ? What child does not live amongst others by the aid of his own self-discipline ? And what adult, surveying the history of his social relationships, can say that he has never needed and will never need the background of external law and external force to reinforce the discipline of self, if his conduct is to be acceptable to society ?

Abnormal men will remain on one side of the balance in various of these antitheses of character. Normal human nature certainly takes an inherent bias of the individual on each antithesis, and also a bias imparted by the fantasy life built up in infancy. And then it swings widely between the one side and the other according to the external stimuli received. Provocation appears to be the cause of a very large slice of human behaviour, whether it be of the good in it or of the evil. And the training of a child consists largely in surrounding it with a milieu in which anti-social reactions, such as aggressiveness, jealousy, meanness, and dishonesty are at a discount. A man like the late George Lansbury, who has got it into his bones that human nature is a good and kindly thing, will stand the aggressive buffetings of fortune, personal or social, with an equanimity arising from confidence attained in early childhood. Given an initial bias to kindliness of interpretation, persistent re-discovery that hatred does not come to meet a cheerful countenance will tip the balance so often that in later life it is only with a creaking resistance that such a kindly character will consent to meet harsh events with a harsh welcome.

2. *Manifestations of aggressiveness.*—Now let us consider Dr. Glover's ' normal ' man (Chapter III, p. 97) who was ' not actively warlike but not actively peace-loving '. There can be no doubt of the fact that hostile provocation can turn that man into a violent warmonger. And the opposing stimuli of a stable society may prevent his ever showing to others, or knowing himself, that he harboured such hateful and hating antipathies. We have to study how these provocations elicit the responses which they do.

There is no doubt that the problem of the unexpected aggressive response is near to the heart of the psychology of law and order in society. Glover,[1] following Freud, thinks of the impulse which perverts the normal man in wartime as being a pent up aggressiveness of his infancy, repressed for years by the necessity of winning the love and approval of a peaceful society. With the outbreak of a popular war, such a man's family and friends, and society generally, suddenly approve instead of dis-approving of his ' infantile ' impulses to smash and ruin, provided only that these impulses are directed on to the national enemy. There can be no doubt that the sanctions of group loyalties and national unity tip the scale in which this particular passion of aggressiveness resides very heavily downwards. But Glover follows Freud into believing that it *must necessarily be so tipped at frequent intervals, or there will be nowhere for man's aggressiveness to go*. Here is a point where theory influences interpretation of fact very acutely. If a parent is told that a dangerous tendency in his child has been definitely checked, he rejoices. If an engineer is told that an abnormal stress in a bridge has been adequately met, he is satisfied. If a horticulturist can finally prevent his best roses from going wild, he is delighted. But in Freud's ' libido ' theory *prevention of discharge* leads to *accumulation of tension*, and accumulation of tension to an *increased demand for discharge*. And so on, until bursting point is reached. Now physiologists who study the nervous system experimentally are familiar with provocative stimulation which *excites* a discharge of nervous

[1] Glover, loc. cit. p. 35.

energy, and even with stimulation which *arrests* a discharge, but not with tension which *accumulates in the absence of excitation*. The ' behaviourist ' psychologist follows the physiologist in this, and is able to make the directing and limiting (' conditioning ') of reflex responses of the nervous system a basis of animal training and even of some useful guides to human education.   It is only because Freud has introduced his ' pressure ' metaphor into his theory of ' libido ' that the impression has become current, first among psychoanalysts and then more widely, that there exist spontaneously accumulating tensions which demand their own release, and that, unless certain educative tendencies are *relaxed*, the result will be, not greater security, but an explosion.   While psychoanalytical technique is unable to elicit factual information one way or the other upon this matter, all the available evidences of analogy with other and accurately determinable reactions of the nervous system suggest that emotional responses are in fact excited by provocative stimulation.   Among these reactions is the aggressiveness of normal men.   The provocations may be subtle indeed—a challenge, a sneer, an ideal of service.   But provocations they remain.   And when they operate upon an individual with an inherent bias towards aggressiveness, or with half-forgotten memories of early aggressiveness and the fantasy joys of ' annihilating ', aggressive he becomes.   The explosions are due to provocation, however, and not to its absence.   If we remove the stimulus we abolish the responsive discharge.

It is, of course, true that most men do not live a life in which their aggressive instincts remain totally unstimulated.   They are annoyed, and they show it, directly or indirectly.   Obstacles thwart them and they set their teeth.   Manifold activities of mind and body are used by healthy men to ' work off ' that aggressiveness which is stimulated by the current events of life.   Our greatest annoyances are often due to the many psychological prejudices and misconceptions which we all harbour.   But healthy men have little or no difficulty in dealing, by a judicious combination of activity and repression, with the aggressiveness which comes to them in normal times.   Some men may occasionally be the better for a fight ; and then a punch-ball should be available in the absence of a like-minded brother combatant. But few of us are better for a war.   And all available observations appear to me to show, not that accumulating aggressiveness leads to war, but rather that *certain artificially provoked conditions which precede war lead to the ' sweep ' of aggressiveness—fully justifying Glover's emphasis—which is apparent in normal men in time of conflict.*

What more does direct observation show us about man's difficulties with his fellows ?   I think this : that, besides being provoked, the aggressiveness of man is temporary, and limited in a peculiar way.   Some men admit to bad tempers.   They are usually half-way towards conquering them. The really tempestuous, touchy, and aggressive people tend to repudiate or minimize their fault. It is plain enough to others ; but to them it is other people who are so repeatedly difficult, or their own circumstances so constantly peculiar. The reason is that they very much dislike their own aggressive outbursts. The rest of their mind *does* repudiate this reaction ; their social feelings dislike the wave of hostility which sweeps through the mind, and the mind as a whole, seeking harmony, forgets, or explains away, or even apologises for each successive outburst, without admitting the fact that these reactions are as much a part of the individual as his more kindly and less dangerous responses. Our attitude to our aggressive and ' baser ' passions is very much that of Conrad's ' Lord Jim ' to his self-preserving and dishonourable caution ; ' his thoughts full of valorous deeds . . . as if some conviction of innate blamelessness had checked the truth writhing within him at every turn '.

Society has always recognized the occurrence of temporary reactions which are inharmonious with the personality as a whole. A man ' loses ' his ' temper ', i.e. his usual temperament, for a time. The French make exceptional excuses for *crimes passionelles*. ' He was not himself at the time ', is a plea in social equity, and in some cases in law as well. Outbursts of personal passion are very near to hysteria in mechanism ; and, at whatever age they occur, the external control which they require is such as we give to an irresponsible and passionate child.

We shall discover later (in Chapter V) that the control of individual violence which society exercises is not merely constituted by a ruling majority (or minority) to meet the needs of a small criminal class. In its essence it is a recognition by social man of one of his major needs as an individual. Police-power of some kind is instituted very early in any organized community. Consciously we all think of it as being useful for our own protection against others. But, again, how many adults who can and will be honest with themselves on the matter could guarantee that their own conduct throughout life would be free of violent physical aggression against others, if it were not for the ever-present knowledge that behind their infuriating antagonist there is, within reach of a whistle, a shout, a bicycle ride, or a telephone message, the force of an unassailable nursemaid who will find their violence wrong and set in motion an inevitable corrective ? Directly effective police power is withdrawn—as in remote districts or disturbed times—the impulse to implement sudden passion with violence enters formidably into men's heads. In the remote west of Ireland minor differences on the way home from market are still settled by resort to the ' ash plant ', and it is comparatively easy to be threatened with a good hiding in County Mayo.

In the ordinary individual we find *the cardinal characteristics of aggressive violence to be* (1) *that it is a well-nigh universal potentiality,* (2) *that it is spasmodically excited, often by means unaccountable to the individual himself,* (3) *that it is generally unacceptable to (and tends to be repudiated or forgotten by) the social self of the individual,* (4) *that it requires at bottom external force for its control.*

In warfare men unite to share their prejudices ; the opposition of the social self to violence is converted into approval—for society approves. The place of selfish anti-social force is then occupied (so it is felt) by ' corrective ' force, of which all societies and nearly all men recognize the need. Repeated observations make us reasonably sure that a society is unwilling to face the physical rigours and the mental stresses of warfare, unless its conscience is clear. National warfare is always seen by the participants as ' the only way left ' to correct some great error, to save a culture, or to establish a ' good '. To a few ' leaders ' a war may be a gamble justified by ambition or fear. To the mass of men who support it and suffer by it, its cause is always ' right '. And since two opposites cannot both be right, and human nature is the same in these matters wherever we turn, it follows that this ' rightness ' is always a figment. If anyone will study the history of any big national war which has needed the approval of peoples for it to be fought, he will see by what steps prejudice and complacency are fed, so that the errors of judgment of a few become adopted by the many, and the faults of a few become attributed to the whole. With increasing tension, blinder eyes are turned upon the faults of the loved ' nation ', and sterner reproaches fall upon the object of hostility and fear. It is then that aggressiveness begins to mount the throne of men's minds ; persecutions of hundreds by tens, or of thousands by hundreds, become attributed to the villainy of millions. There then arises the desire to unite in something very strong (say fifty million strong, and therefore surely unassailable !), and then to be justified in smashing, if in the last resort the increasing infamy of the foe will not yield to a national policy, which it is felt was so reasonable and gentle, if it had only met with a kindly encouragement ! It is like Freud's ' normal ' man for ever unable to take the first step of being generous himself on the impossible assumption that his opponent might be decent. The highly selective propaganda which always characterises 'isms and 'ologies heightens the story. And for months before a war actually breaks out the personal psychology of Freud and Hobbes becomes that of the group as a whole. It is then, indeed, an impossible task to convince any considerable number of members of the one community that the members of the other are very like themselves, a little bolder here, or a little more credulous there, but not passing outside the ordinary laws of human nature,

by which men are susceptible to kindness as well as force. Above
all is it difficult to convince them that they themselves are so
easily deluded over ' right ' and ' vital interests ' that they are
invariably in process of sacrificing these to their own illusions.
In group passion, as in personal passion, the greatest loss is that
of the realization that others are like ourselves. But passion
once over, in both cases our cherished loss is the memory that
we were ' ever like that '.

II. OBSERVATION OF CHILD PSYCHOLOGY

We have before us for everyone to observe the varied natures of
men, the variable nature of each man, and the distortion of both the
individual and the group which aggressive passion produces. Hobbes'
theory of man's fundamental un-sociability of temperament in the
presence of an economic need for society comes appropriately to the
fore in times of social stress and national strife, particularly in
minds that contain an initial bias towards selecting the aggressive
in their observations and interpretations of conduct. Freud's
additional theory that all man's deep aggressiveness is built up in
childhood, then repressed, to be unleashed with the dogs of war, has
led some observers of human nature to look for the actual evidences
of Freudian mechanisms in children.

1. *Klein*, herself a psychoanalyst, introduced Freud's
methods of study and treatment to ' problem ' children. She
was able to support a number of his deductions by direct observation. She traced the roots of the ' obsessional ' character more
clearly than ever to infancy. For instance, she observed a well-
established combination of exaggerated goodness and uncontrollable naughtiness, anxiety in play, intolerance of frustration,
etc., in a girl aged two and a half years, and then traced this back
to oscillations of affection and jealousy over the parents, which
preceded it from the first year of life. Her observations tended
to support the theory that the abnormal attitudes of these cases
to their parents originate in fantasy. For she found that it was
less a real than an invented parent that caused the earliest anxieties
of the child.[1] Her deductions suffer by her acceptance of Freud's
mechanisms, thought, and language, with all its topsy-turvydoms
which are sometimes right and sometimes wrong. For her, any
child that doesn't like sucking is thought to be suffering from
' an internal frustration derived from abnormally increased oral
sadism ', which in its turn is evidence of ' the polarity of life-
instinct and death-instinct '. ' We *know*', she writes, ' that the
destructive instinct is directed against the organism itself. . . .
In my view it is this danger which is felt by the individual as an
anxiety springing from aggressiveness.' She thinks the conscience
(' super-ego ') starts by the mobilization of one part of the self-

[1] Klein, *Psychoanalysis of Children*, pp. 24–28. (1932.)

destroying forces against another, thus dividing the ' id ' (deepest self), and that the resultant anxiety over the self is later projected on to an object, the mother. The child then rages against the mother, and in particular ' wishes to destroy her frustrating breast '. Freud is echoed in the extremity of language which the writer feels it necessary to use to depict infantile sadism, ' coming from every source at once and raised to the highest pitch of intensity ', so that ' anal, oral, and urethral attacks on the mother are desired '.[1] That such emotions are actually detectable in the child affords very precise confirmation of the astonishing mechanisms of the childish mind to which adult obsessional patients return in their psychoanalytical sessions. Klein believes the whole to trace back to ' over-strong sadism, or rather to sadism which has not been successfully modified, and which has led to excessive anxiety '.[2] By these alternative origins she leaves open the question of how abnormal the original aggressiveness of these characters is. But she shows how very clearly and how very early abnormal aggressiveness may take its place in the lives of obsessional children and so necessitate the stressful and complicated mental gymnastics with which they attempt its mastery. The mastery is seldom complete. But by thwarting and disciplining themselves, often to the point of living lives either miserable through anxiety or unremitting in service and self-sacrifice, these same aggressive and hating characters succeed in becoming acceptable to society, and are often classed among its mainsprings. On such findings one might be inclined to regard a ' self-destructive ' instinct as reactionary to the imperious demands of a ' social ' instinct upon an aggressive character. For what are we to call this urge which transcends all others, the one which demands that we shall be acceptable to our fellows ? Examine it where we will, from the grave back to the cradle, we find this need to be accepted and to be well thought of—now by our neighbours, then by our parents. If necessary, we erect a phantom parent in our minds, to school us and to secure that, individualistic and aggressive or no, we are brought back ever and again, with whatever pain to ourselves, to our need for the consolation of a clear conscience in the presence of our fellow men.

Klein's mind follows Freud's in a tendency to assume that the same conflicts as she finds in obsessional children occur in the normal child, but remain undetected because adequate solutions are found. Normal people, she says, ' get constant reassurance against their anxiety '. Why not substitute ' never need to have this anxiety ' ?—Throughout her work we find the same tendency to generalize about ' every girl ' and ' every boy ' that we found in Freud. In general, she confirms his discovered mechanisms. But also she accepts his extended inferences.

2. *Mrs. Isaacs* made her observations in a little school of

---

[1] Klein, *Psychoanalysis of Children*, p. 138. (1932.)   [2] Ibid. p. 225.

normal children. These observations are just what are needed in any survey of the development of human behaviour. Here in her diaries we find, not little excerpts, but the whole mixture of human nature and also the peculiar aspects of it which have produced some of our social theories.

Isaacs shows us children of two to four years of age, threatening, bargaining, bullying, making love, endeavouring to work out conflicts which arise from personal aggressiveness combined with a need for love. First the early megalomanias appear— everything centring round the interests of self. It is a sufficient excuse for hitting another child that ' he opened the door and I didn't want him to '. Force is readily threatened. ' Will you be my baby, or shall I make you cry ? ' Destructive urges are often sudden, e.g. against another child's superior craftsmanship. They ' usually enjoy their first experience of disturbing another child. They laugh if they accidentally knock over a child's bricks, or trip him up or hit him while wielding a spade '. But ' very soon their sympathy and understanding grow to the extent of making them refrain from laughing at the discomfiture they have accidentally caused. They stand and stare in silence, looking somewhat perturbed themselves. Some children have reached this stage by the time they enter school.' [1] Of the bully, ' some of the bigger children find it irresistible to knock about and fight the smaller ones. It gives them such a delightful sense of power. But with the help of reproof and suggestions from the teacher, this feeling of power comes to find ample satisfaction in protecting and helping the smaller children instead of bullying them.'

These are common character traits undergoing a general development. But great variability is noted. There are early differences between the sexes. In one series of abnormal reactions, the boys showed aggressive reactions which compared with the girls in the numbers and ratio of eighteen to seven, the girls showed attacks of fear, anxiety, or night terrors which compared with the boys as forty-three to twenty-four. There may be periods of acquisitiveness and defiance, of anxiety or brooding. A sense of general jealousy of others often appears, e.g. ' It's better for me when there aren't any other children about, isn't it ? ' But really destructive impulses may cause alarm to their possessor at a very early age. Frank, about to bang a cup on the piano, was full of distress and anger, crying, ' I'll break it '. Asked what was the matter, he replied : ' I don't know ', and, weeping, turned to the grown-up for comfort. When the children began to co-operate, a sense of justice appeared, such as in holding a balance of turns for two younger children with the communal tricycle or showing collective resentment against Tommy for snatching a basket of flowers from Alice.

[1] Isaacs, S., *Social Development in Young Children*, p. 44. (Routledge. 1933.)

Sharing naturally offers difficulties. This is the sort of observation Isaacs makes : ' Jessica and Lena fought for a quarter of an hour for possession of the tricycle. Mrs. I. suggested sharing. Each refused, saying " *I* want it ". Mrs. I. walked away saying " If you won't share it, there's nothing I can do, is there ? " At which one and then the other shouted : " Oh ! come *back* Mrs. Isaacs. We *will* share." Then they each wanted to have the first go as an excuse to break the agreement and ride off with the tricycle. But at the renewed suggestion of Mrs. Isaacs they finally settled down and kept going round happily in turns for the rest of the morning.' Here we see the essence of passionate man's attitude to his ' vital interests '. Nobody gets the tricycle because nobody can give up the tricycle, until they are threatened by the greater calamity of losing the guiding presence and care of Mrs. I. The children next demonstrate their need of impartial authority by their readiness to break their agreements. Finally, assured of the authority which will secure justice for them both, they lose their enmity—and share their tricycle. It may be noted that the value of the third party in securing a settlement is heightened when that party appears unwilling to assist. Mrs. Isaacs comments on a series of stressful and hostile incidents : ' There were countless minor incidents of mutual helpfulness and common activity which could not be recorded, and long stretches of quiet constructive work which do not show here.'

Mrs. Isaacs has more of interest to tell us about the fundamental social behaviour of children. Although when they are first put together they do not combine readily, their individual fantasies soon begin to overlap and co-operation follows. ' As the children get to know each other, and build up a common history, the mutual adaptation of fantasy occurs more and more often. They gain the experience of doing things together in the same way and in the same sense, and discover the benefits and delights of mutual support, both in imaginative play and in real achievement.' [1] The children need others from the first. But they need them partly for reality and partly to fill a fantasy picture which is only gradually and partially adapting itself to reality as life unfolds. It is, says Isaacs, when other people refuse to conform to their fantasies that children come to recognize their individuality and the need for conformation on their part.

In group play, a leader does in fact ' create ' the group. The others learn the pleasures of subordinate co-operation. Nevertheless, few children accept a passive rôle all the time, or in relation to all their playmates. Some even of the oldest will occasionally agree to change rôles and become subordinate for a time. But there are some children who are hardly able to enjoy

[1] Isaacs, S., loc. cit. p. 215.

free play with others because their feelings of rivalry are too acute and too fraught with anxiety. They have not themselves the qualities which make leaders, and they are unable to tolerate being followers. They despise their playfellows and call them silly.[1]

Considering the environmental factors in the abnormal children, Mrs. Isaacs records that ' on the whole, the crudely aggressive children were those who had been whipped at home, though there were exceptions to this in both directions '. But ' *every one of the children was hostile to the others in some degree and some form at one time or another* '.[2] She separated a simple ' aggressiveness for possession, power, and rivalry ' from ' aggressiveness with moodiness ', the result of internal conflicts and tending to be periodic and accompanied by superior or inferior feelings. The former is very strong, and its suppression (e.g. in having to ' take turns ' with a toy) is ' one of the most difficult lessons for a child under five to learn '. They have ' ages ' to wait for their turn, and they do not at first trust the other child to give place to them, knowing that they themselves would not want to do so. Here is a link with the partisanship, built out of suspicion and desire, which makes us adults such bad judges of our own cause. And there follow three very important observations for the sociologist : (1) *Neither of the children was willing to accept arbitration of a dispute until she had proved to herself that she could not gain her point by her own efforts. Then* (2) *each fought for equality in the sharing. ' We must be equal.' But* (3) *all the children knew how often teasing and bullying would have passed over into real cruelty if it had not been for the presence of Mrs. I. or Miss B.* In this birth of the desire for law, we see ' *justice* ' starting as the next best bargain after a sense of reality has removed the hope of complete possession. Fear of the violence of others and of self leads to a welcoming, or at least an acquiescence, in external control. The consequent satisfaction and security of the change from aggression to co-operation and sharing provide the conditions in which ' justice ' becomes symbolic of the social solution of individual claims. And from childhood up all of us delight in applying this solution to the affairs of others, giving them at once what will secure society and what should satisfy them.

On the vexed question of ' primary ' aggressiveness, Isaacs writes : ' It can be said, taking all our evidence together, that in the earliest years all children (with an intensity varying according to inner conditions and outer circumstances) feel other children to be actual or potential rivals. . . .[3] There are children who show little if any open hostility to the new baby in their own family, and much less than the average to other children generally. . . . The variability depends on . . . home circumstances,

[1] Isaacs, S., loc. cit. pp. 218 et seq.   [2] Ibid. p. 219.   [3] Ibid. p. 231.

earlier experiences . . . 'the psychological constitution of the child.' ' Moody hostility ' is evidence of ' trouble at home.'

Group loyalty allows hostility to be shown with impunity for it can be focused *outside* the group. Groups once formed showed general but evanescent hostility to newcomers (' Shall we hit him ? ') and even to new clothes. There tend to be two groups at least whatever the number in the classroom—another very important point for the sociologist.[1] A quiet statement by an adult of things as they appear to the other side excited sympathy, however, and was often the surest way of settling a dispute.

Turning to instinctive social reactions, Isaacs considers that no ' social instinct ' develops suddenly, but rather that there is a steady development of social reactions between the ages of two and seven years. She quotes Bridges on three phases of normal social development: first, dependence; second, self-assertion (aged two and a half to three); third, co-operation. Children don't show a ' herd ' but a family response as the basis of their social reactions. She notes very mixed and fluctuating attitudes (ambivalence) to parents.[2] After reaching six or seven years of age they become more sensitive to the praise or blame of their fellows, and from that time less confidence is shown in adults.

Mrs. Isaacs carefully noted the observable sexual development of the children in her school, confirming a great number of Freud's previous discoveries of the child mind made through the analysis of adults. Like Klein she finds the ' obsessional ' type of child, with its undue emphasis on aggressiveness and on excretal and erotic (or ' sexual ') matters. Like Klein she inclines to take many of these mechanisms as mere over-emphasis of those of normal development. She fully accepts the ' hard ' doctrine that ' certainly by the end of the first year of life children are jealous of their fathers' (sexual) relations with their mothers, and also have some intuitive awareness of their nature '.[3] Then, having observed a number of actual behaviours of great technical interest to the psychoanalyst and having set these forth with many wise comments, Mrs. Isaacs turns to the relationship between social development and the fantasies and fears arising in connexion with these early family loves and stresses which are soon repressed into unconsciousness. She notes how a little girl is reassured by her mother's return (accompanied by a life-sized doll) that her own emotions had not driven ' Mummy ' away, and that she then changes at once from a ' difficult ' child into one ' loving, co-operative, and tender with the other children '; and how a boy who had been both unduly aggressive and clumsy at school as long as he was pursued by fantasies of the ' bad parent ' (Freud's patriarchal father), was redeemed in both his faults by a reassuring adult love which believed in his power to

[1] Isaacs, S., loc. cit. p. 250.   [2] Ibid. p. 388.   [3] Ibid. p. 298.

be skilful and sensible. Here is a beneficent circle in which
security frees co-operative impulses which in turn increase the
security itself and thus also the reasons for co-operation. Environmental factors are thus of the highest importance for social
development throughout. Mrs. Isaacs gives no reasons whatever for believing that any fundamentally destructive core remains
from the stage of ' defiant self-assertion against the world in
general and its parent in particular ' which she nevertheless
believes to occur very early in the life of every healthily developing child.[1]

Cautions and very good advice are given by this author both
to parents and to educationalists. For the latter : ' Freedom
from repression ' may mean just leaving the child at the mercy
of a very harsh super-ego (conscience) which he has had to build
up for himself. ' We must respect his early efforts at independence and individuality, and at the same time help him to control
his more crudely destructive impulses. . . . Children help each
other . . . companionship in play is one of the greatest needs
of childhood.'

In her review of the conduct of the young children in her
school the author pays her tribute to Freud's theory ' which
serves to make these records intelligible '. But the picture she
has painted is a much fuller, more natural, and altogether more
encouraging record of fact than the selected residual fantasies
which Freud's intuition seized upon and placed at the fundament
of human motivation. Isaacs sums up her book as follows :
' We have seen these children playing out their private fantasies
and trying to impose them upon their companions. We have
heard them quarrelling for the possession of a coveted tool or
toy, revelling in the sense of power over others and furious when
occasion denied them this pleasure. We have seen their miseries
and hatreds when rivals claimed a place in the love and attention
of playmates or grown-ups, and their unscrupulous efforts to
turn such rivals out of favour. We have noticed the moody disaffection of some of the children, and how little any of them could
ever bear to be inferior to others in skill and virtue. We have
seen how naturally they show suspicion and dislike of newcomers, how severe their strictures upon weaker brethren can
be, and how even the adults, just judges and defenders of the
weak, may incur the united displeasure of the group when fellow-
feeling is strong.' But ' we have seen, too, the charm of their
friendly ways to their playmates and to grown-ups, their generous
appreciation of each other and unstinted warmth of love. And
we have watched their eager interest in making and inventing,
their pleasure in song and dance and miming, in exploring the
world of things and arguing about the world of people.' Finally,
' we have also seen how the younger children will bite or spit

[1] Isaacs, S., loc. cit. p. 257.

in playfulness or in anger . . . chant about excretory products
. . . display their bodily parts for admiration . . . (show) un-
mistakable signs of sexual desire and excitement and . . .
glimpses of sexual loss . . . quaint notions of marriage and
birth . . . guilt and shame'.

These children are the raw material of society, and Mrs.
Isaacs' book is a study of society in the making. It will give a
better idea of the mixed nature of man, of the fine balance
between his co-operative and egocentric instincts, and of how
that balance is swayed, than any reading of technical works on
' deep ' psychology. And in Susan Isaacs' description of her
young children we see the need of and the place for external
authority and control—to win their confidence in the security
which comes with co-operation, to confirm their distrust of their
own suspicions and enmities ; but also, when they relapse into
their passionate primitive selves or join in persecutory ' sadistic '
groups, to act in their restraint with whatever of firmness be
necessary. *In all these matters the child is father of the man.*

III. PSYCHOANALYTICAL REACTIONS AND REAL LIFE SIDE BY SIDE

*But how do people behave during adult psychoanalysis ? And,
among the rather exceptional characters which are submitted to this
process of mental exploration, what is the relationship between
behaviour in the analytical setting and behaviour in the outside
world ?*

We have reminded ourselves of the variety of human conduct
of which we are aware in our daily lives. We have drawn attention to the less frequently noted range of potential variability
and actual variation of conduct in each one of us, the strange
twists and turns of our characters, which we are inclined to forget
or to repudiate, but which do in fact belong to us, and which
are liable to return to claim their places in our minds. We have
seen the first clashes and combinations of our human qualities
under skilled observation in the nursery school. And now we
return to the clever but ailing personalities in whom no simple
solution has offered itself for the direction of pride, or aggressiveness, or lust, or fear, and in whom, in consequence of external
mismanagement or of internal misapprehensions, these stressful
emotions are producing symptoms.

In Chapter III we described the general setting of psychoanalysis, its method of procedure, and the presenting disabilities—
hysterias, phobias, obsessions, arms paralysed through fear,
voices lost through doubt and fear, the apprehension of blindness
from guilt and fear, loneliness, inadequacy, panic, and *always
fear*. We know that when we probe the fear we find it is fear of
the consequences of selfishness, often, though not always, of
aggressive or sexual selfishness, which is repressed as dangerous,

inadequately repressed and thus doubly dangerous. And the fear is the fear of loss of esteem. For the simple adult neurosis— e.g. the shell-shocked soldier—it is loss of the esteem of fellows, of society. In the deeper infantile roots of most neuroses it is less the loss of love of fellow-children, brothers and sisters, than of guardian adults which is feared, and in its first setting and its ultimate analysis the fear is usually of the loss of the love of mother or father. The ' normally aggressive ' little child of Mrs. Isaacs' book will decide either that wayward impulses can be mastered, or else that they are not too bad. In either case parental love and care can be retained, and a normal and reason-ably sociable child faces the outer world. The child who, through mishandling by foolish or wicked parents or through its inherent inadaptability, becomes the ' moody aggressive ' child, needs special help if its youthful misconception that it is impossible to be oneself and be loved is not to lead to the neurotic tempera-ment and the neurotic symptom. It is this latter stressful group of citizens whose psychology we are now to study.

The neurotic citizen is in a minority. But he and she are a very important element in the life of society and of the state. Neurotics may have an endowment of undue aggressiveness or sensuality ; they certainly develop unusual abilities. Our knowledge is sufficient to say that there is probably much truth in Freud's linking together of mental ability and original emotional strength. Repression of a direct and simple expression of energy is certainly related, though often by means obscure, to the elaborate and diverse manifestations of energies useful to society, which neurotics so often achieve. Physical energy, not drawn upon in manual work, produces out of the sedentary student the straining athlete. A psychological reinforcement of an aggressive or orgasmic energy will press him perhaps to physical or else to mental efforts of high attainment. And when we remember that these ' nervous ' types have a further emotional stimulus of fear that they will not achieve, it is not surprising that the plodder who will not be stayed, the shining genius, and the insatiable careerist are all likely to be in or near the category of mind that becomes the special province of the psychoanalyst. We say ' in or near ', because there may be as much difference between so managing one's life as to avoid symptoms, under whatever pressure it is done, and having to run crying to the reassuring ' Mummy ' element in society, as there is between climbing a cliff and falling off it. Certainly our most successful men do not usually come to doctors for treatment, though perhaps many of our best do. Some absolutely ' nightmare ' personalities come as well ! How do these various and striking people behave, (a) in psychoanalysis, and (b) in real life ?

I will now describe a dozen neurotic patients seen by me at the Tavistock Clinic, London, noting the sort of people they were and also the types of unconscious thought which underlay their neuroses. Three of the cases (A, B, and C) I will then describe in detail sufficient to give the reader some insight into the aggressive and co-operative motives of their minds so that these may be compared with their actual behaviour in society.

1. *Twelve case notes summarized.* *Case I.*—An artist, aged twenty-four, suffered from tempers, panic fears, and feelings of inadequacy. He was the only son of separated parents, had lived a varied life of isolation, hardship, and some want as a boy, had hated his drunken father and lived with his mother until the time of our first consultation. A dull job in industrial art bored him, and his own art refused to come right. His analysis showed underlying dissatisfaction with his rather wayward mother, a great deal of hatred and a still deeper love for his father, strong 'Oedipal' situations, with 'identifications' with both parents, much infantile erotism, guilt, and reactionary 'sadism', and 'masochism'.——In real life he was attractive, witty, uncertainly modest, kind and exasperated by turns in society, generously loving and passionately sadistic or masochistic (self-torturing) with his loved ones at home. His is Case A below (p. 130).

Case II.—A housewife, aged twenty-four, was unable to cross a road or be seen in certain ' exposed ' places (e.g. an open heath) unless accompanied by her husband or certain other reliable people. She had been worse since her engagement and the death of her grandfather when she was about nineteen, but she had feared exposed places on and off since she was five, when crossing the playground or the hall at school had upset her. She had a rather spoilt upbringing as the only child in a difficult household composed of alcoholic father and grandfather, weak mother and a dominant grandmother. In analysis she traced her fear of exposure to fear of her own infantile passions and erotisms. She showed the aggressiveness of obsessional characters, of which she was a good example, reviving in analysis memories of intense demands upon the emotions of others, and fearful jealousies and fears of retribution. She showed both sadism and masochism.—— In real life she was quiet, virtuous, domesticated, intellectually keen and masterful, and anxious to resolve her doubts and fears of maternity. She made emotional demands upon her near relatives and exacted attention and care from them, a trait which opened the pathway to her interesting and sympathy-arousing symptoms. (Case B, p. 132.)

Case III.—A specialist engineer, aged forty, could not travel by Underground train for the previous four years without an agony of mind as to what would happen if the train got stuck in the tunnel. His relief was in hurried visits to the lavatory at each available station. He was the youngest son of a happy family, and ' happily ' married. His analysis showed a deep distrust of others, and a fear of the ' battle of life ' with its ' survival of the fittest'. This was accompanied by an intense aggressiveness against all who would delay or thwart him, which was traceable to 'Oedipal' situations.——In real life he was reliable and popular, he 'killed others with kindness', and only occasionally reacted spitefully when too much was demanded of him. He indulged in sly sadistic remarks, however, and made his phobias and obsessions trying to his wife. He was highly valued in his firm and given posts of responsibility, where energy and unique knowledge were required. (Case C, p. 135.)

Case IV.—A manual labourer, aged thirty-six, had feelings of tension when at work (as a fitter's mate) which made him feel it would be a relief to 'get the sack'. He wandered about alone, brooding over abstractions of 'conflict', and plans of self improvement. He had had a motherless and very hard childhood after the age of nine, with a father who was sometimes drunken and brutal and at others emotionally inaccessible. He both went to sea, and left the sea, because of diffidences and stresses in dealing with his fellows. His analysis showed a withdrawn emotional life, with much detached and symbolic ('schizoid') representation of emotions in clouds, figures, and diagrams, and an intellectualization of his problems which had made him a wide and a deep philosopher. Many of his diagrams resemble those of Freud himself (e.g. he visualized the 'ideas borrowed from others' of Freud's 'super-ego', with 'below and on another plane my real self'). He saw his problem as 'Fear'. By analysis he was able very gradually to face conflicts between desire and fear which seem to have started in early misapprehensions (again at the 'Oedipal' period of life). His deeper mind had great difficulty in accepting human nature as he believed it to be. He feared and hated the 'primitive impulses which are the real motives of men'. He envied those 'whose parents love each other'. He had aggressive impulses, but a fearful search for love dominated his emotional life, and despair of love had numbed his feelings.——In real life he was reserved, cautious, with a slow kindly smile and a pugnacity which was purely reactionary to real or imagined slights ; a helpful, honest citizen, full of social and patriotic idealism and loyal to his friends.

Case V.—An electrician, aged thirty-four, had feared blindness since about the time of his engagement nine years previously. He had chosen his wife rather than her sister because of the latter's need for spectacles, and his fears—which extended to cataclysms of various kinds, earthquakes, strokes, visitations of God, sudden death—were traceable early in his youth and boyhood. On analysis he was found to have developed in childhood elaborate anatomical notions connecting his emotional tension (1) with tension in the head (which might burst) and the eyes (which might 'pop') ; (2) (during adolescent sexuality) with loss of brain substance through his spinal cord with a consequent draining of vital substance from the eyes at the top (the reverse of (1)). He had come to believe that God punished sins by an affliction of the organ sinning ; and as a ' voyeur ' he felt much guilt at many innocent and natural pleasures which his eyes had brought him. Characteristically enough his fears of things swelling and bursting were accompanied by desire for these same things to happen. The anatomy of the human calf fascinated him as it swelled upwards to pass out of sight under the skirt. Red faces like his father's, apoplectic and bursting with passion, attracted frightened looks from behind his shielded eyes. By free-association we discovered the horrifying and compelling ideas of the ' Oedipal ' situation in his infancy, when he shared a poor room with his neurotic mother and drunken father,[1] whom like Patient No. 1 he both feared and loved. Sadistic impulses to ' smash heads ' he certainly had. But in an analysis of over one hundred hours these reactions were meagre compared with those masochistic (self-torturing) ones through which his social instinct attempted a combined punishment, prevention, and cure of his selfish erotisms. The manifest needs of this patient were : (1) religious sustenance, (2) dispersal of the fantastic notions built up by his sense of guilt, (3) an adult revaluation of the demands of self and society where they appeared to clash.——In real life this man was quaint, modest, friendly, and lovable. His work was painstaking and reliable, except when he was ' ill '. He had secured a very wise wife for himself, though in some of his wild searches for cure she had had to upbraid him with ' marrying her to a bottle of medicine '.

Case VI.—An insurance clerk, aged thirty, had not been able to swallow liquids properly since ' panicking ' on choking himself with iced lemonade five years previously. He also wanted to discuss his fears of physical suffering. His imagination dwelt on affairs of honour where he might prove unworthy, and he soon described such a fight at school when he was thirteen. Underneath, he liked fighting and as a younger child he had shown this. But it was un-Christian and alarming to-day. The relevant early misconception of this man's mind was that people of certain physique (his own) were always weak and cowardly, while ' leaders and natural people ' were quite different. These latter had receding chins, jaws which ' locked properly ' and ' large swallows ' (like his mother and his *fiancée*). His own facial peculiarities included a small mouth, unequal jaws, large tongue, awkward swallow, and prominent chin. The latter he would feel gingerly and pronounce ' very thin '. His father resembled him physically. Again the fear was traceable to a fear of emotion —first to the ' lynching atmosphere ' when a bully was half-

---

[1] If the reader will count the drunken fathers in this series of cases it will give him an idea of the significance of this phenomenon in causing infantile neurosis.

drowned by ducking in the school wash-house (the scene of his own ' cowardly ' fight and flight) and then to an earlier fear of his own passion if it were let loose. He remembered his rage against his (drunken) father's stupid annoyance of his mother, and then, in an agony of apprehension, he realized that he wanted to attack—burglars, bullies, and in fact his own father, by blows directed to this fatal weak spot of the jaw. Alternatively he wanted to throttle or duck him in a way which his imagination seemed to have developed out of composite memories of the asphyxia of whooping-cough and of his father holding his head under the tap when he had a fish-bone stuck in his throat as a child. This was the jealous conflict with the father of which Freud speaks so much. He had now discovered his reasons for repressing his aggressiveness, for, probably like all little boys, he loved his father too. Also, he had accounted for his cowardice. For, in all the violent encounters which he feared, he anticipated death, no less, and that without being able to loose his own so dangerous aggressiveness in self defence.- —In real life he was very tall, broad-shouldered, strongly though lightly built, shy, witty, readily embarrassed, full of high idealisms of personal and social service. He became temporarily though awkwardly aggressive with his colleagues during one stage of his analysis, and by the end of it his swallowing troubles had practically ceased to worry him.

Case VII.—An advertising manager, aged fifty, had been ' in a panic all his life '. Early hopes of entering the Diplomatic Service had vanished at seventeen, a well-to-do American marriage had later got into difficulties, and ended finally in the insanity of the wife. He had had a rigid puritanical upbringing from a powerful mother and austere (when not dipsomaniac) father. He had a clever elder brother and had been the dunce of the family. Wanting his mother's love, he was forced by her austerity to try to win his father's respect through successes at games, which he hated. Analysis showed an early notion that all pleasure was sinful, *a fortiori* sensual pleasures of all kinds. A tendency to play passive and pathetic rôles in search of love had been fostered by his petting and kind treatment over a broken leg when five years old. Imagined joys of demonstrative love from father and mother traced back through the classical Freudian epochs of development and had led him to fearful and anxious posing for affection in adult settings. It was difficult to find any aggressiveness in this man : his positive attitudes were quelled early in boyhood.——In real life he was on the whole austere, drank a little to excess, and found that alcohol put him more at ease with his awkward social feelings. He was careful in his dress, careless about money matters, scrupulously tidy, and deeply interested in religion, in which he sought the satisfying love which he had seldom experienced in mundane life. He was very anxious to be a good and happy citizen.

Case VIII.—A journalist, aged thirty-four, wished his mind cleared of instabilities, and inability to concentrate, and difficulties with people. He had read too much psychoanalysis, and claimed to have a ' mother-fixation ', when he really suffered more from the lack of an effective father and certain of its ill-consequences in adult relationships. He was afraid of men and despised women, but was filled with sexual and intellectual curiosity about both. He was brought up in a slatternly way, his father paralysed, his mother supporting the family, often by manual labour, and himself sensitive and anxious for social progress and cultural assimilations against which a deep sense of ostracism militated. He wanted to ' love everybody ' but was quickly suspicious and resentful of others and alarmed at affection.——Socially, he might well be the most ' difficult ' personality in this series. Yet he was devoted to international peace, thought deeply and worked hard for a number of societies which aimed at social service and reconstruction, and restrained certain personal passions which had got into confused relationship with his search for ' friendship, comradeship, things one can never have with women, things devoid of all self-seeking . . . God-likeness . . . God the Father. . . .' One can imagine that his personality was not unlike that of Jean Jacques Rousseau.

Case IX.—An orchestra conductor, aged thirty-two, had panic fears of collapse when conducting slow passages, especially under certain conditions (e.g. of artificial lighting). He was reassured against his fear of falling by having people grouped round, and particularly behind, him. His first attack was at eighteen, when he had had rapid promotion to the leadership of his orchestra, and was playing a solo passage on his violin, a passage for which he had been praised and during which he made a rival colleague remain ' tacet '. At that time also his father had just died. He had a much-loved, quiet, easy, reliable, and loving father, and a violent and hysterical mother, whose physical attacks against himself he had had to dodge and parry since childhood. He loved her too, and so had quite repressed an answering rage against her wayward cruelty. He had leant on his father for support, metaphorically ; and in fantasy and infantile memory he also felt his physical support behind and beneath him. Lack of support, or attack from behind, had always been alarming contingencies, and during an attack of diphtheria as a young child he had been frightened, though unresisting, when silent doctors and nurses came to his bed, rolled him over, and gave him injections without any explanation. At the age of five he had had a panic when his father, returning unexpectedly from the trenches, offered him a stick of chocolate. By analysis, he discovered that his aggressive rage against rivals or against his cruel mother all ' came back ' on himself. Another emotion produced the same ' paralysis ', namely enthusiasm. In both cases ' the emotion starts low in my body, rises, comes up against something with a bump, can't escape, and comes back on me and knocks me out '. Whether arising in anger against his mother or in desire for his father, the paralysis was due to fear. In the end it proved to be a fear of the consequences of his own emotion, a fear of abandonment. In self-protection against this emotion : ' I want to shrink, to get into myself, to efface myself altogether '. Under an intravenous narcotic he was told that his fears were understood, and groundless. He went under his anaesthetic murmuring ' Awful ! awful ! ' and returned to full consciousness saying ' I needn't worry about any of them. I've been at peace. Peace with the world ! ' It must be confessed that he added ' To hell with them ! '——In reality a vivacious, debonair, ingratiating, and frank young man in the middle of a very successful artistic career, this patient went off cheerfully to tour with his orchestra though his isolated professional situation still gave him qualms from time to time. Only occasionally, and in one field (though that an important one to him) had personal aggressiveness or desire come into conflict with a stronger social instinct in force sufficient to cause a battle. The conflict resulted on every occasion in the rout of the former, which took defensive cover behind the neurotic symptom.

Case X.—A bank clerk, aged twenty-three, had sudden uncontrollable shaking of the right hand—a sort of ' writer's cramp ' —when he was pressed by his chief and a string of waiting messengers to complete certain daily ledger entries from cheques. As the pile of cheques was placed in his basket and the grumbling messengers clustered round, his hand shook and sweated, his heart beat fast, he became flushed and hot and his thinking powers became dulled. He was thus forced to ask for a transfer to another department, which represented a set-back in his career. He envied the older clerks, as he had envied his four-year-older brother, whom as a boy he could never equal, though by adult efforts he had at last surpassed him in all athletic achievements. Even now that brother was unassailable in his easy self-confidence. The patient came from an undemonstrative family : his father never showed personal affection ; even by his mother he was never ' picked up and cuddled '. As the youngest of four brothers he became ambitious, a climber, for he felt love to be out of the question : ' There was nothing in me for them to like '. Aggressiveness, obvious against the senior bullying clerk in the office, had of course been present against his brothers in the home. Once he nearly choked one of them, always ' lost badly ', and kicked till he got things, wanting always to be first. As a boy he insisted upon dominating his little friends and when he ceased to do so he became worried. He must never be left alone, and, unsure of approval, he ' spent time and money to get people to mix ' with him. But he only wanted to overcome their opposition, mental or physical; actually he disliked them. He 'didn't worry' when his favourite brother died. In fact he early decided to search for power instead of love : he chose friends for the ' leg up ' they would give him, sought and copied ' better off ' people, to ' improve his self-esteem '. He ' never mixed with people just because he liked them '. He preferred the company of women to men, because their minds were more easily dominated. Once dominated, friends bored him. Sometimes he bullied them ; usually he dropped them. And few or no real friends could he find. He tried to content himself with superficialities, liking people to come and sit round his desk. It was the approval of men that he really valued, ' because they are better judges than women, and I want to foist on them the idea that I'm a decent bloke '. Although afraid of the dark as a child, he did not dare to cry for fear his father would say, ' What a child I've got ! ' He feared that his father thought him a ' wash-out '. When he recounted this, out came the aggressiveness he had felt against his father for slighting him. It linked up with the harboured hatred against all his colleagues. He imagined himself killing all of them who thought him a weakling, which he had really always felt himself to be. Very soon after this he began to realize that there was no reason for others to look down on him, as he had imagined his cold parents and all his big brothers had done, and also that, if there were no hostility between himself and those messengers, his hand would cease to tremble. This happened ; and he applied for the first available reinstatement in his banking career.——In real life this man was cold and suspicious in manner, until he discovered in himself the abnormal power-drive which derived not from fear of loss of love, but despair at ever winning it. Here at last is an unsociable neurotic ! But his individual aggressiveness was not of strong enough fibre to stand an unloved life, and he was able to swing his whole attitude into one of general sociability in a far shorter time than most neurotic adjustments take. Within ten visits to the clinic he discovered that people liked him more for what he was and less for what he did than he had believed possible. His eleventh visit was his last.

Case XI.—An advertisement designer, aged twenty-seven, was a very miserable man, worrying over trifles and with much lack of confidence. He believed, however, that his ' muddled ' mind was capable of great things if it could only be ' directed '. An ' Intelligence Test ' (Terman and Merill) supported him here with a quotient showing ' professorial ' ability (143 per cent.). He had come ' up ' from a ' lower ' social class through scholarship. His father had died in his infancy, and he had had his ' ego-ideal ' moulded by his mother's desire for neatness, tidiness, and cleanliness ; and perhaps some of his trend towards his ' betters ' came from her as well. Certainly he left his old friends behind regretfully, and then became stranded, with moderate artistic powers and aspiring but uncertain social standards in a whirl of London cosmopolitanism which passed both of them by. He had come to distrust his instinctive feelings for right and wrong and to look to be told what to think and feel. As he won his way into each new group, he envied the next ' above ' it ; all with a shrewd suspicion that the better as well as the bigger portion of mankind lay behind and not in front of his social progress. Then he got stuck in a nasty job, designing covers for cheap journals, lost it, married a girl who must have found it difficult to be as good as his mother, and earned a precarious living in certain commercial art work where he felt he was prostituting both his talents and his morals. Finally he set out to exploit an idea that he was good at mechanical things which he had cherished ever since his mother marvelled that he could mend the kitchen mangle, and with the help of a vocational psychologist became a dental mechanic.——Competition and dis trust were naturally strong in this man, who had struggled so hard to apply his abilities to goals approved by the scholarship boards. But he was fairly ready to realize that aims of his own choice well pursued might now be better for him than those borrowed from his mother and her antitypes. A nice, amusing, refined man, he set out to try to conquer his resentment at the stupidity of other people and to employ what aggressiveness was necessary in the pursuit of a career which would use his powers and satisfy his ambitions.

Case XII.—A joiner, aged fifty, had tears and depressions and a feeling of weakness on the right side of his chest. At seventeen he had had pneumonia and his chest had been thought to be weak afterwards. At forty-two the pneumonia recurred, and ever since he had felt there was ' something wrong with that lung '. There was not. In analysis he found that really his illness had merely allowed an underlying feeling of physical inferiority to others to appear. He was a strong man, but superficially humble, paying his workmates ' undue respect '. He had wanted to follow his father in a full career as a skilled joiner. But after a short apprenticeship he had become a clerk at seventeen. At thirty-two he was a dock labourer, and only at thirty-five did he ' pick up his father's tools '. His inferiority and sense of guilt as an untrained man with false pretences, together with his taking future illness for granted, led us to his underlying notion that he was going to suffer a retribution for ' the brute ' in his own character. His present monotonous, unskilled work in the basement of a government office had brought his discontent and fear to the surface together. The chest was merely the site chosen by his unconscious mind (on the strength of his medical history) for his coming retribution. The ' brute ' in his character had been repressed with energy. He was mild, hated violence, 'could not understand' the embitterments of individuals or of nations, had strict principles against taking life, and had been a conscientious objector when asked to do so. Underneath all this pacifism was an intense aggressiveness, which had escaped somewhat in close domestic settings and engendered much guilt in him. He had now given up hope of his wife's affections, and until recently his depression of spirits had found consolation in informed and skilful playing of the flute. He came to discover how much he cherished aggressive designs upon others. In his psychoanalysis he first imagined the 'joyful realization of administering punishment', then pride in giving 'blows to kill'. Both in aggressiveness and in sexuality he felt that 'conscience is opposed to nature'. Reviewing his position together we concluded that his ('conversion') symptom of weakness in the right side of his body represented three things : (1) a justification for recent relaxation of effort towards success in his career, and (2) a justification for demands for sympathy. At the same time it was (3) a threat held over him by the conscience which he finally decided to continue (though less stressfully and ignorantly) to obey. He valued his home, 'even as things were '.——The striking fact of this man's social life crystallized in his refusal of military service. He instinctively felt that call upon his aggressiveness to be wrong. On the whole he was mild and subservient. But repressed aggressive impulses (based no doubt on early conceptions, of which at his age we do not attempt the analysis) were liable to bring dangerous stresses upon this man's sociability. He did *not* love his fellows very much. And if his fears of punishment had been removed by society's approval of his aggressiveness in war, he might have become a very 'nasty customer '. As it was he returned to the flute, beginning with the composition of a minuet.

2. *Fuller Records of Cases I and II.   Case I.   Mr. 'A.'*—I have said that this artist was an attractive young man. Socially, he wanted to please and knew how to do so, except in boorish society where he was very sensitive that his bright remarks were looked at askance and himself stared at 'like a train going by '. Loving variety, and easily bored, he feared that marriage would bore him as his bare companionless home and his parents had bored him. Intensely affectionate himself, this boredom with dull virtuous life had worried his childhood. For, if he satisfied his many pre-artistic leanings, such a grubby little boy as resulted would surely lose the love of his elegant and fastidious mother! He imagined himself reduced to the mud in which her dainty evening shoes trod. . . . And an appearing streak of sadism told him that, if coming up to her level involved too great a renunciation of self, he might alternatively somehow degrade her to his level, or at least make himself felt through the contrast.

This eternal tussle between trying to be worthy of his immaculate mother and trying to persuade her to countenance his own aesthetic vagaries may be called his *Anxiety No.* 1.

But degrading his mother—and in adult life it became the woman to whom he was attracted—had yet other roots in infancy. His father and mother had lived on ill terms since shortly after his birth. The man became disappointed, neglectful, selfish, and drunken ; the woman disappointed and flighty. At five years of age A. loved his father, valued access to his woodshed, and delighted in the boats which the retired naval officer made for himself, the bow and arrow which he made for his son. But temper (and probably suspicion of the mother's influence on the child) made the father glower and cuff, and break the new bow in two—and the boy would fly back to his mother. She inevitably taught him to hate his father's pathetic figure and lonely, debauched ways. But the desire to be ' like Daddy ' was already strongly implanted. And so, in adolescence, whenever he found in himself any trait or mannerism of his father he feared he would become a ' horried little fat man ' or a ' Don Juan '. But he still loved his father, and had nightmares of drunken assaults or bizarre love from him. And thus in adult life to be what he wanted, a great painter, meant becoming a selfish neglectful temperamental man. This was *Anxiety No.* 2.

A. offered opportunities for the study of sadism and ' masochism '. He suffered from fantasies not only of degrading his mother and his fiancée, but of torturing them. He imagined himself a sultan and women suffering endless indignities for his gratification. In reality, though he once partly smashed his fiancée's flat, his attacks were usually directed against himself. In tortures of rage because his goaded loved ones did not respond either with suffering adequate to arouse his pity or with the masterful control of himself which he would have liked as an alternative, he bruised his head, cut his wrists, threatened and contemplated suicide. He linked the ideas of intense pleasure and of suffering, both for others and for himself. And to secure sympathy he cried as he cut his arm : ' You can't understand my mental suffering, but you *can* understand that ! ' There was no doubt about his pleasure in imagining himself beaten by his father ; a pleasure which passed on to ' that awful horror of being tortured by stimulating as pain what would naturally be pleasure ' (cp. Mrs. B. below). Then there came a ' feeling of the indignity of it, and I want to cut his life off from mine '. In fantasy, it was this feeling of being made an object of contempt which excited his reactionary sadism. Imagining that, he then imagined himself inflicting ' terrible agonies ' upon a little boy, thus taking his own father's place and even finding himself (in imagination) with his father's suit on. In another group of fantasies his father was injuring his mother. First he counter-

attacked him, and then, reidentifying himself with him, introduced the phallic sexual component of sadism. Thereafter he
found the idea of hurting people distasteful, once the element
of sex was removed. Though apparently 'reactionary' rather
than 'primary', A's sadism came out vividly and was utterly
disproportionate to any actual thwartings which he recollected
from childhood. In each thwarting he feared and anticipated
loss of love ; and whether the neglect was from his mother
or his fiancée he retorted : ' Because you've lied to me about love,
I'm going to smash you up completely '. Such passions, directed
outwards, would naturally have led to the loss of love which he
feared. Demonstrative self-torture thus remained the safest
way of dealing with sadism, and the one most rapidly productive
of sympathy and love. It was as if A's masochism (like Mrs.
B.'s, q.v.) had a primary root in imagined suffering at the hands
of a loved father, of pleasure stimulation which reached ultimately to a painful height. But the final inward (masochistic)
directing of sadism certainly appeared to be derived, or
' secondary '.

For those who like such a division, Case A affords evidence
in favour of masochism being partly ' primary ' (through pleasur-
able sensory stimulation) and partly secondary to sadism ; the
sadism itself remaining ' reactionary ', though it is often an over-
reaction. In such a difficult early environment as fell to the lot
of A no amount of psychoanalysis would determine whether he
had an original constitutional endowment of undue aggressiveness or not. Nor, reduced to these terms, does this controversy
carry a significance for sociology which is of any great importance
at the present time.

But the reader must here be reminded of the immense significance which Freud's arguments attach to the place of masochism and sadism in human nature (Chapter III, pp. 74–78).
He is then asked to read this case in conjunction with Case B.
below.

Case II. The masochism and sadism of Mrs. ' B.'—There
follows a greatly condensed summary of those parts of my
analytical notes in which Mrs. B. traced her sadistic fantasies to
feeling-conceptions of her early childhood.

In her adult life, the child-beating fantasy [1] from which this
lady suffered occurred, among a number of other cruel imaginings, as dreams and day-dreams. Any account of cruelty—e.g.
a vivid wireless description of natives being thrashed—excited
her in an unpleasant and sexual manner. In childhood, either
the idea or the actuality of physical punishment had had a similar
effect. One occasion had been when she was herself bound with
string and locked in a shed by other children. At four or five
she had suffered intense excitement on hearing a playmate's

---

[1] Freud's analysis of this fantasy will be found in Chapter III. p. 76 et seq.

screams as she was spanked by her father in the next house. She had excitedly beaten her own teddy-bear with a ruler.

In this patient I again encountered the feeling that ' pleasure and pain must come together at the highest point of pleasure '. Judging from the infantile memories to which she was led by free-association, these feelings were at least reinforced (as Freud would have expected) by an early idea of an inevitably sadistic element in domestic sexual life. This is a conception to which most obsessional characters advert during their psychoanalysis, and one which seems to play a very important part in the development of their minds.

We have mentioned that infants set a value on excretory pleasures equally with those of ingestion. For ' narcissistic ' and obsessional characters, these interests often retain power sufficient to disturb the repressive forces of development and education, and the phenomena of being in love with one's own bodily sensations frequently contribute to the symptom-formation of neurotics. Strong interests in the parts of the body (the buttocks) which share some of their anatomical nerve-supply with the excretory organs appeared in this patient, were traced back to pleasures of infancy, and there associated with painful excitement in a way which in effect she summarized as follows : ' The excretory functions give me pleasure in that part of my body which is being beaten in this fantasy. Somehow I feel guilty about that. I am, however, jealous of other people getting pleasure in such a site, and that jealousy is exciting.' Deeper associations (including dream-analysis) led the patient to conclude : (1) ' I want to share my bodily pleasures with someone I love, and particularly my Father. I want petting and cuddling from him in these important parts of my body which want pleasure and hate pain.' (2) ' There is pleasure in the idea of damaging others in this site, because of (meaning in consideration of) the threat or the actuality of being hurt there myself. I want gentle and supporting stimulation there. But *if it hurts, I want to hurt back.*' (3) ' I am frightened at being thus hurt by my Father. But I love him, and there is a mixture of pleasure and fear according to how hard he smacks me.'——The patient had entertained certain infantile confusions common to these cases. To the young child the buttocks had resembled breasts and so had gained importance for those parts of her mind which still valued the oral pleasures of infant feeding. Thus was added another important association at once of bodily pleasure and anxiety of mind.

The most detectable origin of this patient's masochism was that she was beaten (in reality or in fantasy) by a loved father. And when the pain of that beating preponderated over the pleasure to a certain degree, she *reacted* with sadistic desires to reverse the process of hurting, by herself assuming the active rôle. In imagination she vented her rage chiefly on her mother's anatomy, against which she had an earlier grudge which had aroused both rage and fear : ' She didn't feed me. It was loss of that love which I felt.'

This patient's family had been full of drunkenness and quarrel. Her ' best sensations of all ' in these memories recovered from her infancy were when she could feel that her mother and father were in harmony with each other, and together wanted and loved her. *Her sadism was a reaction to thwarting : her masochism perhaps an attempt to avoid sadism, but certainly an effort to accept a fusion of pleasure and pain.* Later in her development she transferred the idea of pain away from herself, and beat her teddy-bear, keeping the while the sensations of pleasure, now and thereafter of a ' genital ' nature.

Psychologists who are familiar with psychoanalytical records will recognize that in the above notes I have both greatly condensed and paraphrased the repetitious and often child-like language of the original record. These two cases are offered here, not as an adequate technical summary of a phase of psychoanalysis, but simply as evidence and comment upon Freud's reading of the child-beating fantasy. *For the theory of primary sadism from which his social theory directly derives relies on his arbitrary reading of the psychopathology of this and a few allied obsessional situations.* I have already said that these obsessional cases exhibit such a wealth (or welter) of unconscious reactions, aggressive and voluptuous, that it is tempting to hold that they contain an initial overdose of imperious desire. But as is again so often the case with such characters, the early environment of each of these two only children was unfavourable to a healthy and confident reliance upon their elders for love. Nor was it calculated to resolve their doubts about the aggressive element in the ' primal scenes ' of parental relationship.

Having implanted upon the minds of his followers his own instinctive reading of the correct relationship and significance of sadism and masochism as he had discovered them in an insignificant number of people with an abnormal type of mind, Freud announced that he had thus achieved a driving principle of life which these characters share with ' normal ' men and women because it is universal. If he had been content to accept a universal ' pleasure-principle '—man's urge in all varying situations to gratify as far as possible the varied aspects of his nature—he would have left his followers free to study man's social and selfish natures unfettered by the ' necessity ' of deriving the former from the latter. It is that unnecessary ' necessity ', imposed by a theory which was dictated to Freud's intellect by his feeling self, of which psychologists have to rid themselves if they are to begin to see social man as he is.

3. *Case III. The life and misconceptions of a consultant engineer. Introduction.*—Necessary as it has been to expose the incompleteness of Freud's observations and the fallacies of Freud's arguments, we shall never succeed in grounding a psychological appraisement of human nature upon an alternative assertion that sadism is largely a peculiarity of obsessional characters and that its appearance even in them often favours its classification as ' reactionary ' rather than as ' primary '. I consider that the short case summaries which I have quoted do in fact constitute good psychoanalytical evidence against the universalizations upon which Freud claimed to base his gloomy opinions of mankind, selfish and hating, ' forced ' into co-operations from which it for ever seeks the escapes of destructive group warfare. But from psychoanalysis we have more to learn than that its founder was erroneous in his judgment of normal human nature and that its subjects, whilst *expressing* aggressive individuality, do actually *live* co-operative lives. Important as both these facts are to my argument, we need to know further *how* men come by such erroneous views of their kind as were held by Freud. To that end we will now consider a patient of mine whose views of human nature resembled those of Freud, and recount at some length how those views came to be explained during his psychoanalysis and how they became modified by an increased knowledge of himself.

(i) *The case history.*—Mr. C. was born forty years ago in a quiet village in Surrey. He had a sister six years older than himself and a still older brother. His mother was a ' bonny Yorkshire woman ' of thirty-two ; his father a ' cocky little Cockney ', a little her senior, who had done well in establishing himself in charge of a riverside saw-mill. C. was the baby, with round face, sharp eyes, and lovely dark, curly, long, girlish hair. He was much admired, and his mother doted on him. ·C. wanted to be loved ' as much as possible may be ' ; but he was also self-willed and lazy. He loved country things, wandered in the fields, played truant, pushed another little boy into the pond, and ran home, always sure that mother would defend him against the outside world. Seeking and expecting admiration, he was deeply hurt when the girls next door played at chalking names on the pavement and laughed at his inability to spell. This spelling weakness became a trouble at school. Derided by the master in comparison with his clever sister, and laughed at by his schoolmates in class, he developed much skill in dodging spelling classes. And, with nice little notes to the headmaster about colds in the head, his mother aided and abetted him.

And so C. went on being beautiful and relying on Mother. At first there was little that this healthy woman could not defend him against. But as time went on he detected an alarming fact. There were things that Mother herself was afraid of, or couldn't always put right. She was alarmed by travel ; and he remembers to this day an early journey on the Metropolitan Railway, in which he cowered by her side, as with uncertain finger to lip, and frequent eructations, she showed her lack of confidence and ease. But the chief source of Mother's anxiety lay nearer home. When the dinner came on to the table, the finger went to the lip uncertainly until Father had pronounced upon it. When C. had been naughty and Father was angry, it was a difficult task that Mother undertook in his defence. In the evenings, at some minor disagreement, off Daddy would stalk ' up the road ' and both Mother and child waited anxiously for his return.

In his teens C. found evidences of lack of sympathy in the world at large. At seventeen he was summoned by the police for having no lamp on his bicycle. At eighteen he was ' attested ' and whisked off into the army, where doctors stripped him in front of half a dozen other recruits, and he was abruptly admonished for having dirty feet. This stripping was a serious business. To C. his body had been a sacred thing. He felt it must be superior to others although it was so thin. At the school baths he had shrunk from exposing it because he thought certain parts were less well-developed than those of the other boys. In fact, C. had begun to find doubts as to whether he was the perfect little boy he had thought himself to be, or whether, by the tests of the big world, there were some radical defects somewhere— ' like a beautifully painted post rotten at the base '.

Then came business and its rebuffs, doubts about young ladies, and matrimonial hesitations till his mother died, when he married a reliable wife who admittedly resembled her. He felt business competition to be very keen. He was in a big concern and ' the higher you got, the more fellows were waiting to pounce on you if you made a mistake '. His policy was to ' kill them with kindness '. But how he wished he could relax his self-control and tell some of them what he really thought !

Early in his career he used to be sent travelling. It was a great strain. He needed the constant reassurance of friends around him, and a journey to an unknown job at a distance was ' like travelling into oblivion '. Once arrived at a destination he set to work with grim efficiency to discover the engineering defect for which he had been called, and also to conquer a place in the hearts of those with whom his business dealt. That should have led to popularity. It did. But always underneath he felt that resentments and competitiveness were present in his colleagues though they were suppressed from view. For himself, he felt that, if it weren't necessary to keep their goodwill : ' I'd be a swine ! '

Then came a business crisis. His own very big firm was ' merged ' with another very big firm, and that meant rationalization and the discharge of many men. C.'s friends said : ' You'll be all right ! They're short of engineers.' But he sat in his office every evening waiting for news as to how he stood.

At about the same time, two other incidents occurred. One day he was standing in front of a lorry talking to a colleague and feeling quite secure, when suddenly it moved forwards, caught him in the stomach with its starting-handle, and over he went. He was very little hurt, but so frightened by the unexpected attack that he could hardly write a telegram home, and lived through the experience repeatedly in his dreams. For the second event he was in his best plus-four suit at a football match, yet he was rebuffed with contumely by rough-looking men when searching for a w.c.

He retained his place at the business ' merger '. He suffered little enough from the motor accident, nothing but loss of self-esteem at the football match, for the police came to his assistance on that occasion. Yet after these events he could no longer stand the strain of his long business railway journeys, nor was he happy far from home—or from a lavatory. He was worried if his wife left him for any length of time. He continued at work however. They found him a good job in the central office. He was meticulous about it. But he still felt the ever-present envy of colleagues, and longed for quiet country days of fishing up the river. There remained moreover his weak spot, spelling, and the further he was promoted the greater exposure he felt it would be if it were discovered how heavily he leant upon his typist.

C. redoubled his efforts for security. He became the mainstay of the manager—' even down to mending his umbrella '. He was the wit of the staff mess : no reunion dinner was complete without ' dear old C. ' who was by now a tall stoutish man, a little bald, whose face settled into an anxious expression when the smiles left it. He always came forward to assist anybody in any predicament in which he found them. He did everybody else's work as well as his own. He felt there should be far more co-operation in the world, ' pulling together like a crew on the river '. He did his best to bring men together as friends.

Still his symptoms grew worse. His daily journey to the office by ' Underground ' became a nightmare. He stood with one hand inside his trouser pocket. If the train stopped a panic came upon him : ' Shall I make it ? Can I get out in time ? Can I hold out to the lavatory at the junction ? ' Every day he visited half a dozen such places on the way to work. And he would hang about to secure some companion or other to talk to in the train, preferably a ' hefty fellow ', so that ' if I should break out in any way he can hold me '.

If C.'s career had been just a little more successful still it is possible that he would never have come for treatment. Efficient, conscientious, skilled in verbal argument and diplomacy, considerate to colleagues and subordinates, capable just occasionally of ' snapping a head off ', and with the home-life of a recluse, he would be regarded as a great success and a very pleasant fellow with a few idiosyncracies of genius. As it was, he worried his doctor about his mild ' asthma ' at thirty-eight, confessed his story at thirty-nine, and came up for treatment in his fortieth year.

What was C.'s underlying attitude to his fellows? How did his unconscious mind view them? Were there reasons for it all? Were his views alterable?

(ii) *Mr. C.'s social theory.*—The psychoanalysis of C. was by ' free-association ' and the venting of the ideas to which that process led. It lasted 200 hours. From the presenting symptoms we had to follow such matters as the fear of being left alone, of being trapped, of losing his wife, together with the peculiar significance attached to the lavatory and the reassurances he got from visiting it. We had also to follow his character trends, to discover why he had to be so impeccable in his work, why so nice to everybody, when he realized that he often wished to behave quite differently to them. Furthermore, behind an initial and conventional assurance to me of a ' happy ' married life lay a number of troubles, the chief of which had left him and his wife a childless couple twelve years after they married desiring offspring. These matters had to be uncovered. It will be realized that for C. to ' break down ' through fear in the middle of a career which would have afforded the greatest reassurances to many men, and when he had incurred so little apparent thwarting either in it or in his home life, meant that there were unconscious influences at work distorting his view of things around him. So that, as much in the dire competition of office life as in the menace that lay hidden in the stationary ' Underground ' train, *he was dealing not so much with realities as with bogies.* Or rather, he gave to realities a fictitious valuation, as a connoisseur will to a piece of old glass. *We all distort the power and malignity of our adversaries—in one direction or another. We will now describe some of the ways in which C. had come to do it.*

This psychoanalysis divides naturally into three phases. During each of them C. freely expressed his views of society and his relationship with his fellows. In reading these notes of his case through now we must remember certain things. First, we are dealing with a man of simple origin and humble schooling, but very marked talents. In addition to an almost unique mastery of certain technical subjects, he had become the man of choice for interviewing difficult customers in his department and for explaining technicalities to laymen, indeed in a number of business situations he was called upon for his ability to ' put things across ' verbally. Secondly, we are dealing with a man who was so pressed upon by troubles of imagination that he found no choice but to retire into neurotic symptoms. Thirdly, C. had a social theory, bits of which he was in the habit of expounding to audiences of colleagues and messmates—audiences attentive or unwilling as the case might be. He expressed it to me piece-meal amidst much other matter during our earlier conversations, and amended it as our analysis of his emotions proceeded through its three phases to its solution. Naturally various emphases changed to fit passing moods and the stages of understanding at which he successively arrived. I append what he said on these particular matters; and the stage of his analysis at which he said it. The figures indicate the number of the session. Each session was approximately of an hour's duration.

Finally, the disjointed nature and apparently confused order of C.'s remarks is due to the fact that he had learnt to ' free-associate ', and his convictions are being spoken in the order and the manner in which they occurred to him without the intervention of a critical and logic-chopping intellect.

Extracts from analytical diary. Case C. Stage 1. Sessions 1 to 141.

(References to the ' state of nature ' in italics.)

6. I get hot and bothered waiting for people. I want to help everybody. We must pull together like a crew on the river. I've tried to be straight. *But people who do all the wrong seem to get all the sweets of life. The wrong 'uns seem healthy : if they threw weeds in my garden they'd grow !* And those who never kill a fly, like Dick Sheppard, suffer from asthma and die at fifty ! Even a deformed plant *I have to help.* Do they impose upon me ? I used to put big jobs right till I got my phobia. At my firm's merger lots were sacked, but C. was worth keeping.

16. Every shopkeeper cuts every other's throat. Why do people scramble, fight for tube trains ? I've got to do it too ! I'd rather go out along the river, catch fish, and throw them back. We must have done a lot of wrong at the first, according to the Bible, to have got into such a mess.

17. I don't think people are really bad. It's the breeding's wrong ; or they've been badly treated.

25. *In nature the fittest survive.* Our wars thin out the wrong people. We control nature instead of letting her control us. *We're doing everything against what our inner selves want to do.*

29. I treat people kindly because they're of use to me.

34. I want sincerity, to be natural. But one's always worrying about being caught out. There are too many traps about. *People are all individualists. But none of them will admit it. Underneath there's something that doesn't ring true, as if they were all play-acting.* If you know there's enough food in the world ! . .   I'm not searching for Utopia. But if we could think of helping instead of retarding each

other, life would be a pleasure to live. We'd wake up happy—not expecting burglars to steal the last 1s. 6d. from the mantelpiece.

The insecurity of this ' security '! . . . Germans and Chinese should be safeguarded by the same things as ourselves. Yet *on nature's footing, you'd use your fists or your feet.*

36. If I hadn't to stop at the end for fear of what would happen to me *I'd be a swine, sticking little porcupine pricks in all the time.*

39. At the barber, I have to be nice, in case he cuts a chunk out of my head. With all people, with all animals, I have to gain assurance that they won't do me an injury. You never know when your office-boy is going to be your governor. But we *ought* to be a happy family !

42. *In nature we'd all be scrapping, everyone an individualist, all afraid of each other. Live! Eat! Kill! And carry on! Bump anyone over the head directly they didn't agree with you! There'd be no trust. And to-day there's mass war ; and individuals set traps for each other, within the law. The only reason they don't still kill each other is fear of being hung. It's nature's way—to fight, defend, shelter your off-spring. But only up to a point. Then it must support itself, and be ready to defend its own young.*

I don't want to hit anyone at all. And so I'm repressing a natural instinct. If nature had its way it'd say : ' *You're big. You're going to survive. Push! Climb! Get on!* ' . . . But I may be from a stock that's endeavoured to restrain that, that's always aimed to take the weak ones along with it ? . . . Why do the good suffer so ? Why are we prevented from fulfilling our purpose ? Somebody must have done wrong ! It was *meant* to be all right. Think of animals, beautiful swans fighting to death ! . . . I'm so disappointed in the lack of co-operation, the back-biting ; instead of all living together. One long big scramble ! *I* don't fight for any kingdoms ! But where are our standards ? Whom shall we use ? What we want to do we have to do.—Until we become afraid. *I* can't be certain. So I run away.

Note 1.—C.'s two conflicting themes are : (1) the savagery of natural man, which ought to be controlled in the interests and pleasures of co-operative life ; and (2) the thwarting of the natural passions of man, which civilized life does in fact impose. The first he infers from the conception of people all ' wanting to do each other an injury ', which conception he will later be able to trace to certain infantile fears of his own father and mother. The second springs from his own feeling of frustration both of his aggressive impulses (which are at once fortified and quelled by his fear of others) and of his voluptuous impulses. The latter have remained unsatisfied through twelve years of married life for reasons which we shall presently discover. The ' natural savagery ' which rightly requires the control of *other* men, and the ' natural demands ' which are wrongly frustrated in *himself* make the ' state of nature ' at once repellant and attractive to C. The claims for personal freedom of action are neutralized at their every emergence by fear of the results of the freedom of others and also of losing the ' someone by my side ' which his need for love demands.

44. In nature you fight : in civilization you get frightened, and repress. Better get rid of aggressiveness somehow, instead of having to shake hands feeling all white and spiteful.

53. If I wrong someone else, they're hurt. Then they feel like chewing me up. So that's why I don't do it.

56. Would anyone stand in front of *me*, to shield me from the glare of other people ?

59. *What the body wants to do is right !* I think *I* should soon be able to chase and swim. And if I slipped and brained myself, well, off I'd go ! But in spite of what I've said, I doubt my abilities !

60. We're a rotten lot of blighters to each other. There's no unity : we don't care a damn about each other really. Half of us are waiting for the other man's job. Only on the farms are 70 per cent. of the troubles gone. They might fight ; but it would be a simple affair, driven off, or winning. . . . ' Thou shalt not covet they neighbour's wife ! ' That's all hooey ! I could have snatched Smith's job ; only I must always have somebody by my side.

61. I want to live cleanly and be at peace with all.

71. My advantages are balanced by my disadvantages.

74. In our success in the last war we set a trap which nearly hit back on us last week (September 1938). Directly the trouble's over, though, they'll all shoot out their necks again, and that'll be the end of our ' all standing together '. Every man *is* an individualist at heart.

76. *In the state of nature, the weak ones would have gone. We wouldn't want them !* But then I feel ' *Here's* one you mustn't get rid of ! '

77. How dependent we all are on other people !

79. The worst punishment is to be stamped as rotten.

87. *We are all individualists, only converted by strength from the other side.* Love is hooey : we want our goal ! (Is every man against his fellow ?) Yes, definitely ! Socialism would be impossible without the reconstruction of all of us. (*The whole human strain is such that you can do nothing with it.* Take a big rubber and rub it out ! Tear it up, and start again !)

88. It's a wonderful world ! And occasionally very clever men find out more about it ; and hypnotize the people in consequence. There is something in myself which is reverting, perhaps, to a simpler pattern ?

95. I try to live happily and naturally. But I'm a fettered slave to other people, and have to deceive myself. I've done everything but trust. And why should I ? But you *must* have trust !

100. (Regarding his wife's neuralgia.)   Best not show much
sympathy.   Girls pretend they've got a headache to make love to you.

101. If they knew what a rotten beggar I am when I've *got*
security ! . . .

104. A fellow plays merry hell with everybody else in his own mind.
But put me in a train, and I have to keep friends with people who
ought to call me ' Sir ' !

111. Rather than be trapped in a desert alone from everybody,
I'd take a little dose, and chance the other side.

119. What a person feels they want to do is right.   But *I* would
soon be in Bow Street !
The whole world has my phobia !
I must correct a nasty mistake :   I want to help people because I
don't want to be left alone.   My whole being demands their presence
. . . the women for sexual intercourse and the men to produce more
women and be beaten in the fight.

120. I'm a snake in the grass.   Even with you I'm nice to you,
but it's myself I'm trying to help.

121. I'm afraid of all things.   (Is all the world like you ?)   Fifty-
fifty !   *They've got daggers and I expect them to use them !*

122. But why have such pretty flowers ?

126. *Human nature deep down is revolting : to be on top of others.*

128. I'd like to take my dog to Crufts, because *she's* so kind to me.

129. Others won't believe they do things for themselves only.

131. I want to be comforted, have assistance, somebody to be with
me when I die.   Real confidence and companionship, to know they
won't do anything against me.   I know that's all against my theory !

132. I see what I, and everybody else is doing.   They want to
strike, and will when you're weak.   I want friends to fight for me.
And then I talk of them behind their backs !   If we could only go
parallel !

141. If there were any hundred per cent. trustworthy people, C.
would compare very badly with them.

Commentary upon Stage I of the analysis.—First anxiety (6),
(16), is expressed over human life and especially over competitive
human relationships.   C. has a sense of injustice about the rewards
of virtue, and annoyance at his own compulsion to be kind.   He
enjoys achievement and a sense of being valued above others :
the ' state of nature ' would give special prerogatives to him.
Mutual hostilities are the result of sin (cp. Catholic theology and
Milton).   A theory of original virtue is considered (17) ; a ' state
of nature ' which rewards the fittest (Darwin), as opposed to a
society which punishes the fittest (25).   Man's social life opposes
his instincts.   He recognizes a selfish motive for his own kindness

(29), and infers similar selfishness in others (34). This is a source of anxiety. The perils of mutual aggressiveness and the advantages of its obeyance (39).

The ' state of nature ' emerges as one of universal aggressiveness and 'survival of the fittest' (Hobbes-Darwin) (42). This makes C.'s own lack of aggressiveness abnormal, especially in one so well endowed. Nature ought to be different ; but, as it is, each man must be his own law. C. begins (36) to admit his own aggressiveness and to vary uncertainly between two systems of thought, one running : ' I wish them well : do they wish me the same ? If so, I must preserve that state ; if not, I must create it ' ; and the other : ' I wish them dead. They mustn't see it, or they'll wish me the same.' Note (42) his regret at the absence of rules for the guidance of conduct. We act on a balance of the emotions of lust and fear.

When his own aggressive self becomes clearly recognized by C. (44, 53), it is justified by his believing others to be the same (56, 87, 121). He attempts to reassure himself of his ability to survive in a Hobbesian state of nature (59, 76), but tends to pass on into Rousseau's idea of rural rectitude (60). And, alternating with a recognition of his aggressive individuality, is a desire for social love through co-operation (61, 79), accompanied by a realization of his lack of secure advantage in a rough world (71, 77). He sees how men reach temporary social solidarity through union against something outside their group. He passes through doubt (95) and suspicion (100) of the motives of others, to a recognition that his own aggressiveness is distasteful to him (101, 120, 126, 132), and yet that its restraint is equally so (104). In reality his own aggressive ' nature ' can't be followed (119) because of his absolute need of the help of others. He sees the beauties of the world (122), fears loneliness through lack of human love (131), and finally begins to feel unworthy and inferior to others because of his aggressiveness.

Note 2.—Throughout this first stage of the analysis the patient had been seeking, by free-association, enlightenment as to his unconscious attitudes in other spheres. We do not wish to delve into the technicalities of the sexual neurosis which ran parallel with the disturbed social relationship which we are here studying, except to indicate the essential stages of enlightenment which mark the three stages of the analysis. At the point we have reached, C. had discovered that his adult fear of women was derived from a fear of his mother's love in his infancy, and the excitement which this had aroused in him. Her attraction for him (though subsequently forgotten) had been overwhelming at the time. He had felt that through this power over his emotion she might overwhelm him and reabsorb him into herself. The rediscovery of these long-forgotten thoughts and feelings produced a sudden revolution in his matrimonial life. For his mother had become the prototype of womankind, and though the original thought was archaic, the attitude of fear had remained and had cast an inexplicable but inescapable shadow over his attitude to the whole female sex from his youth up. Arrived by a long and trying path at its origin, he lost his physical diffidence with the wife whom he had chosen for her motherlikeness. A ' real honeymoon ', twelve years overdue, came to bless them with very great relief and mutual understanding, and at the same time a fear of having children, which in this case was present in the husband alone, vanished. We resume his history at this point.

Stage II.   Sessions 142 to 164:

146. My wife has taught me about human nature by her sacrifice, that none of them really want to stab me in the back. I really want to help people and understand why I'm helping them, and not just help them to protect me. I don't want to be against religion. There's something in it : faith anyway. I still think there must be some Being behind it all.

148. We're out of step with the Germans. But really they're as anxious to be friendly as we are. If the political people could lose *their* phobias, then the houses could spring up again. There's my own fear of ' encirclement ', fear of being beaten. And when I get it I'd like to tear people to pieces. If I'm wrong about the fittest surviving, well then we're in Utopia. But I ought to be able to sow my seed and walk away !

149. I want to get free, find completeness, socially as I have sexually. There the shackles are off now. I can't believe that there ever were any ! I don't believe I was ever frightened of getting stuck. How could I have been ?

150. I want to feel like the little country minister, going round helping people. Everybody's friendly ; or he thinks they are, with faith in Providence behind him. I'm like a sheep-dog that expects the flock to revolt.

151. They don't think I'm genuine, and I don't trust them.

152. My faith in my wife is now implicit.

153. I really want to give others a square deal, if they'll give me one. (And what do they want ?) The same thing. But others would have to give up so much ! If anything happened it would be to me. Gradually I am realizing I am only one of millions. There's fear in my heart—and in every man's.

154. Socially I must open my account now. Every time you twist somebody, you are breaking the law of decency by which you want to live. Yet we do want to get a little dig in sometimes, even the parson does. Getting the best of others is corrected by our code of decency. We peg ourselves down from being carried away. We're

afraid of ourselves. When individualism comes in you may as well
give up the game. If only we could collaborate like doctors. (You'd
like ? . . .) An island ! No !—to work in this society we've got.

157. Need black, yellow, and white races be separated ? It's when
somebody starts to covet, when we're unsatisfied with what we've got,
that things go wrong. If I never coveted, and weren't deceitful, I'd
be afraid of nothing.

Instead of ' get rid of the old 'uns ' we should be doing things to
save life, help one another, better one another.

156. With my wife, I can now do what I want. But when it's the
survival of the fittest, I ought to hit and can't. I feel as if I'd a skeleton
in the cupboard, had murdered somebody years ago, and fear always
that a hand will be laid on my shoulder.

160. If I want to shoot others up under cover of being nice, I must
expect them to shoot me up.

164. If I felt I could do things for people, without a come-back,
I'd go through anything. If nobody harmed me, I'd do nobody harm.
It's the uncertainty !

Commentary upon Stage II of the analysis.—Reassured about
the love of others through his new understanding of his wife (146),
C. finds a generous response in himself. The principle of love
is supported, and extended internationally (148). His own
aggressiveness depends on fear of others. But he feels a restraint
still present on certain aspects of his nature. His distrust is still
present (151) ; others are still liable to be aggressive (153). The
problem he is solving is every man's problem. The problem of
social obligation is restated (154) ; a guilty social conscience (156) ;
the need of a Christian philosophy (157), (160) ; lack of faith
(164).

Note 3.—Once C. had discovered and lost the fear of his
mother, he found that he had also ' identified ' himself with her
in *her* fear of his father. She had often communicated her
domestic perturbations to him. And a sensitive young child
can not only sense connubial difficulties, but builds up his own
very alarming fancies about them. ' They always appeared so
happy : yet something was wrong . . . I hid behind Mother.
But I wanted to kick or clump him. He was always the victor,
giving us both a phobia so that he could control us for ever and
ever ' (160). He discovered that the ' phobia ' his father had
given him had awakened in him an aggressive hatred that could
not be shown, because ' if we tantalized him and he stumped up
the road, we wanted and needed him back '. But in the young
child's mind wishes can kill. In this second stage of his analysis,
C. discovered alarming ' death wishes ' against his father, then
fears that those wishes would execute themselves. He discovered
suddenly that his fears of being left alone by a loved one or a

companion to-day derived partly from fears that, ' tantalized by me, Father might have jumped into the canal '. Finally he exclaimed in great excitement : ' Sir ! I've got it ! If it's my wife, or Johnson, or you that's late, I wonder if they've met with an accident which will be charged to me ! " (i.e. as murder) (160).

Stage III. Sessions 164 to 176.

164. (After rediscovering his death-wish against his father.) Relief of the fear of these forty years ! Wilkins, Johnson, even Barratt —I no longer suspect a trap !

167. Our core of energy, the fighting spirit, could be used for pumping the waters of life. And if the screw were never put on, the aggressiveness in man would lie dormant.

164. There's a perfect mixture of gases necessary to run the world. A wrong mixture causes an explosion.

168. Niceness and aggressiveness should be balanced. People do help one. But (relapsing) the other man *still* has the whip handle !

170. Father would only be spiteful when he felt let down. He helped people, was very good to Mother. She wanted too much ! I've transferred to Father's side now. For forty years I believed Father was going to attack Mother, and was going to attack me. I'm not afraid to lose the phobia because *there is sincerity in Father's kindness to others. And in mine.* That aggressiveness won't be too strong. I'm not afraid of it now.

171. Father and I were pals underneath, and just like each other. But I took over Mother's attitude to him, lock, stock, and barrel.

173. My attack was to anticipate their attack ! Father's great rapier against my little dagger !

174. Father was an enemy formed by me. I wanted to fight up to the level of Father. There's nobody else I wanted to murder. An alibi for Father ! That's why I must never be alone ! Really he was a beacon, a standard.

175. I wanted to be a dictator. It's nice to be nice. To be a bit ahead is fine. To be horrid is terrible. Now I've got them, Mother and Father, both locked away where I wanted them ! It's a terrible thing to say ! Sex is O.K. now. The bigger problem is to kill and be kind.

176. Are *you* just using me ? How can I be a friend with such doubts in my mind ? Faith is at the bottom of everything.
All my life has been lived among enemies who had to be made friends. And *really they are friends all the time ! Until C. can say to himself : ' These are not enemies, but like my wife, changed over from enemies to friends', I'll never be right.* (Can you ?) I'm trying. But some people *do* shoot you up ! (Is the world full of these, or of nice people who are occasionally nasty ?) Well, faith should be based on

THE ACTUAL BEHAVIOUR OF MAN

facts. Those fellows are afraid too, or they wouldn't do it. We should find out *who* has been trying to stab us in the back, as in courts of law. You've got to believe that you're going to have a run for your money. Minds get distorted by lack of faith. (Lack of faith leads to . . . ?) Aggression! All that mighty reserve wells up. '*I'm going to attack them before they attack me . . . take my sword and fight my way out.*' *If I've no faith, I'm welled up with aggression!* Give me faith, and the aggression can lie dormant until someone else *is* aggressive! But we must have a way of discharging our aggressiveness. I wanted Father on my side to fight my battles. I chase Father till I get rid of him. Then there's something left. I'm afraid there's always *someone* better than I am!

Note 4.—In this, the final stage of his analysis, C. discovered that in infant fantasy he had feared an actual attack upon him by his father. A very informative dream enabled him to separate ' aggressiveness ', his own and his father's, from the individual and to regard it as a *property*. He imagined a man as a seed. The husk is the ' veneer ' of niceness we put on. When this is stripped the aggressive substance appears. Even this can be mastered ; and at the core is a kernel, a source of energy which can become aggressive upon thwarting or misunderstanding, but which can also be used (varying the metaphor) for ' pumping the waters of life '(167).

In these last sessions of his analysis, C. was engaged in discovering that his father had become the prototype of mankind just as his mother had of womankind. As Freud puts it : ' What began in relation to the father ends in relation to the community '. And the fear of their onslaughts—a physical fear which had actually caused him to make self-protective movements with his hands in his adult panics in the tube train—was complicated by the underlying love which he found deep in his heart, and which had made him desire his father's presence, support, and contact. His agony of mind in the tube-train was in fact a composite picture. That scene represented, at once : inability to escape (from Mother), sudden exposure to attack (from Father), a desire for reassurance, contact, and love in a dangerous situation (from both Mother and Father) and a fear that an attack upon him would prove fatal.

In fact, while C. stood hanging on to his strap, panic-stricken under the eyes of his fellow-travellers, and quite unable to determine why, an unconscious, infantile, but active and directing portion of his mind was grappling with a terrible problem. First of all it feared a threatened and imminent physical attack— the product of his own aggressive and fearful misconceptions about rivalling his father and defending his mother and himself against him. Secondly, he loved that same ' threatening ' father and (as we found with the masochism of Mrs. B.) he would welcome his attacks up to a point, if indeed that point could only be separated from one of fatal injury. The gates of the citadel might thus be opened from within. For though it took us over a year to discover the fact, this man had carried deep in his mind the nightmare conception, utterly fantastic to the daylight of our adult thoughts, that both his passionate love for his mother and his passionate desire to be loved by his father threatened his own existence, the former by his being sucked back to the annihilation of the womb, the second by his succumbing to an assault combined of love and anger, such as young children too often imagine their mothers to suffer in the dark hours of the night.

It was while elucidating the second of these fears that C. concluded his discussion of human nature, after having recognized the unconscious alignment of his views of men—his colleagues, the analyst, and the world at large, and of women—his wife and all others—with his forgotten sentiments for the essential proto-types of all man- and womankind in his developing life, his own father and mother. That alignment with fantastic falsifications of the true rôles of his parents in his life had involved him in an emotional conception of human nature which was wrong from start to finish. It had led him to endow human nature, masculine and feminine, with aggressive qualities which were the product of his own entirely irrational fears. It also led him to develop an aggressiveness of his own, which was far in excess of his social needs. Painfully he repressed that aggressiveness in order to secure social approval. But he retained his fears ; so that the starting handle of a lorry could bowl over his self-esteem, and an imagined breath of criticism could awaken a nightmare of appre-hensive effort at self-habilitation. For C., intelligent, kindly, successful, and witty, human nature was selfish, aggressive, and threatening, not because of his observations of men, but because of his interpretation of all the ' battle of life ' by the measure of a series of fundamental misapprehensions of infancy. Where do Freud's views of mankind stand in the face of such a discovery ? Where do our own ?

(iii) *Symptoms and needs.*—Fearing, as in the end such patients do, to be denuded of his symptoms, Mr. C. had at last to analyse what advantages his fears and his policy of ' veneering ' his aggressiveness had brought him. First (and we must remember that these were *unconscious* motives), ' You can dodge anything. " I'm a weak inoffensive bloke ! Don't kill me ! " They gather round and comfort you, and (said the patient, nearly weeping) you laugh up your sleeve.' Then, ' it gives me a controlled area to work in, protecting me against strange people, and bringing sympathy against the harshness of the world. They try to make you happy. And under cover of that you have them disarmed and can get at them. If I'm a " lame duck " no decent man would attack me.' Those were the contemporary values of symptoms which caused great misery and inconvenience in this man's life. They all depended upon the underlying conception of the 'harshness of the world' and the aggressiveness of man. That conception was traceable to a fear of the effects on his welfare and life which the infant C. imagined his own emotional reactions to his parents (as he conceived them) might have. We cannot say what view he would have taken of the world if his mother (like Rousseau's) or his father had been early removed from his life. We can hope for light from the analysis of such cases of neurosis in motherless or fatherless children. *The significant matter for social psychology seems to me to be that here is a man whose view of natural life was similar to that of Hobbes and Freud. He believed himself hedged about and threatened by the continuous aggressiveness of others. Though he reacted openly and defensively with kindness, more deeply he wished to be hostile and aggressive in return. But when he discovered that his fear of the emotional pull of his mother was a logical antecedent of his fear of women he lost that fear. And when he traced his fear and aggressiveness with men to a reactionary aggressiveness against a fear of his father, those symptoms too were immediately and durably lessened.*

In our psychoanalysis of Mr. C. we found the links between his fluctuating but on the whole cheerless adult social sentiments and the web of fact and fantasy which the infant C. had woven and on which he based his desirous, fearful, and hostile attitudes to his parents. He had an 'Oedipus Complex', some traces of which are probably to be found in most of us. His was characterized by a wealth of fantasy and fearful imagining, in the throes of which his various emotions struggled in interminable warfare. We might say that the battle was between desire and fear, or between personal desire and social desire, or between two personal desires—a Freudian desire for aggressive domination, and a Suttian desire for love. This last appears to me to sum up the conflict most clearly. For, if he had had a clear preponderance of a desire to be loved, Mr. C. who, unlike Mr. A. and Mrs. B., had a favourable family and social setting, had also a mind which was skilful enough to have secured abundance of affection and regard from his earliest domestic setting until he was ripe with age. He very nearly did so. The trouble was his discovery that 'one must find channels for one's aggressiveness', and his fear that 'other people would keep their phobias, even if I lost mine'. In fact he would have to be content to be *merely* loved, and would win no place of distinction in the competitive world. If, on the other hand, he had had no fundamental instincts except aggressiveness and lust, he would not have worried about securing love by kindness, but would have pursued power first and foremost. For there is every reason to think that C.'s aggressiveness would have conquered his fear, if it had not been for his need of love. As it was his heart had been too soft to go very far in that direction. Thus it was with a preponderant awareness of his need of others, their approval, their assistance and their love—an awareness which we may surely call his *primary social instinct*—that he was faced with his growling, protesting, and powerful *primary aggressive instinct*, not easily to be disciplined from the first, but fortified by much secondary aggressiveness, the product of the fantasy formations of his infancy, and because of those same fantasies, abnormally repressed.

(iv) *Lessons of our case material.*—(i) *General.*—Of twelve diverse and unselected persons who came to me for advice and treatment for nervous stress, I have summarized, first, their underlying motives and mental mechanisms, and, second, the presentation of themselves which they made to the world. On the one hand we have the unconscious urges and fears which are susceptible to Freudian psychoanalysis. On the other, we have the actual social behaviour of these people, the part they play in society as they live their lives. What is the relationship between the two ?

The twelve case summaries (pages 122 to 130) may be placed in two groups. Nine of the cases (Nos. 1, 2, 3, 5, 6, 9, 10, 11, 12) had outstanding problems of repressed aggressiveness : three did not. Of the former, all showed well-marked obsessional traits of character, though only two (*Case II*, Mrs. B., and *Case III*, Mr. C.) appeared as fully developed obsessional neurotics. In seven of these nine cases—and among them the two obsessional neurotics—the aggressiveness was repressed adequately from the point of view of society. In their daily lives the conduct of these people was co-operative and socially acceptable. Of the two exceptions (Nos. 1 and 12), in *Case I* (Mr. A.) the aggressiveness was liable on occasion to vent itself destructively. The vast preponderance of these outbursts was turned upon the patient himself, the remainder upon his loved ones. In *Case XII* domestic cruelty had emerged, and had caused the patient a great sense of guilt. Of the three cases of the second group (Nos. 4, 7, and 8) i.e. those which did not disclose repressed aggressiveness upon analysis, two (Nos. 4 and 7) were ' schizoid ' [1] and only one (No. 8) obsessional. The two former had little aggressiveness, either overt or covert. The third, the obsessional, was overtly aggressive in his surface reactions. What he had repressed were ' passive ' sexual traits. His analysis was uncompleted.

With regard to the relationship between obsessionalism and repressed aggressiveness, two points require to be made. The first is that, in this small but consecutive series, *all the cases of repressed aggressiveness showed well-marked obsessional traits of character*. That finding would meet with the general confirmation of practising psychoanalysts. But the second is *that all but*

---

[1] Abnormally withdrawn, tending to separate their deep emotional life of fantasy from a superficial, mechanical, and dazed life of contact with the real world of men and things ; verging towards the ' split-mind ' of schizophrenia.

two of these ' aggressive-obsessional' patients were helpful and acceptable members of society. The two exceptions were oppressed by guilt because of their failures. The majority, who had made good, though often individualistic, *citizens*, had however become questionably successful *family* men and women. The *self-assertive instinct* had taken full note of, and full licence from, the securities produced by love and care within the home ; while the *social instinct* had, in their social life, exacted the exhausting tribute of a slavish conformity.

(*ii*) *Special lessons from the long cases.*—Cases *I* and *II* are inserted because, though to a layman the subject with which they deal may appear both unduly technical and somewhat unwelcome, their material bears directly and antagonistically upon the theory of primary universal sadism and secondary masochism, upon which Freud draws so heavily in founding his social theory upon the mutual hatred of men.

Case III (Mr. C.) is recorded at length for two reasons : (1) in order to give those who are asked to take psychological findings into their social philosophy an outline of the development and yield of a long psychoanalysis, (2) to indicate how social theories—with which the patient was well endowed—can appear as intellectual emanations from the turmoil of unconscious feelings which are the heritage of man from his infancy. It is a new way of looking at the theories of our philosophers, to consider not so much whether there be hidden truth in this obscurity or that startling departure from consistency, but rather to what unconscious motive we may attribute the obscurity or the departure in question. It is instructive to have from such a thorough-going Hobbesian as Mr. C. once was, the assurance of a recent letter, written a year after his analysis terminated, that ' others are not going to attack me in any way '. I do not say that this is C.'s unvarying attitude in the world in which he finds himself to-day. It is not. But it does represent such a change of attitude as might have greatly modified the writings of Hobbes, or of Freud himself. In the end C. held the view that *most of our aggressiveness is due to fear arising in the fantasy life of childhood, and that fear and aggressiveness are built up both in the individual and in the social group as a vicious circle of distrust and determination not to be beaten.*

On psychoanalysing a group of patients such as that which I have presented above, one can hardly escape the conviction that, if the additions to the aggressive self-assertiveness of character which are produced by infantile misconceptions were eliminated, we should have much less aggressiveness in the world. Aggressive characters awaken counter-aggressiveness. They ' would try the patience of Job '. Sympathetic aggressiveness too is as infectious as panic. We know how one powerful speaker can secure the approval of thousands for ' decisions which no

normal mind in any circumstances could have assented to'
(Trotter).[1] And such eloquent speakers are not uncommonly
the possessors of pathologically aggressive characters.

IV. TWO ' PRIMARY ' INSTINCTS

In our summary of Case ' C ' (p. 150) we referred to a ' primary '
social instinct in conflict with a ' primary ' aggressive instinct.
For the purposes of sociology I can see no better division of
man's instinct than into these two groups. The *primary social
instinct* serves that need of others which is fundamental to man's
nature. His *primary aggressive instinct* serves his equally fundamental need to assert himself. It might equally well be called
the *self-assertive instinct*.

These two instincts are ' primary ' in that they are part of the
original endowment of man. They are inherent in that they
appear in the infant's responses to the first situations where
character can show itself, and they are fundamentally incorporated
in all human relationship throughout life. It is in the proportions
of the endowments of these two instincts that the character of
man as a whole, and of each individual man, is set from the start.
What these proportions *ought* to be can only be a matter of
speculation. The theological dogma to which we have seen
Milton subscribe held that the collective organization of law and
force which characterizes established society to-day would not
have been necessary if Adam—and therefore we may perhaps say
if man—had exhibited less self-assertion. And indeed we may
well consider the ideal of social life to be the minimization of the
external government of man in favour of his own self-control,
so that, at the point of the mythical ' golden age ' of the past or
the shadowy ' millennium ' of the future, the self-assertive instinct
will be found to be entirely disciplined to the service of the social
instinct. That will not be in our day ! In every man the primary
social instinct is nicely, though not equally, balanced against the
primary aggressive instinct. The variations of proportion mark
primary variations of character. The secondary accretions which
the experience of life gives to these instincts are determined
partly of course by adult experience. But to a large degree the
adult has ' decided ' what mankind is like and with what responses
he will meet the affairs of his life, which consist so largely of old
situations in new guise. It is chiefly in childhood and infancy
that important events—some real situations and some imagined—
impinge upon the primary character, and give it its secondary
endowments of an increase of one or other or both of the instincts
—greater confidence in love, or more aggressive self-assertiveness.

There seems little doubt that a fortifying or mishandling by

---

[1] Trotter, W. : ' Panic and its consequences '. *British Medical Journal*,
vol. i. p. 270. (1940.)

the parents of the jealousies of the ' Oedipus situation ', at a time when the young child is inclined to have aggressive and self-assertive demands awakened in it, may cause a great deal of secondary aggressiveness to develop. From such evidences it is not possible to say that the reactions of childhood *cause* the reactions of adult life. They are certainly associated in type, and linked in the deeper associations of the patient's mind. But, given an entirely abnormal early life—e.g. without a mother to care for him—my patient, Mr. C., might still have reacted to adult social life in the way he did, or in some similar fantastic way. Rousseau, most certainly a neurotic, is a case in point here. His mother died at his birth. Yet his *Confessions* [1] show us that by the age of eight he had developed a sado-masochistic complex of the ' child-beating ' type (like those of Patients A and B of my case series), by eleven he had a divergence of the impulses of sexuality from those of tenderness, which to-day is technically known as a ' split libido ', and he entered adolescence with conceptions of adult connubial relationship which were ' hateful and disgusting ', a well-developed sense of injustice and persecution, and a sexual perversion which he does not closely characterize. All these deviations many psychoanalysts would wish to derive from Oedipal love of the mother and consequent hatred of the father ! We await the results of psychoanalyses of people with such abnormal histories of infancy : for we may thus gain new insight into how essential the specific Parental Oedipal Situation of Freud really is as a determining point in character development. That environmental influences, whether they be those of parents or foster-parents or nurses, or the later relationships with other children, are of the greatest importance, we see from observations of sympathetic psychoanalysts, from such studies as those of Mrs. Isaacs in her nursery school, and from direct observation in everyday life.

But the most significant social fact about the operation of these two main instinct groups—the social instinct of self-realization through others and the self-assertive instinct of self as against others—is that, whether in a happy normal personality, or in the self-restrained individualist, or in the repressed and unhappy neurotic, *the social instinct nearly always wins.* Except in the case of the conscience-free bully (with whom a stable society can readily cope) *the troubles of modern society spring less from the individual self-assertiveness of its individual members than from its failure to master collective aggressiveness.* Partly by its power over the conscience of the individual through his social instinct itself, and partly by the provision of means of control external to him, society has mastered the problem of the aggressive instinct in the individual—though that still remains a problem for the individual himself !

[1] Dent : Everyman edition, No. 859, pp. 11–17.

Society has learnt to control its individual members. But it has done so pragmatically, using law and force without understanding the most fundamental reason why law and force are necessary. For the most part, we have made our laws, in theory, for other people rather than for ourselves. We have done so because of a constant property of the human mind by which *we judge others differently from the way we judge ourselves*. It was through such passionate judgment that Freud was able to complain with great bitterness of the treatment he received from others, and to make his estimate of that treatment a basis of his unfavourable theory of human nature. And thus it was that Freud missed the solution, which we must attempt to find, of the problem of the aggressive impulse in society. *That solution lies in a further understanding of the emotional relationship of the aggressive instinct to the social instinct in each man, and also of his intellectual responses to this perennial conflict of his emotional life.*

In the following chapter, on the *Psychology of Law*, we shall consider how it is that society has achieved its mastery over the individual. For *it is upon a fuller understanding of the conditions and control of individual aggressiveness that our coming mastery of collective aggressiveness will depend.*

PART II

V

A PSYCHOLOGICAL THEORY OF LAW

1. FOUR FACTS OF HUMAN NATURE UPON WHICH LAW IS BUILT

THE facts about human nature which matter most for our essential control of human behaviour are four : (1) *the similarity of human nature which underlies the diversity of men's conduct ;* (2) *the potential and actual diversity of each ' normal ' man ;* (3) *the established misconceptions of the minds of men upon which prejudice is built ;* (4) *the vagaries of the ' aggressive ' self, and our methods of its repudiation.*

Upon each of those points our study of psychoanalysis throws light : upon none can it give us our verdicts unassisted and unchecked by our observations of actual man, actually behaving.

1. *The similarity of men.*—The diversity of men needs no recording. It strikes the eye of each of us. It has been noted that the developing child observes properties which are common to objects (e.g. that both balls and oranges are round) before it appreciates their points of difference. Where that is true, it is because the child is enquiring and learning his way about the world, bringing the unknown into the known, generalizing and classifying his observations. But when once anxiety or fear is aroused, it is the new and different thing which becomes significant. Adult man has long taken for granted the most obvious similarities between himself and others. And, because of the more advanced stage of his judgment of familiar objects, and also because of the prejudice of his judgment of those which are unfamiliar, political man has come to stress not similarities but dissimilarities. The striking thing about a tramp or a foreigner is that he is different—steals where we would not, perhaps, or has different eating habits. It is a revealing experience, the implications of which we can never quite succeed in generalizing, to discover that Italians (say) fish, or climb mountains, or dig gardens or enjoy music *like ourselves.* We may be sure that underneath they love and hate and fear more like ourselves still. Psychoanalysis of diverse individuals of diverse nationalities has shown the balance between the various social and self-assertive instincts to be set at different angles in different individuals, owing partly to inheritance and partly to experience. But it also shows us that, in the vast and impressive majority of us all, those balances are set within certain limits of normal, despite the fact

that they are ready to be swayed so greatly by the weight of passing events. We may remind the reader of the common psychological plan of man's mind (see Chapter III, Introduction), and also of the basic common physical and emotional needs of men and women (far transcending any type reactions of nation or race) of which a little honest contemplation will make him aware. Here we may recommend the psychoanalytical dictum that ' at bottom they are all alike '. *Both emotionally and in practical life the diversity of men is superimposed upon a far greater and more fundamental commonalty of man.*

2. *The actual and potential diversity within each normal man.*— The first striking experience in psychoanalysis is the revelation, in patients who have utterly dissimilar ' obvious ' characters, of the common properties of the unconscious mind. The second is the diversity of those common properties. The whole great mechanism of repression with which true psychoanalysis primarily deals, constitutes a revelation that the parts of the basic character of *total* man or woman which each of us fails to show overtly, we carry within us in every essential ingredient. Alive within our minds is man loving more than we can trust ourselves to love, hating more than we dare hate; man generous to a fault beyond our faults; man mean and cruel, lustful, cowardly, and brave. No human power can ' free us from the body of this death ' or from the tremendous possibilities of this our human life. Whenever a man becomes ' converted ' to new religious thought, or freed from such a phobia as was suffered by my patient Mr. C., or whenever a nation alters the general attitude to life which we call its ' character ' (under the leadership it may be of a great man, or of a base idea) there occurs a tilting of the balance of human character a little one way or the other in the minds of those concerned. That tilting, decisive enough it may be to great events, is small compared with the power of becoming the hero, the saint, or the brute, of which an adequate analysis of any man's unconscious mind will show him to possess the germs.

3. *The established misconceptions of man's mind.*—We have here to deal with the *formation of prejudice from fantasy,* a process deeply hidden from all but the most penetrating introspection, and one the elucidation of which constitutes perhaps the greatest debt which society owes to psychoanalysis. We have described the mental processes involved (Chapter III, p. 63). Its two stages are : (1) *the formation of ' fantasies ' in infancy,* and (2) *the subsequent adult ' identifications ' of situations and people with elements in those fantasies.*

(i) *The formation in infancy of fantasies about essential human relationships.*—These fantasies, of ' loving ' and ' hating ' parents, the Perfect Mother, the Quintessence of Evil, etc., are compounded out of (*a*) genuine observations made by the young child, (*b*) perversions of truth introduced by misapprehended observations, and (c) pure inventions of the mind, imposed by the early emotional life of the child upon the real or semi-real figures that hover over and dominate him and arouse his primitive and incoherent passions. It must be remembered that, since they are being formed and modified throughout the huge changes of awareness which occur during the first few years of life, these fantasies of infancy are of very varied strength and definition, ranging from the vaguest associations of certain faces and forms and traits and situations with ' good ' or ' evil ', to elaborate dramatizations of the life of the home. Further, these fantasies are in part peculiar to each child, and in part fundamental and common to humanity. There is a recognized sequence in fantasy-formation, the varied emphases upon each stage of which give indications of the profound influences which are at work therein upon adult character formation.

(ii) The second stage in the formation of the unconscious prejudices of our adult life is the ' *identification* ' which the uncon-scious mind achieves between various scenes and personalities of our adult experience and these same fantasy figures of infancy. Be the fantasies general, or peculiar to us, they bring a distortion of the realities of infancy to bias the tastes and judgments of after life. We meet the persons, situations, and causes, the X Y Z of our adult life ; and to our conscious appraisement of them is contributed a factor from our *unconscious* memories, which judges them as if they were the A B C of some forgotten far-off experi-ences of childhood.

We can draw our examples from as wide a field as we wish. From the psychoanalytical case-material upon which I drew in Chapter IV, we may recall the reasons why Mr. C. was so ready to think that everybody was ' getting at him ' (pp. 137 and 145), how it was that Mr. A. thought—quite wrongly—that if he were himself he'd be a beast (p. 131), and that early fear of passionate abandonment which led Mrs. B. to act as if she were liable to be ' carried away ' whenever she was in an exposed position (p. 122). These are extreme instances. But these three individuals (with the rest of the dozen people whose emotional problems I described) were earning their daily bread and were mixing with their fellows as ' normal ', despite these misconceptions about their relation-ships to others, which in every case we were able to trace to ' identifications ' of adult situations with infantile fantasies. If we pass beyond the consulting room to observe our chosen philosophers (of Chapter I), we may note the fear of attack, and the consequent demand for strong government, which coloured the whole political philosophy of Hobbes, or the unconscious repudiation of the self-assertive half of his character by Rousseau, under the mistaken apprehension that there lay the ' evil ', and that in the surviving ' good ' self would lie happiness and peace. We have seen certain indications of character types among the philosophers : in particular we have linked Hobbes with Freud, and Freud with my patient C., bringing them all into the ' aggressive-obsessional ' group of minds, the prolific unconscious fantasy-life of which has afforded a very great deal of psycho-analytical material. But beyond individual peculiarities and character-types there lie *the fundamental and universal conceptions of primitive and infantile mankind*. It is these that give us the crude classifications, the superstitious awes, the blind loyalties, and the ready identification of enemy and friend which are universal traits of humanity.

In *fantasy-identification* we thus find a fundamental machinery of human distortion. If any philosopher should seek confirmation for his view that things are not as we see them he has it here to hand. We do not see things and people as they are—first of all because of our common prejudices, and secondly because of the special prejudices of each one of us. This mechanism is constantly at work in society, falsifying all situations of life where our emotions are strongly engaged, giving us our predilections in government and our prejudices of class and creed and race and colour. So that in the very act of labelling an experience we must needs go on and identify it with some fantasy or other, and docket it accordingly. The reason why A. thought all fat little men were brutes was because they unconsciously recalled the father whom he had *imagined* to be a brute. Shakespeare's Caesar followed a different subconscious classification : ' Let me have men about me that are fat ! '

We may notice how our language ministers to our identifications of neutral objects with fantasies of good or evil by providing us with virtual synonyms which are also nearly antonyms. According to our predilection we term people ' slim ' or ' skinny ', ' plump ' or ' fat ', ' buxom ' or ' blowsy '. We have the ' robust ' ' brute ', and the ' delicate ' ' weakling '. According to your attitude the negro face has its ' smile ' or its ' leer ', while the white man's is ' clean ' or ' ghastly '. And according to our side of the battle we see the ' gallant charge of serried ranks ', or the ' onrush of savage hordes '. We have our choice of phrase as of feeling according to the identification in our minds. And that identification is ultimately with something afar : and in part at least it is with something that never existed outside our fancy.

Here are the very roots and origins of prejudice ! They are roots so deep within us, that, try as we will, we cannot trace them in ourselves, but only infer them from our most detached and cool observations of others. Sometimes we may do that with great effect, as for instance when we note that death in battle is a murder of madness, in every *other* war than this in which we fight. But in most of our lives we shall live on, fighting and striving to adjust ourselves to reality, in total inability to divest ourselves of the many fixed prejudices to which, as normal men, we are heir.

It is because of its discovery of the depth and universality of these prejudices formed from unconscious fantasy-identifications, that modern psychology can give confident and insistent support to the maxim which is quoted both earlier and later in this book that *no man can form an objective and unbiased judgment of a situation in which he is emotionally involved ; that no man can safely be admitted a judge of his own cause.*

4. *The vagaries of the aggressive self.* (i) *Repression of the aggressive instincts.*—The nature, the strength, and the persistence in adult life of unconscious fantasies formed in infancy depend in great degree upon the place that aggressiveness comes to play in the mind of the individual. We have described [1] the struggle between the *social instinct* (which serves comprehensively man's need of society) and the *self-assertive instinct* which represents each man's interest for himself alone, to advance his desires and lusts at the expense of others, or in their despite. We have described and entered the controversy about the place of aggressiveness in the fundamental instinctual life of man.[2] I hold that, as there are as yet no means of quantitating psychoanalytical findings, there is no scientific way of settling that dispute. The clearer demarcation of fantasies peculiar to individuals, to character-types, to races it may be, and those common to all men offers a task for the future. So also does the whole question of proportioning the claims upon mankind of these two great rival instinct groups, the co-operative and the competitive, self through others and self against others. Here we must be content to attribute to unconscious fantasy much of the prejudice which gave to our philosophers their variously reasoned pictures of mankind—to Hobbes, man's restless desire for power after power, to Bodin, that ' horrid plundering crew ', to Freud and Stekel, those hating infants at the back of the mind, and to Hooker, Locke, and Suttie upon the other hand, those yearnings for loving comfort and union. In our support we have related our patients' fantasies ; and especially would we note the modifications which these have produced in the stressful, distrustful, and anxious social co-operation of the aggressive-obsessional character type.

Let us now take up again a fact which I noted at the end of the analysis of my psychoanalytical case histories [3] and which is open to the widest confirmation throughout our social life. It is that, whatever their ' fundamental ' balance of instinct may be, *most men* BEHAVE *as if* AT MOST TIMES *their social instinct predominated over their self-assertive instinct.* The very existence of society as we know it, the nature of loyalty, and the total of material culled from psychoanalysis all confirm the conclusion

[1] Chapter IV, p. 152.
[2] Chapter III, Sections II and III, pp. 70, 78 ; Chapter IV, Section I (2), p. 109.
[3] Chapter IV, pp. 151, 153.

of Aristotle, that man is *in practice* a social animal, whose adequate
life would break down if his individual aggressiveness were
generally allowed to be victorious over his co-operative social
urges. We have considered at some length the way in which the
effective predominance of the social instinct comes about. But
whatever the nature of the ' instinctual renunciation ' by which
it is accompanied, there is no doubt that *society does in fact master
the individual.* With what would happen in hypothetical contingencies we shall again be concerned when we come to deal
(in Chapters VII and VIII) with the possibility of a new type of
society arising which differs in the nature of its claims upon
human loyalty from those of any that have gone before. But for
existing societies we can say that, as far as their internal organization is concerned, the problem of aggressiveness has been
pragmatically mastered. For the minority of openly aggressive
men the problem of repression is an external one. Psychologically and practically that is a minor problem : for society can
readily recognize, and thus under normal conditions can readily
deal with, the bully. Among the majority of men the bully is
only occasionally in evidence, and that shamefacedly. But *the
general and guilty repression of aggressiveness is an integral part of
the normal ascendancy of the social instinct over the self-assertive
instinct.* In the realm of theory Freud's development of man's
social conscience from ' dread of society ' admits this equally
with Suttie's derivation of it from man's ' need of love '. Our
aggressive impulses would naturally make us assert ourselves
freely and selfishly against our fellows, were there nothing to
fear from such outbursts. But for there to be nothing to fear it
would be necessary that somehow or other love would not be
lost, in spite of the aggressiveness which we vented upon our
loved ones. Only thus would the social instinct feel itself secure
against the primitive violence of the aggressive instinct. In the
sphere of practice, this is the consummation most devoutly desired
by almost all neurotics. Yet of the twelve consecutive neurotic
cases in my series (Chapter IV, Section 3), while ten were abnormally aggressive, only one gave scope to his aggressiveness. The
remaining nine achieved a complete, nearly complete, or usually
successful repression of their aggressiveness, with painful or
disabling results to themselves. *They achieved this repression just
because they dared not venture an affront to the demands of their
social instincts.*

It has been argued that ' dread of society ' can be removed
by the removal of illusions, leaving the aggressive instincts in all
their natural predominance. It is true that much of that dread
of society which *is* based upon illusion can be lost, and is lost by
neurotics under treatment. But under what conditions is an
aggressiveness freed which is able to defy the real power which
society exercises over a man through his psychological dependence

upon it ? Though the majority of neurotic patients show intense repressed aggressiveness, a great deal of which is vented during treatment, at no point before, during, or after treatment do any of these men and women really allow their self-assertive minority desires to challenge the authority of their real need of society. This experience is general. The man who loses his dread of society to a degree which makes him challenge it, does but test its power of social sanction. And if he is not to become an outlaw —which position very few men can tolerate for long—his defiances will be strictly regulated, and very limited.

Psychologists rightly doubt and debate how like 'normal' people are to such neurotic patients as I have described. But it is now generally admitted by psychoanalysts of all the schools that *in as far as the former do repress aggressiveness and hatred* the mechanism is on the whole similar to the one we have described. And, in the event, whether we look at the behaviour of men and women in affairs domestic or social, or in peace or in war, their conscientious adherence to their conception of their obligations is matter for us all to confirm by observation. Be each one's temperament normally balanced or abnormally aggressive, the majority of people choose for repression, not their social selves— which would enable them to free themselves from dependence upon others—but the aggressive selves which threaten that dependence. They do this in the degree which they conceive necessary to satisfy their security in society. But all normal men do it. There is only one major condition which realizes, for neurotic and normal alike, a freedom for their aggressiveness which does not conflict with their need of the approval of their society. That is the condition of warfare, in which the exclusion of ' the enemy ' from a particular society enables its members to become united in aggressiveness and at the same time to feel free of social guilt. To that exception we shall return (in Chapter VII).

(ii) *The manifestations of the aggressive instinct.*—How then do the instincts of anti-social aggressiveness secure any outlet within a disciplined society ? In Chapter IV (page 112) I described the aggressiveness of normal man as being *provoked, temporary, limited, repudiated, explained away, and forgotten*. It is *provoked* by situations which arouse anger, or prejudice, or suggest danger. It is *temporary* and *limited* because its manifestations are inacceptable to the social self which is usually the ruling self, and it exercises its power, like a repressed but virile political minority, periodically, suddenly, and furtively. The political analogy is that of a short-lived regime following a *coup d'état*. It is *repudiated, explained away*, or *forgotten*, for the same reason. For its expression, the aggressive instinct must either seize that rostrum of consciousness which is normally under the direction of the social instinct, or else it must find a short cut to executive action. We all suffer to some degree from a ' split-mind ' on every question about which these two instincts drive us in two different directions. The conscious mind, anxious for consistency and the harmony of social approval, attempts to ignore the existence of the aggressive instinct, except at those times when it is enthroned, as Dr. Jekyll ignored Mr. Hyde. Our major selves are as much the victims of the *coup d'état* as are our enemies. In some sphere and at some time, with or without the obvious aid of external influences, the executive of thought or action, in adulthood as in childhood, is seized by that strong minority, and aggressiveness is vented. It may come as a frontal outburst, or in oblique persecutions, of individuals or of ideas, or as fantasy or dream, which (unless it compels to action) commits no crime and leaves no external injustice to set right. The manifestations are often furtive, eluding full consciousness. And their final relationship with consciousness may be either to elude it altogether, and so *to determine our actions for us without our knowledge of our motivation in them, or else to be repudiated by our consciousness when the occasion has passed.* Often we dodge ourselves so successfully that we remain in entire ignorance of our own major faults of conduct and of character. Brought face to face with them, however, we have our means of repudiation ready to hand. (1) Sometimes we *challenge the facts* themselves. We did not say this, or do that, ' could not have ' implied the other, or started a certain quarrel. With complete candour, we introduce a list of our well-attested vices with the phrase : ' No one could accuse me of . . .' Those qualities are so far from what we wish to be, wish to be thought, or see ourselves as, that, though they come from us, they must not be found in us. The mechanism applies to faults as measurable as deceit, faithlessness, even drunkenness. ' I *did* not do it, because I *could* not do it. It would not be *me* to do that.' So says the major self when again in its wonted seat of executive power. (2) But sometimes we *admit the facts and falsify the motive.* Our object (even to ourselves) was the ' greater good ', or we ' had obligations ', or there was irresistible provocation : ' The woman tempted me '. (3) Most important of all, *we forget.* Graham Wallas has stressed the selective remembering by which we acquire material for our political reasoning : ' All Nonconformists are influenced by their memory of certain facts of which very few churchmen are aware and all Irishmen by facts which most Englishmen try to forget '.[1] Of cardinal importance in politics, selective remembering and forgetting are also vital mechanisms of individual self-esteem. If we remembered the same things about ourselves as we do about each other, not only our major cautions and suspicions, but also the chief excuses for our cupidity and self-righteous aggressiveness would fall from us. The all too rare sympathy of ' seeing

[1] Graham Wallas, *Human Nature in Politics* (1908), p. 136. (Constable's Miscellany. 1929.)

the other man's point of view' is less often an act of sympathy
with sentiments foreign to ourselves, than a recollection of how
we habitually view Mr. Brown's problems when we are in Mr.
Brown's shoes. In fact the competitive and acquisitive aggressiveness which is in us, which harmonizes so ill with our social selves,
yet which will out, is a cause without rival at once of blindness
to our own faults and prejudice against those of others. And,
naturally enough, the more firmly we demand a high standard of
social virtue from ourselves, the more complete has a self-
deception to be in order to allow the egress of our cruel, selfish,
or carnal lusts. The more 'upright' or 'perfect' a man or
woman wishes to be—that is to appear to himself or herself to be
—the more he or she must whitewash their own aggressiveness
and blacken that of their provoking adversary. And, given a
sweeping 'sanction', the crueller to that adversary will they
become. This was the mechanism of hatred of others in my
patient Mr. 'C.' It is also ours.

We have noted the technical psychological term of '*projection*'
for the blackening of others by foisting upon them, in our
imagination, our own unconscious feelings. It is a well-known
finding both in psychoanalysis and in everyday life. 'The world
is such an aggressive place', sighed my patient, A. ; 'Hatred not
love is the primary state of feeling between human beings',
wrote Stekel and Freud in the midst of lives of bitter antagonism
and quarrel. 'I thought I saw all this (nobility) in my native
land, because I carried it in my heart', said the introspective
Rousseau, finding the correct solution albeit for a different
emotion. Both in hatred and in love we tend to endow our
object with our own sentiment. With love, to do so gives us
solace or an excuse for requital : with hate, it gives us all our
justifications for reprisal and revenge. There must therefore be
added to the methods of repudiating our own aggressiveness this
one (4) of *imagining it to be in others*. From the evidences and
examples of the mechanism which we gave in Chapter IV, we may
extract the following reminder : Mr. C. discovered through
psychoanalysis his competitive and aggressive rage against others
—hitherto unappreciated by him. Next he traced this to a
'primary' self-assertiveness, which had been greatly aggravated
by infant imaginings of specific threats directed against himself
both by his mother and his father. We saw what resulted.
As he stood in discomfort in the London Underground train at
the age of forty, the very organs of his body about the functioning
of which he half-consciously sought reassurance were those
which he had imagined his father to have had designs upon ;
while the anatomical centre of his life-long fear of women was that
point towards which he had fancied his mother was drawing him
dangerously towards herself. Upon both his parents the infant
C. had '*projected*' an emotion, aggressive and competitive in

the one case, loving and voluptuous in the other. *He thought these things were in them because he carried them in his own heart.* We may hazard a guess about the unconscious mind of Thomas Hobbes, endowing it with potent infantile fantasy-memories of his father. That violent clergyman, who was forced to flee his parish after committing an assault, was probably demanding through the brain of the adult philosopher the control of ' others like father '. The ' father-figure ' of Hobbes' nightmares would comprise a memory of the real father, together with a fantasy which endowed that father with a further aggressiveness which really resided in the son. The infant imagines others to behave as it feels it would behave if it had the power. And everyone who has heard an angry infant cry can guess what that would be like !

I have criticized the assumption that the mechanisms of neurotic thought can be taken as a general mental process of normal mankind. Freud makes this inference repeatedly—over the repressive mechanism of obsessional neurotics (Chapter III, p. 78), the formation of the social tie (p. 85), the hatred between homosexual siblings (p. 87) ; and at each point I have questioned his justification for doing so. Sometimes he questions it himself. At the same time I have emphasized the commonalty which underlies the diversity of man (p. 156). No one who has studied and practised analytical psychology questions that. I have hitherto avoided attempting to draw a line between the normal and the pathological in mental process. It is in truth a very blurred edge ! But there can be no doubt that this mechanism of projection occurs as part of the self-deception of normal life. We employ it to create mythical bogies. We use it to create situations which justify a certain response which we wish to make. To such a *kind* teacher it is only reasonable to take flowers ; such a *difficult* and *unfair* master surely deserves our stratagem of deceit or our breach of agreement ! Surely it is obvious that *my* competitor is (too often) ready to seize every unfair advantage over me ? The stalwart wife who goes in real terror of a meek and defensive husband is a phenomenon not exclusively confined to humorous literature. The general conviction of rectitude among litigants, upon which we would invite experienced judges to comment, might be attributable to other methods of self-deception to which we have alluded. But I would ask the reader to study others, quarrelling, loving, competing, others easygoing or tense with effort, and see how often these friends and acquaintances are noticeably imagining the pressure of feeling to be inwards towards themselves, when in reality it is outwards from themselves.[1] Then study the discipline of children with Mrs. Isaacs

---

[1] Compare Rousseau's endless projections of his aggressiveness onto others. (*Confessions*, passim). In my case series note Case IV's fear of his own refusal to fight for personal honour, and Case VI's refusal to take life for the state. Both patients really feared the consequences of their own aggressive passion.

(Chapter IV, Section 2), and note how those anxieties and jealousies which require the external regulation of their communities of work and play, so constantly arise out of fear that the other child has planned just the enterprise—e.g. to ride off with the tricycle—which they would like to execute themselves. Last of all study yourselves. But that, alas, is too hard a task ! For unconscious projection is beneath the depth to which introspection normally reaches. In fact it *is* the other fellow's fault : and we can prove it !—Fantasy-identification and projected aggressiveness are universal human traits. *It is the nature of the fantasies and the intensity of the aggressiveness which constitute the normality or the abnormality of the process.*

II. THE PSYCHOLOGY OF LAW

1. *The grounding of law.*—I have said that we ourselves are as much the victims of the aggressiveness which conflicts with our major characters and our ' social solidarity ' as are those upon whom we vent our aggressiveness. It is thirty years since Graham Wallas pleaded that we should abandon the view that ' anger was part of the angry man '. *The prime operative duty of law is the control of human aggressiveness.* In pursuance of this duty, law should proceed against the aggressiveness in man rather than against the aggressive man. And it is the temporary, furtive, and repudiated aggressiveness of the normal individual, no less than those departures from rectitude which are made ' wilfully ' and with the majority of the character, which constitute the lawlessness of man. The characteristic manifestations of the aggressive instinct which I have named above combine with those fixed prejudices of the mind of normal man which render him incapable of executing equity in his own cause to constitute him *always and essentially a potential law breaker.* He cannot see the truth about others. And either he does not recognize or he is loath to admit his own aggressiveness.

I believe that once we have understood the properties of the aggressive instinct which I have enumerated, we can do something which is much more important to our present society than to assess or quantitate it—we can control it, to our own infinite advantage. This control falls in the first place upon law ; in the last it may fall upon ourselves. *It is upon the fact of the potential criminal in every man that I would give to law its psychological grounding.* We can observe, and to some degree we can measure, the diversities of mankind. We can study the causation of a criminal tendency, of the outbreak of cruelty, violence, or injustice, meanness or deceitfulness in a given man. But our knowledge of psychology to-day not only does not tell us who will be the next to depart from social rectitude. It tells us that we cannot tell. Psychologically speaking, it is against the whole field of man's universal potentiality to anti-social conduct that law has to proceed. It is to cope with this fact of human nature that the structure of law has been, however pragmatically, built. It is here that its theory should be sound.

2. *Law and the aggressive impulse.*—It is then a first function of law to remedy our inability to control our own aggressive selves. It is for our new social psychology to inform moral philosophy, which Maine [1] defined as ' the science of the rules governing human conduct ', of this rule governing conduct which makes us unable to remain for ever under the influence of our social instincts, yet equally unable to realize, by anticipation or by memory, the extent (and often even the nature) of our departure from the guidance of those instincts. Our social instinct is in general control of our lives. We *wish* to find it in a control which is harmonious with our individualism ; and it is not. In consequence, we fail to evaluate our individualistic self-assertive impulses where they conflict with our social conscience. It is because of this blindness which turns man's ' natural justice ' awry when he comes to judge his own cause that so few of us realize the fact that in our law-making it is *our own control* which we are planning rather than that of others. Milton was right when he held that if Adam's human nature had been more completely under the control of his sense of obligation (i.e. his social conscience, or Freud's super-ego) we would have had no need to remedy ' the discord and violence that spring from our transgression ' by appointing kings and magistrates as our deputies, but would have been able to execute ' that justice which every man by the bond of nature and of covenant must else have executed for himself and for one another '. If human nature *as such* had been endowed with adequate control of its own aggressiveness, we could dispense with the external controls of law and government as we know them.

Thus it is that *the need of law arises from the similarity of men rather than from their diversity*. But Graham Wallas's forecast [2] that we would come to consider the control of conduct as the control of mental processes rather than of people still awaits realization, and even theoretical acceptance. ' Anger, previously part of the angry man, is now separable from him.' And to anger we may add all man's anti-social impulses. The control of man as an individual exists external to himself because certain emotions require such external control, and to these emotions man, as man, is liable. Such an attitude to its function on the part of those who make and administer the law would enable that discipline to advance much further into the lives of men than it has hitherto done, and to be welcomed by them as a friend and counsellor, as well as a benevolent discipline. We ought to be able to regard

[1] Maine, *Ancient Law*, p. 204. (Everyman, No. 734.)
[2] Wallas, loc. cit. p. 181.

the law as controlling for us those qualities in us which we never really master of ourselves. In performing this function it should as far as possible proceed against the faulty social emotion rather than against its temporary possessor, should ' scorn the vice, but spare the name '.

3. *The detectable origins, authority, and enforcement of law.*— Let us now re-examine the place of law in society, considered in the light of our knowledge of the properties of man's aggressive nature. For reasons given in an earlier chapter (Chapter II, p. 56) I shall take as the definition of law ' *rules for the guidance of conduct imposed upon a society by its sovereign power, which as such is capable of their general enforcement* '. We will begin by noting what the origins of law actually are ; what also its ' sovereign ' source of authority, and its means of enforcement. We shall then consider upon what principles law should be based, administered, and enforced.

(i) *Origins.*—The detectable origins of law are, of course, very varied. Both systems of law and their component laws may be traced either historically—such as to the regulations of the interest of individuals or of groups in primitive societies, as is done by Maine—or psychologically, such as to the ' largely unconscious efforts of communities to realize their material and spiritual ideals ' (Jenks). Laws may originate as rules tyrannously imposed upon a community by an autocrat or an oligarchy. The laws which govern a community may or may not be directed to serve the interests of that community. And the community as a whole may or may not desire them.

(ii) *The ' sovereign ' authority.*—The ' sovereign ' power which imposes and enforces the law clearly varies with the type of community. In an ' autocratic tyranny ' this power resides in the tyrant—that is, of course, for all laws which he can enforce. But under careful examination no tyranny would show a completely successful domination by the tyrant in all spheres of life. The sullen obstinacy of his slaves as they tired would reduce his returns in labour ; their passive resistance would thwart him— even though it led to the execution of the resisters—fear of revolt and assassination would check him. And many a powerful tyrant has failed in the collection of his taxes. The ' sovereign ' power is in fact never absolute, but merely *the preponderance of power effective to the particular occasion.* It may rest in tyrant, oligarchy, majority, or in a ' universal general will ' which meets with resistance only as individuals find themselves temporarily out of alignment with its purpose.

(iii) *Enforcement.*—An essential feature of the rule of conduct which constitutes a law is that it shall be capable of enforcement. The more nearly the alignment between the intention of the sovereign power and the wishes of the subjects of a law, the more can external force be abolished in its execution. The force required for the administration of a law varies in nature and in degree. Against the fixed will of the subjects great force is naturally required, though in societies where one group or class is entirely dominated by another, laws—e.g. of labour or taxation —may sometimes be enforced in spite of continued and un-flinching resistance. If on the other hand a law has the main-tained acquiescence of a majority of those upon whom it operates, its enforcement tends to become an easier matter, for the active resistance is limited, and there is no added potential resistance from the community as a whole. If the law has the support of an active will from the majority of the community its enforce-ment is rendered easier still. For behind the actual force of court and police there lies an available potential force, that of public approval. At the extreme end of the series we find laws which merely regulate custom in the absence of conflict of interest. And these may be both grounded on consent and operated by consent.

4. *Emotional processes in law*—(i) *Law as an extension of self-control.*—But the highest test of law as a social force does not lie in any of the above categories. Because of the qualities of man's mind with which we have been concerned, a law may have the support in principle and in habitual practice of *all* those for whom it operates, and yet require the sanction of force. For, as we know, a rule may be accepted and supported by a subject in certain phases of his life, and resisted in others. In modern states the regulation of road traffic, the laws governing the sale of alcoholic beverages, and nearly the whole range of legislation against personal violence, are instances where men are not content to protect themselves and limit others, but can be seen to be *preparing a discipline for themselves*, securing society in their more co-operative moments against their own actions in moments when they are liable to be less co-operative and more selfish. It is this aspect of law which shows it as not merely regulating affairs between people, but as maintaining one set of moral values against another, the product of human decisions taken upon one instinct against the impulses of a contrary instinct in the mind of the same subject at another time. It is thus that the law becomes *an external support for a man's social instinct against the anti-social activities of his self-assertive instinct*. In this function law and government may truly be regarded as an *extension of self-control*.

(ii) '*Projection*' *and law-making.*—It must be remembered that, because he represses, repudiates, forgets, and projects on to others his own aggressiveness, the ordinary man is only dimly and occasionally aware that in legislating and approving legislation to secure equitable assessments of rights and obligations, or to prevent deceit, or to arrest violence, he is legislating for the control of himself by the principles he wishes to follow, against the practice to which he is liable. But let anyone examine himself candidly upon his attitude to the law governing the moral sphere in which he believes himself, though perhaps erroneously, to be weakest—the licensing regulations, the traffic regulations, the elaborate police control of brawling, the control of financial integrity, the protection of contract, the enforcement of humanitarian obligations—and see if, scanning the past, he cannot discover reasons why his social instinct should glory in the law as one means of its triumph over the keen if occasional and even more occasionally remembered thrusts of his self-assertive and anti-social impulses. Next let him note that there is far more of this beneath the limits of our normal powers of direct introspection. When Hobbes asked for laws and government to protect himself from the aggressiveness of bad men, he was not aware that a great deal of his apprehension probably sprang not from the burglaries his own house had suffered, nor from the personal or group violences of which he had heard during the English Civil Wars, but from an unconscious fear of his own aggressiveness. With the aid of psychoanalysis Mr. C. came to this very clear understanding of his Hobbesian philosophy. It is possibly the mechanism of ' projection ' which has done most to prevent man from realizing that in law-making he has been legislating for the control of emotion within himself. He wants those emotions controlled ; and his unconscious mind has approved and demanded his laws to that end. But he cannot bear to think of himself as in need of restraining law. Did Hobbes, did Locke, did Rousseau not need law ?

5. *The prime function of law is to implement the social instinct of man.*—Ideally, where men make laws for the government of themselves their object may be defined as *to express and to implement their own physical, mental, and spiritual needs by preserving that balance between the demands of their self-assertive and social instincts which they have agreed upon as necessary to their common social life.* Where men's laws are made for them, the object should be the replacement of an internal by an external setting of this balance.

6. *The source of the obligation to obey the law.*—The definition of the ideal function of law as an extended self-discipline of man points at once to the psychological source of that obligation to obey which has long concerned the philosophical lawyer. The obligation is certainly a ' moral ' one, i.e. the imperative comes from within. But it is also an intellectual and emotional one. It is the urge of man's ' conscience ' that he should maintain self-control of his aggressive and self-assertive instinct in the over-riding interest of his social instinct. This instinct is in its turn based upon his social dependence. His ' conscience ' is his estimate—largely an unconscious one—of what that dependence requires of him. It includes both ' dread of society ' (Freud) and

' fear of loss of love ' (Suttie). It is the authority which his fear
of pain and his need of love combine to give to the social environment of the individual, which fastens upon him his social instinct,
as surely as other demands of his body and mind fix in him his
instinctive awareness of the needs of nutrition or of sex.

7. *The emotional aims of man.*—The social instinct of man
welcomes law as a means of extending his control over those
aggressive instincts which, useful as they are to him in group
warfare, in solitary defence, and in so many of the achievements
and acquisitions that satisfy the ego, are nevertheless felt to be a
danger to that social well-being without which there can be no
secure happiness. It will be remembered that we spoke
(Chapter IV, p. 152) of man's need of others and his need of
self-assertion as ' equal ' in importance, and of the struggle for
the control of our conduct which goes on between the social and
the aggressive instincts as being so deep as to justify the division
of our instinctual life into these two components as ' fundamental '.
Psychologists must come to accept as ' fundamental ' the needs
that all men show as fundamental. We must give up deriving
all social qualities from thwarted aggressiveness, with a subsequent
' self-identification with the object hated '. Equally must we
renounce the opposite error of deriving all aggressiveness from
thwarted love. Love and hatred of others undoubtedly get
deeply confused together within the psyche. The chief cause
of this seems to me to be the simple difficulty of satisfying at once
the love of others and the love of self. But however that may be,
to whatever ' depth ' we conduct our analysis we always find these
two instincts, of self *through* others and self *against* others. And
the attempt to find a balance between the two in the truest interest
of the ' Pleasure-principle ' runs through the whole length of the
emotional life of man. Attempts at law and justice are but
examples of his search.

8. *The fluctuating standards of the Pleasure-principle and the
stabilizing influence of law.*—When I say that the balance of the
psyche is usually so fixed that co-operative reactions usually win,
I do not affirm a general law-abidingness of men. Nor is it true
that the periodic departure which each one of us makes into
selfishness each himself deplores. We do not anxiously seek to
correct our wayward passions by submitting ourselves to the
external discipline of law. A man does not deplore what he is
unaware of. And, as for conscience, there is every degree and
variety of voluntary departure from social behaviour according
to the varied interpretations by which men have decided that
their love of self and security will be safeguarded ; how far they
shall pursue self-satisfaction through others, and how far through
self-assertion. We must remember too that our ideas of what
will bring us happiness are fluid and fluctuant. Satisfaction of
the ' Pleasure-principle ' may be defined as the goal of every man.

But this all-embracing demand can only be met by the satisfaction of a variety of instinctual demands. The instinct we desire to satisfy at any particular time is that one which presents itself with greatest insistence at that time. And, group our instincts as we will, in effect they are a very mixed lot. Desires for power, achievement, love in its many forms, approval. Desires distorted by unconscious misconceptions ; desires perhaps to suffer or cause suffering—they clamour with their various voices, and every man has his own collection and proportioning of them. Out of the mixture, and as a result of experience working upon inheritance, there crystallizes a strong but peculiar sense of certain obligations to society, without the honouring of which happiness is felt to be impossible. With however common a start, no two infants reach childhood without each acquiring the first edition of his own peculiar ' conscience '. It is his own cool interpretation, in the light of his own experience, of what will bring him happiness. It may be a desire to be loved ' as much as possible may be '. Or it may be a desire to achieve a supposed ' freedom ' at all costs of betrayal of friendships. Or he may be hag-ridden by fears of imagined powers arrayed against him and be for ever seeking the propitiation of, or protection from, the strength of others. It is on account of our experience of the actual behaviour of ' average ' men in ' normal ' times that we affirm that in them the conscience is so set that, in the words of A. D. Lindsay : ' Most men usually wish to obey the law '.[1] The law in fact remains stable by virtue of our desires, while we who create and obey it do not. It should be an expression of the major wish of the majority. If it represented the *constant* wish of the majority it would lose its greatest value.

9. *Law, liberty, and welfare.*—Allen [2] has posed again the question ' whether law exists for the sake of enlarging or for the sake of restricting the liberty of man '. It clearly achieves both. But ' liberty ' is a word of deception, and the idea which it connotes, attractive enough when we feel ourselves to be fettered, is never an ultimate ideal. To ask whether life should be ' free ' or ' restricted ' is as if we tried to determine whether a ship's helm should be fixed to turn it to port or to starboard. We are freed *from* certain things and *for* certain purposes, never ' freed ' *in vacuo*. However ' free ' we may be, we are always directed by some influence from somewhere. When Pollock [3] writes that duty and right are not more divisible in law than action and reaction in mechanics, he leads us to think that the distinction between the two is unprofitable. And when we say that law gives liberty or takes it away, we are making no more fundamental

[1] Lindsay, *Essentials of Democracy*, p. 62. 1929.
[2] Allen, C. K., *Legal Duties*, p. 156. (Clarendon Press. 1931).
[3] Pollock, *A First Book of Jurisprudence*, p. 73. (3rd edition. Macmillan. 1911.)

a distinction. ' Liberty ' to go to the devil ?   Or a life ' fettered '
to high achievement ?   The law may bring either of these things
to us.   It may free us from ' economic slavery ' or bind us to it,
and still be, not only ' good law ', but law which is good for us.
It is not the liberty which matters, but the influence that is brought
to bear.   In his law-making and law-keeping frames of mind,
the demand of man is not for freedom but for justice, for equity,
for a balance to be maintained.   And it is only because the actual
law so often fails to meet this demand that we find that ' firm
distinction of the layman between law and justice ' which is so
rightly deplored by Jenks.   Good law should externally guide
and internally oblige us towards a just proportioning of our
instinctual satisfactions, to enhance at once the *welfare* of our
fellows and ourselves.   Grotius recognized the operation of the
social instinct (with its agent, man's conscience) when he wrote
of natural law that ' no one can deny it without doing violence
to his own nature '.   But at the same time he tried to stereotype
its behaviour.   Allen himself shows the same inclination in both
respects when he writes of ' a growing doctrine of Common Law
that, at least where human life is at stake, the impulse to purely
altruistic conduct is part of the morality of the average man ',
and anticipates that the law will come to require of us a ' minimum
altruism, the plain man's duty '.   If democracy is to be admitted
a psychological possibility, then in securing this minimum
altruism the law should find that it is implementing the plain
man's major desires.   To be grounded in democracy the law
should at once have the approval of the average man, and be
for his control.

10. *Five partial theories of law integrated.*—At the end of
Chapter II (p. 58) I grouped under five headings certain expressed views of the function of law.   Law was variously described
as existing : (1) to maintain the state, (2) to enrich the community, (3) to protect the individual, (4) to express duties, (5) to
regulate both duties and rights.

Law does, or should do, all these things together, none of
them exclusively.   For the first, if the state is the executive
organization chosen by a society to express its own will, the
society will naturally set the balance of its agreed demands upon
its members in such a way that both the structure of the society
and the power of its executive are maintained.   If, however, the
state is imposed by a few persons upon a community of men
without meeting with their agreement or strong support, the
laws and the force of such a ' state ' will be directed more consciously, emphatically, and exclusively to this function of state
maintenance.   Austin fabricated a ' sovereign ' source of power
' absolute, unlimited, indivisible, uncontrollable, inalienable ',
and found that power in the state.   We know that no repository
of power is in fact sovereign in this sense, even when, as Austin

imagines, it is backed by a law-abiding people. It is easy, or difficult, to enforce certain laws, at certain times, upon certain people. But it is only where the state and its laws are imposed upon an unwilling community from without or by a minority of its members that it can be said that the essential matter is the support of the law-making agent, the state.

As for the other four functions variously allocated as paramount in law, if we regard the object of law-making as being to express and to implement the physical, mental, and spiritual needs of the members of a community, laws made with such an object should at one and the same time enrich the community, protect the individual, express his duties, and guard his rights. The needs of the individual include the preservation of his society and the control of himself. The ' state ' decreases in significance proportionately as the community comes to see itself and to govern itself in this way. For the ' state ' is then seen as the mere machinery of government. As Jenks points out in his opposition to Austin, it is the law which matters, not the state : ' The state as it is now thought of will cease to exist '. To think of law as existing to maintain the state will ultimately become as anachronistic as if we now claimed that the law existed to maintain the City of London.

To claim, as did Duguit, that law consists ' solely of duties ' is to miss the essential regulative function of law, to substitute a task-master for a friend, and to introduce a sermon in place of a summing-up. The reason he gives—that to encourage ' rights ' is to encourage individuality—places in our hands a key to the mental process of the author. We have seen that the real business of the law is to hold that nice balance between our social and our individualistic instincts of which we have written so much. Duguit thinks that man is inclined to be too individualistic, as of course he sometimes is. In consequence he throws his whole weight into the opposite scale. The decision would be just and the sermon would be applicable to most of us at many times, but it does not state the position of the law. A magistrate who finds a motorist has driven too fast says so. But it would not aid the cause of justice to have a gramophone record of his strictures played as a judgment at all trials of road offences. Duguit really wishes to strengthen our consciences, to fortify that ' superego ' which makes us desire to perform our duties, and which urges us to devise our laws and support our courts against the time when, in violence or in prejudice, we ourselves or others like us shall start to encroach upon another's rights. But if we are taught that we have no rights ourselves, it will not be our co-operative social selves that will be strengthened ! Rather will it be our aggressive instincts that will rise in wrath and self-assertion. For the most favourable condition for revolt is oppression ; and this can apply to instincts as well as to peoples. That

' individual liberty exists in order to develop social solidarity ' is not any more true than would be the counter statement that social solidarity exists in order to foster individual liberty. Our instincts make us desire to be both independent and united, both free and bound to others. There is a right place in our lives for each instinct, just as there is for activity and sleep ; and there is a right degree for each of the impulses—towards others, with the protection and comfort their approval can afford us, and away from others, in freedom and realization of our personal integrity. Some of us have minds which feel that we need more of one or other of these conditions than we get ; and if we are philosophers we foist that feeling upon the world. Others of us struggle to rationalize conflicting impulses and conflicting thoughts upon the subject. But the business of the law is to find and hold that balance which will first give us ' social solidarity ' *as much as need be*, and then will free each one of us, to develop, in the light of the freedom that comes from the security of our society and the clarity of our consciences, that variety of life and achievement which will both integrate our individual lives, and diversify and enrich the communities in which we dwell.

Throughout the ages of discovery and social thought there have been constant alternations of emphasis upon the community and upon the individual. The contrast of ' control ' and ' mastery ' upon the one hand with the community of free-willing men upon the other has always been in men's minds. And because political theory has never been subtle enough to express the complicated and fluctuating desires of man upon this subject, there has been this swing of dogma from side to side of the truth. Communal devotion, private property, self-sacrifice, selfishness, joy through and with others, joy in defiance of and in contrast to others !— Emotionally normal men desire all these things *to some degree*. It is the function of the law of a society to attempt to realize for its members the conditions under which they can live the best possible life. The best life may be defined as one in which *each of the natural instincts of man is allowed to make the contribution required of it for his life to be one of happy association with his fellows*. It is in pursuit of this ideal that the social instinct of normal man urges him to associate himself with others in attaining a permanent security against the disruptive tendencies of his own aggressive instinct and theirs. I hold it established that such security is the major instinctive aim and interest of normal man ; and I hope that to ground our law upon it will be found to meet the plea for a revived theory of ' natural law ' which is made by Laski.[1] ' Natural law ' thus derives from that instinct of social man which urges him to submit himself to the necessary rule of his fellows in extension of his own self-control.

[1] Laski, H. J., in *Modern Theories of Law*, p. 52 (Section on Duguit). (Oxford University Press. 1933.)

But if we claim as 'natural law', law arising out of the natural
dominance of the social instinct, we must remember that the
self-assertive instinct which it dominates is no less natural.
Perhaps that passage of man from a 'state of nature' to a state
of organized society and of law which has bulked so largely in
earlier social theory might be described to-day as his passage
from an *imagined* life of freedom to obey each of these natural
impulses as it attained temporary ascendency within his mind,
to a state of prevision of the need for external control of his
aggressive impulses in the major interests of his social life. That
is a state of realism which he has as yet barely achieved. For the
most part he has projected this need for re-enforcement of his
own self-control onto others, legislating to control them, and
rejoicing in the 'security' which he himself has thus attained.
What we may call the 'Rousseau Fantasy' was perhaps a necessary
stage in man's analysis of the need to bind himself to law. It
told him, correctly, that good would come from the binding.
Unfortunately it also told him that his group would necessarily
enshrine his own best self. It does nothing of the sort, as the
individualist has not ceased to protest to the 'Idealist' philosopher
ever since. Men are *always* fallible, whether single or in groups.
In attempting to judge their own cause, they are *always* misled
in their judgment. When they are in groups their misjudgment
is likely to be greater than when they are alone. A 'general will'
which represents a partisan judgment is a veritable snowball of
error.[1]

Let us then recognize our law of order as grounded upon the
fact that most men at most times desire it, even if—indeed
because—it frustrates their anti-social self-assertive impulses.
But we must also recognize that, though the joys of the social life
of any well-ordered community will secure for that life the
support of most men who have experienced them, the support
of many such men would never have been secured had the
initiation of the community rested with them. Most of us learn
the value of a law-bound community only by dwelling in it. Men
skilled and practised in an established community can view it as
did Locke, savour it under the tongue, analyse it as a free and
easy affair, and readily support a generous theory and an efficient
practice in its further prosecution. Far fewer men are capable of
taking the step of voluntary submission to others whom they
have no reasons to trust but those of theory or of faith. Hobbes'
counsels are stern and desperate ; for his mind saw the *creation*
of a community out of warring factions. Adults have to learn
by experience like the children which for the most part they still
are. And it may be that, as in the past so again in the future, the
balance between self and community will have to be fixed upon
men from without—at however great a risk of being fixed wrongly

[1] See Chapter VI, p. 207, on 'The validity of an analogy'.

—before they can understand what they really wish to do, and so take over for themselves the administration of that ' natural ' law which teaches each of us, not only his need of his fellows, but his constitutional inability to regulate his relationship with them unaided.

VI

THE STAGE OF SOCIAL ORGANIZATION REPRE-SENTED BY PRESENT ' INTERNATIONAL LAW '

INTRODUCTION—A FRUSTRATED COMMUNITY ?

IT is customary to think of our social life in terms of the existing organizations of our society—' domestic ', ' civic ' or ' municipal ', ' national ' and ' international '. These divisions are largely matters of convenience. Even administratively considered they overlap. The most important official in a matter of educational administration in Scotland may be found, according to the aspect of the question under consideration, in London, in Edinburgh, or in a remote Highland county. Psychologically, they overlap still more. A schoolmaster may be more of a ' father figure ' than a boy's actual father. Men's loyalties flit and hover between these various units, guided by their material interests and also by their emotional and fantasy life. So that one man's entire sense of community, whole object of ambition and total fantasies of greatness and of strife may appear to be bounded by his parish, while for another a passionate and exclusive interest in cricket may fix him eternally to a ' county ' loyalty. For one Kentish man Kent is larger than the British Empire ; for another the Empire is the sole symbol of significant loyalty in his life.

At the boundary of the Nation or the Empire the material for most men's loyalties stops. Only a very few cultured Englishmen declare themselves more European than British. After all his journeyings, physical and spiritual, André Maurois felt that when he landed in France he returned to reality. In the very heart of Europe, few Germans yet feel themselves Europeans. Where interests begin to reach beyond the boundary of the nation-state, the pro- and contra- which loyalty demands seek to set a limitation to allegiance. The ' English-speaking peoples ', ' Democracy,' the ' New Order ' arouse a fluctuant loyalty in the breasts of some of us. But that loyalty depends very largely upon their being set over against an external opposition— ' foreign-speaking ', ' anti-democratic ', ' pirates '. For the vast majority of men and women everywhere the multiplicity of cultural strands which weave a sense of community do not reach beyond

the nation. Ignorance and prejudice about the unknown and the
different prevent the cultures developing. Propaganda cuts the
strands which are there. And the absence of common law means
the absence of the sovereign corrective of our fancies, that cold
douche of fact-finding reality.

' I'm glad I'm *British* ', said a shop girl in Dumfries in the
middle of 1940. ' The Germans and French seem to be terrible.'
The lady named a unit for her loyalty which would have met
with the shocked repudiation of many an ancestor even since the
unions of the kingdoms and the parliaments of Scotland and
England. But she named the largest unit for her loyalty that she
knew of, the biggest power unit to which she could claim to belong
in a struggling world. After an altercation with an awkward
English customer, or on the occasion of the annual international
football match at Hampden Park, her loyalty might contract and
her ancient racial antagonism swell again. But although she said
her worst against the English, that worst would meet with only
such general sympathy as is born of general experience, plus the
evanescent sympathy of prejudices *most of which are open to
factual correction*. She might meet with as much if her indictment
were directed against mothers-in-law. If you live in common
law with people, you will not carry your neighbour far with you
when you unjustly suggest that those people have criminal
propensities. For the touchstone is there. How comes it that
they are still at large ? If I say that Manchester men steal, I can
expect only a limited assent from my London neighbours. But
if I say that you can't trust the French, or that Germans are brutes,
I awaken a mass of uncorrected prejudice and uncontrovertible
rumour, and a second-hand story which could be culled from the
criminal assize records of any city or the court-martial books of
any army in the world will meet with grave assent, and be added
to the collected ' evidence ' of my hearers upon the national
character in question. For there is no corrective, except perhaps
some distant memories of courtesy and kindness, integrity and
self-restraint, in a far-away student holiday. For most of us there
is not even that. Above all there is no fact-finding commission
to put right our accumulating prejudice. Few of us are in a
position to analyze the criminal court records of domestic or
social violence and misdemeanour, or the breach of contract
suits within another country. If we did so, we should find that
(with certain minor and particular differences here and there
which form interesting enough ground for the speculations of
sociologists) they were the same as in our own land. As it was,
the absence of facts and the collected prejudice of twenty years
of life in Dumfries had led the shop assistant to believe that,
while only the duller bits of the world's news and achievement
were now limited to Scotland as such, outside Britain and the
British character all was fraud and violence. In her judgment

the 150 million neighbours of her 45 million compatriots dwelt in
' chaos and old night '. They dwell it is true without a law in
common with ourselves. And in the absence of such law between
us and our foreign neighbours much significant ' information '
about their characters is likely to belong to a species of misinformation.

High among the causes of international misunderstanding it
is common and right to place ' propaganda '. But the significance
of political propaganda is itself a subject upon which our collective
judgments are often much in error. It is our opponents who set
off their ' propaganda ' against our ' information '. The Germans
use the former term without any implication of intention to
mislead, and so can indulge in a ministry with that title. But
that does not except them from falling into the same error as
ourselves about the intentions and the morals of contrary and
unfavourable propaganda in neighbouring countries. The object
of issuing information from any such ministry is of course the
same as the object of ' writing up ' a patent medicine. It is to
select favourable news and present it convincingly. No partisan
information bureau is ever there to evaluate and present the
whole truth. But on the other hand *all* information bureaux are
run according to some standard of morals. With the lowered
moral standard which Grotius observed as characteristic of warfare, the selection of information may of course amount to a
selection with intent to defraud. Doctrines which claim the end
as justifying the means add grievously to the evil ; but not more
perhaps than the prejudice which imagines the enemy to be
totally devoid of all scruple. In warfare a myriad lies are told,
explicitly or by implication by all agencies of national propaganda.
That fact soon comes to be generally understood by the peoples
who receive the information. What is not so generally realized
is that originally, and often persistently, most main currents of
propaganda are believed by their authors to be essentially and in
substance true.

In individuals, subnormal standards of veracity are often
accompanied by persuasive eloquence of tongue or pen. Men
with such equipment have early made the discovery that for them
truth-telling is not essential to happiness. And such men may
find themselves in exercise of their talents either upon the political
stage or in remunerative journalism. The machinery of political
propaganda may be influenced or even directed and fed by men
of such character. Probably it often is. But these men seldom
initiate policy. They are the possessors of arts which minister
to the convictions of others. The initiators of trends of political
propaganda are men honestly and profoundly convinced of the
need of their mission, however wrong-headed and fantastic that
mission may seem to others. If that fact were more often
appreciated other means might be employed in dealing with

defamatory propaganda and policies of persecution than to meet abuse with a counter-abuse which occasions cruelty and suffering on a far greater scale than that which we set out to correct. To characterize propaganda as the cause of national misunderstanding and quarrel is to mistake an agent for a cause. *The cause is misinformed prejudice.* Rage, folly, abuse, and ' information ' which poisons kindly feeling in the breasts of kindly folk are the results.

Prejudice, then, remains our quarry. But we may observe that simple people appear to be less easily provoked against masses of fellow men than are the educated, despite the greater corrective knowledge of the latter. A predominance of ' obsessional ' psychological mechanisms among the wise may be a reason why they more readily abandon their greater wisdom for distorting prejudice. Their sympathetic imagination, fed by the machinery of ' identifications ' and ' projections ', falls a ready victim to stories of tyranny or discrimination ; and the deeper humanity of kindly clever people is readily sapped by such convictions as that ' we enslave our children's children when we compromise with Sin '. Simpler folk will accept the identification of an established national enemy with ' Evil '. But even so that enemy remains the ' Evil One ', either an abstraction or an enemy leader, and is not readily confused by them with millions of people like themselves. Perhaps, too, such resistance to abusive national and racial propaganda as is shown both by city labourers and tillers of the soil, and which takes the form of expression : ' I don't believe they are like that really ', is fed by a conviction that, since folk in other countries are for the most part also labourers and tillers of the soil, they feel they know the basic nature of most folk.

Some people may question whether the growth of such feelings of community as might bridge the gulf between the nations and weaken prejudice, is materially retarded by the absence of a common law. We have answered that question in general in the essential function which we have allotted to law in regulating the social life of man. We must nevertheless consider the particular question of how much international community is possible in the present state of International Law. For no friendship, no ' community ' is secure against aggressive misunderstandings unless it is under the regulation of effective law. In the domestic sphere we know that even the constantly renewed emotional bonds which characterize the happy blindness of love are frequently found to lack adequate security in the absence of the stabilizing influence of law. All larger communities need fact-finding law to settle their inevitable disputes. And among the nations, history records few long-standing friendships between equals. In this present century alone, a quarrel between the British and American peoples was ' unthinkable ' in 1918, and fortunately equally so in 1938. But in 1928, when the United States was insisting for the first time in history on a naval equality which the British Admiralty felt to represent a virtual superiority, that exasperation between friends which easily foreshadows a quarrel sprang up as a mushroom growth on both sides of the Atlantic. Nor was this the only crop of the kind which grew between these next of kin within those twenty years. Again, the Scottish condemnation of the two great peoples of the European Continent which I quoted at the beginning of this introduction would probably have lost its sweep by one half if I had taken my opinion in May 1940 instead of in August of the same year. We shall see that the relationship between peoples who are not bound by common law is like that between individuals in the ' state of nature '. Their association depends upon feeling, the feeling of the moment, which is insecure, unpredictable a moment ahead, and certain in the long run to be swept by sufficient passion and prejudice to set at risk whatever of community has been established between them. Among the causes and occasions of man's prejudicial and aggressive passion we shall find no grounds for attributing less passion and more self-control to men in a group than to man as an individual. Rather is it the reverse.

I. A STATE OF ' NATURE ' AND OF ASPIRATIONS

In Chapter II (Section III) of this book we reached the conclusion that, because there are no means of their enforcement, the present rules for the guidance of the conduct of nations are correctly described by Smith as mere ' pious aspirations '.[1] How came it then that a body of rules which has taken the title of ' International Law ' was built up, and that not a little deference has been paid to the majesty of this great illusion ?

The answer appears to be that men desired two incompatible things—that their nations should be at once bound and free, the combination which Rousseau desired for himself as an individual. The untrammelled freedom of the ' sovereign state ' bulked large in theory from the time of Vattel onwards ; but at the same time both lawyers and statesmen desired an orderly and a peaceful relationship between states. Whether these two conditions were compatible with each other has been a matter of dispute from the time of Grotius to the present day. It is worth recalling certain points of Grotius' own analysis,[2] for it exposed the dilemma clearly.

Early in the seventeenth century Grotius had set out to discover laws for the suppression of international warfare, because of the destruction war caused and because, once a war had

[1] See Chapter II, p. 52.   [2] See Chapter II, p. 48.

actually commenced, it was ' as if an edict had released a madness driving men to all kinds of crime '. Just what alterations of behaviour do occur in individuals, leaders and led, when the general human law which forbids murder is withdrawn and replaced by the edict of war, psychologists will have to study more fully than heretofore. Grotius generalized his own observations by saying that, once arms are taken up, ' no reverence is left for divine or human laws '. There is a lowering of moral standards, as there must be if it becomes recognized as right to kill. But there is also a specific weakening of the moral imperative in ' human ' laws so that treaties and contracts are more readily broken, and deception and fraud tend to be practised wherever their practice is both profitable and possible.

Grotius' original search was for effective legal instruments : (1) to prevent; (2) to limit and control warfare. Any such effective legal instrument would require coercion. For, though ' love of justice is a part of the social nature of man ', ' counsels and instructions which enjoin what is honourable but do not impose an obligation do not come under the term statute or law '. In limitation of warfare, only ' just ' wars should be undertaken and only justice sought in their execution. ' Just wars ' could perhaps be defined : Grotius chose as definition the defence of person or property and the punishment of offenders. But how to judge the case ? And how to find the coercion ? The problem proved insoluble and Grotius had to be content to bequeath to posterity three things : (1) the faith that the social nature of man was striving to establish security and justice in the world ; (2) the intellectual conviction that man's natural sense of justice must somehow be implemented by law to prevent the injustices of war ; and (3) his melancholy observation that resort to war lowered just those moral and social qualities of man's nature, against the decline of which he as a lawyer had nothing but exhortation to offer. All that now remained in the attempt to control warfare between sovereign powers was to appeal to the *appetitus socialis* of the parties concerned before the demoralization of war actually commenced. As Brierly comments, Grotius did not thus supply new law, but rather a didactic philosophy opposed to that of Machiavelli. Many other writers have done that. But Grotius is worthy of especial note to-day because, as a lawyer who made a specific attempt to find a law controlling war and completely failed to do so, he indicated the nature of the difficulty. Effective law *is* external control. Words addressed to others, whether by precept, counsel, or the drafting of regulations, do not constitute regulative law, unless what they say can be enforced. Grotius rightly found that *as between ' sovereigns ' there can be no law*, because, whatever rules for their conduct are made, these cannot be enforced by means external to the parties concerned. If the alternatives of promise and contract were spontaneously effective, it would mean not only that men were always honest with each other—a state which exhortation might conceivably produce— but also that they were always consistent within themselves, which we know to-day they cannot be. Such may be the 'law' of man's ideal nature : it was Milton's Paradise ! It is not the man-made law by the aid of which society has freed itself thus far from the bondage of human passion.

(i) *The desire to be 'free'*.—It was in 1625 that Grotius failed to establish international law because he could not find any means of enforcing it. With no judge, no jury, no court, and no police force, why then did men go on writing down rules for the guidance of conduct between the national parties ? The reason was that men incline ever and again to hold that rules drawn up and supported by a purely moral appeal to the social instinct *ought* to be capable of guiding their societies in peacefulness. They do this because of their self-deception about their own aggressiveness ;[1] so that law is seen by men as being primarily for the control of others who are less moral than they. In a large community it is relatively easy for us to accept the hypothetical and apparently distant control which the law of order will exercise upon ourselves. But in such a small community as is constituted by the sovereign states of the world as such, we are forced to come nearer to perceiving the reality, that effective law, if it existed, would be there to limit ourselves. And national statesmen, as such, like it less for that reason, though they find this difficult to confess. ' Let us rather rely upon promise ' they say. ' And then let those of us who are honest men hold close together against the knaves.' By so substituting promise for compulsion we achieve at once three desirable feelings : (1) that law does in fact exist ; (2) that we ourselves are free (to exercise our virtue) ; (3) that others will either remain bound or will hardly find themselves upon the side of the angels. It was only to one who could either stand aside from current passion, or who examined events historically, that it appeared futile to say with Grotius that in behaving as they usually did behave men were ' doing violence to their own natures '. Breach of contract, by others, always tends to be regarded by us as such a violence. The moral doctrines of Grotius must have been preached by moralists in the caves of our ancestors. But with nothing but moral precept for our guide, should we ever have passed from cave to commonwealth ? The answer of moral philosophy and of psychology is ' No ' !

The idea that the individual should dissolve his personal freedom in the freedom of his state grew with the passing centuries. The political theory of mutual association common to Hobbes, Locke, and Rousseau gave rights and duties to individuals within the state, but no human right to a good life in the world at large.

[1] See Chapter V, passim.

In the earlier days of an imagined contract between a monarch and his subjects the king could do wrong. The Scots of the fourteenth century, for instance, declared to the Bruce that if he broke his contract they would depose him (Acton).[1] But the new Sovereign Peoples were impeccable ; and the new philosophies which sustained them led citizens to believe that, while they must expect limitations of their individual happiness and ' freedom ', any limitation of their corporate ' state ' represented an affront to them all. Man is brought up to individual frustration from infancy : a large slice of his practical education consists in finding out when and where he has to give way. But the ' Fantasy of Omnipotence ', as psychologists call it, is hidden in the breasts of most people—a survival apparently of early fancies of ' his majesty the baby '. Such ' sovereign ' powers, ' absolute, unlimited, indivisible, uncontrollable, inalienable,' we may perhaps experience in a fleeting period of our infant lives. But the idea is attractive and tenacious, and our minds remain ready to accept such sovereignty as our due, if ever it should come our way again. In adult life it never does—except in fantasy. Nevertheless, for all the supporters of a ' national sovereignty ' which has such fantastic epithets as these attached to it, there has been, as there was for Rousseau, an identification of the irresistible and righteous Self with the righteous power and wrath of others, in a fantasy of the greatness of the group equivalent to that of personal perfection and power which nourishes and sustains the fragile and dependent infant. And all the personal aggressiveness which has had such poor and diminishing outlet, between the stage of the kicking two-year-old and adult life in each one of us, is thus enabled to rise and unite in violent self-assertion against any insult, offence, or limitation of our *corporate* good, which can never be shown to us to be wrong—except historically.

The idealization of the Collective Self which emerged from Rousseau to turn the heads of the people-states of modern Europe is thus a doctrine which awakens an emotional echo in normal men and women. It forms a strong quality of group psychology, and offers an appeal which has withstood the checks of much opposing realism. Small states still cherish the illusion of ' sovereign independence ' in international affairs, though they are often demonstrably dominated by larger states in the world of reality. Large states cherish such ' sovereignty ' in their turn, though their power is always challenged by other states or groups of states. It is patent to all of us that no nations in the world have been able to give as good a life to their peoples during the past fifty years by remaining ' sovereign ' as they could have given them by being bound to regulative international law. Yet nearly all state governments and most state nationals still seem to

[1] Acton, *History of Freedom*, p. 36. (Macmillan. 1907.)

regard national sovereignty not only as a rallying point of honour, but also as a means of securing ' freedom ' and ' power '.   In addition, there has been a ready confusion of thought between the necessity (as it was felt) of basing law *within* the nation upon state supremacy and the entirely separate claim of the state to sovereign independence of judgment and action in external affairs.   Actually, of course, the success of the former was in itself a refutation of the claims of the latter.   Judgment adequate to maintain order must come to us in each case from outside ourselves.

Such considerations as I have enumerated placed behind the governments of the eighteenth and nineteenth century states enough of the will of their peoples to maintain the theory of sovereign independence intact, whilst ignoring the repeated practical demonstrations of national limitation.   And whenever wars broke out between the sovereign states of the world, the self-righteous corporate self of its citizens rose to express anger and resentment, under conditions which fulfilled for each citizen something near a psychological ideal for the discharge of rage. For that rage could be vented (1) in righteousness (which salves the conscience); (2) in strength (which satisfies the passion to destroy); and (3) in apparent safety (the safety of numbers).

That went on until 1918, when a world-wide public in revolt against the horrors of a Great War supported a demand for a legal machinery to abolish warfare.   Even then there were few to confess, like Smith[1] and Hall,[2] that the conditions for such a machinery did not exist, and that the search for them would have to be resumed where Grotius had left it three hundred years earlier, at the attempt to distinguish between the lawful and unlawful use of force, to define and adjudicate between just and unjust wars.

(ii) *The desire to be bound.*—We have said that somehow and sometimes politicians wish to feel that they are bound to rules in the conflicts of their national interests.   Brierly[3] thinks that it was ' unreasonable ' for writers and statesmen to have concentrated their attention upon the ' laws of war ', where no true law existed, rather than upon the improvement of the ' laws of peace '. The explanation may lie in that sense of responsibility, fluctuating yet real, which keeps this subject alive in the minds of practical statesmen.   Peoples, secure behind the ' representative ' govern-

---

[1] Smith, F. E., see Chapter II, p. 52.

[2] W. E. Hall, *International Law*, p. 82. (8th edition.   Oxford University Press.   1924.) ' International law has no alternative but to accept war, independently of the justice of its origins, as a relation which the parties to it may set up if they choose, and to busy itself only in regulating the effects of the relation.   Hence both parties to every war are regarded as being in an identical legal position, and consequently as being possessed of equal rights.'

[3] Brierly, *Law of Nations*, p. 27. (2nd edition.   Clarendon Press.   1936.)

ments of to-day, fear war, regard war as inevitable, are excited and enraged by the course of war, accept defeat or victory, and then hate and renounce war. That is the normal cycle for them. It does not seem so far to include a sense of responsibility for war. We have passed the detachment of mind with which men viewed a war to which they were called in the paid service of a master. But we have not yet reached a flexibility of democracy in which the people may be made to feel that they share moral responsibility for a war in which they are involved. In a modern ' democracy ' a statesman five years out of office can be blamed in full, though in historical retrospect, by us whose votes put him in power ten years ago ; and we feel able to accuse subsequently the policy against which we never raised a breath of criticism at the time. Education, improved representation, and a liberal use of a referendum may remedy this cardinal blot upon ' popular ' government, that it is irresponsible. The truth is that the ' liberal democracies ' of the world to-day appear to be at a stage when neither statesmen nor people take adequate responsibility for policy—a fantastic stage in which a Prime Minister, while enjoying the plenary power of a huge parliamentary majority, can insist that it is the business of the young men outside the elected government to reverse a fatal trend of his own foreign policy, while those same young men, when the light of understanding ultimately reaches them, can retaliate by cursing the inept policies of a retired and impotent ' leader '. During the eighteenth and nineteenth centuries political leaders could not transfer or evade responsibility in this way. A knowledge that, despite increasing ' democracy ', the franchise was farcically unrepresentative meant not only that an ear had to be kept close to the ground to detect the realities of popular sentiment, but also that real responsibility was felt, not a whit by peoples, but very definitely by their leaders. Pitt, Fox, Palmerston, Disraeli, Gladstone, Salisbury, and Grey never doubted that they led, and that as leaders they often stood alone with heavy responsibilities to God and man. Responsibility for the deaths of men weighs heavily upon a con-science—until that conscience can be cleared. A clear conscience is obtained by being on the ' right side ', and—such is the habit of man's thought—by ' obeying the law '. Whatever the rationale of the conviction of rectitude—and it is always there, on each side—with which statesmen approach an ' inevitable ' war, it will be found from a study of the documents that big, evenly-balanced, and consequently dangerous wars are preceded by a strong and convinced recitation of the moral case of each pro-tagonist by himself. The *intellectual weakness* of the enemy's position is seen, and appeals are made to his reason. The *moral strength* of our own position (which conceals its intellectual weak-ness) is felt and affirmed. Statesmen who are embarking upon a war need to convince themselves either that they have kept the law or else that, in the specific instance in question, the law is unjust and therefore no true law.[1]

When the issue of war is actually joined, conscience makes a wider demand upon all of us who voluntarily participate in it that we keep upon the ' right ' side. In the early stages of war there is great emphasis upon international ' law ', convention, and even courtesy. The play is begun as if under the eyes of a nurse. Attempts are made to secure symbolic victories and spare enemy life. Enemy crews are warned, rescued, and even landed as near home as possible, or at least given good position and compass bearings. Enemy airmen receive funerals with ' full military honours '. Assurances are asked for and accepted from enemy governments whose word no one would think of relying upon at later stages in the same war.[2] The ' rules ' of war are run over and reaffirmed, later to be broken with curt references to *clausula rebus sic stantibus* and amid fierce and exultant denunciations of the enemy for making such breaches necessary. The deteriorations are those commonplaces of war which disturbed Grótius and which also have reason to disturb us to-day. But the initial value set upon these ' rules of war ' must be attributed, in part to the conscientious desire of statesmen and peoples engaged in warfare to be keeping as close to the ' rules of the game ' as possible (and at least as close as their enemy keeps), and in part also to the unconscious need of war-making statesmen to feel that, in the field of dangerous passion into which they are venturing, there *are* rules, that there will be some limit set by some external means to the violence which they unleash. The child within them must be reassured that his passion will not wreck the universe.

The conception of an international law which left our own state sovereign and free in the pursuit of its good works, but which would bind others to virtue if they could only achieve a sufficient morality, survived and secured general approval until this present century. In times of peace governments both show

---

[1] It would be unwise to generalize too widely the attitudes to such matters as subtlety and the valuation of the justifiable in politics of men as divergent as, say, Bismarck, Campbell-Bannerman, and Balfour. On the political stage minds like those of Hooker or George Lansbury, in search for brotherly love as a solvent of man's aggressiveness and villainy, meet those who follow more closely the recipes of Machiavelli for playing upon those same qualities in a search for power. The political ' leader ' probably has on the whole a readier aggressive challenge than the average man, both in his personal and national dealings. At whatever point it operates, however, he never lacks his conscience ; and it may be presumed that, in general, his psychological type lies well within the two extremes named above. In this I am at variance with certain authors in their assumption of a mere ' lip-service to morality ' on the part of the statesmen of civilized governments. See e.g. Mowat, R. B., *Public and Private Morality*, p. 48. (1933.)—Modern psychology affirms at once the universality of Conscience, and its universal social inadequacy.

[2] See e.g. the exchange between the British and German Governments about the use of Gas, in September 1939. (White Paper Cmd. 6115, Germany. No. 1. p. 25.)

their goodwill and facilitate their interests by adhering to conventions and signing trade agreements and treaties of conciliation
and friendship. Non-aggression and war-renunciation pacts
follow, expressing in their turn the earnest desires of both
statesmen and peoples to feel that war between themselves and
X. is unlikely or ' impossible '. And lawyers draft ' Gentlemen's
Agreements ' between states and club-like regulations for members
of the world community. Each provides pledges for his own
patron as far as in cool blood and comparative innocence of mind
his patron wishes to go. That is not of course where in the
outcome of an unexpected development of self-interest, passionate
controversy, or actual warfare he will go—but where he intends—
subject always to the faithfulness of his potential antagonist—to
go. It is like business men drawing up rules of association and
of dealing in the absence of municipal law. It is true that these
rules are promises. They are also ' pious aspirations '.

Such pious aspirations, which are as certain of disappointment
as men are true to their real nature, are all we have of ' international
law ' to-day. ' Sovereign ' units, be they men or states, are units
which by definition cannot be controlled from outside ; they
can only behave according to their own nature. And their
nature, whether they be state or individual, is to emphasize their
own good social qualities, those of which their consciences
approve, and to disregard, disown, or underrate the manifestations
of their own faithless and aggressive qualities, of which their
consciences disapprove. The result is the varying misjudgment
of our relationship with others from which all human units suffer,
and which can only be corrected by external judgment backed
where need be by external force. I have suggested that it was
because of these psychological facts that man had to introduce
law into his social relationship. He did so pragmatically and
with many strange and interesting explanations of why he had
done it. Often he had not done it for himself at all, but had merely
carried on the wisdom taught him by a tyrant. He has not yet
begun to do anything of the sort for his world community. Until
the wars of this present century, with their consequent degradation and misery for nearly all mankind, the ordinary citizen
appears to have taken wars as they came. For the most part he
identified himself with his sovereign protagonist (wherever he
was) while the war lasted—or at least when it commenced—and
forgot it long before the historical documents of its rights and
wrongs appeared. ' We are right now, and the past is history ',
was felt to be a generally sufficient attitude to foreign affairs.
That was until 1914, when public approval of a war brought to
each person concerned a considerable chance of suffering death,
disability, personal loss or financial ruin in it. Men then began
to remember, to count the gains, and to try to offset them against
the losses. The process continues. Alongside all the emotional

factors we have catalogued and which still operate conclusively, there does at last appear to be a *homo sapientior* at work, watching himself and his social organizations, and wondering why it is all so difficult, and why things always turn out so differently from what he is led to expect. It is for all of us who think we can see reasons for this to try to help him to a solution. If we do not do that, someone with yet another unit, larger in reality or in idea than the national one which is falling into discredit to-day, will seize his loyalty yet once more, and direct his antagonism against some new object for him to hate, find ' unreasonable ', load with abuse, attack and graze his knuckles, bark his shins, and dent his skull upon, as always heretofore.

II. PROBLEMS OF THE ' INTERNATIONAL ' LAWYER

Grotius and Hobbes both found the nation-states of the world in a lawless ' state of nature '. But they offered very different remedies for that state. Grotius attempted to apply the only existing ' law ', the moral ' law of nature ', which was counsel as to how men ought to act to men who could not do so. Hobbes realized that the creation of new and binding law was essential to the formation of a peaceful community between princes as between men. Throughout the following two centuries the lawyers, anxious to buttress state ' sovereignty ', followed Grotius and ignored Hobbes. We might be tempted to call this the period of the sycophants. But the idolatry of these lawyers was for the most part quite genuine. Their consciences made them pretend there was a law : but their ideals held them loyal to the nation. There was nothing to make them loyal to civilization. Great poets like Goethe and *littérateurs* like Voltaire absorbed the culture of the civilized world, valued its variety and felt constricted by an exclusively national limitation of their loyalties. But the jurists of those days, however well informed they may have been of the thoughts of foreigners (expressed in Latin) in their own subject, had no legal system, no legal institutions, no machinery outside their states to which they could be loyal. They had not even a theory of supernational government to inspire their imaginations. When the evils of monarchic sovereignty gave way to that magic ' sovereignty of the people ', the lawyers stood inside, not outside, the loyalties the new states inspired. Vattel advised his state to substitute force for law in all its vital external dealings, and his language in doing so shows him as a patriot, but not as a jurist. Austin excluded the possibility of law emanating from a source higher than the state, which he well knew to mean that he excluded the state from the controlling process of law altogether.

We come at last to modern times. Since the institution of the League of Nations and the Permanent Court of International

Justice, matters have somewhat changed. We now have with us lawyers who have drawn up international laws for the submission of disputes ' liable to threaten the peace of the world ' to the League at Geneva, and judges who have sat at the Hague in a court empowered to settle disputes between nations. More important, we have lawyers who have observed the trend of events and who have begun to imbibe the spirit of a wider justice and a surer law for men than the small justice within a large disorder which is ours within our nation-states to-day.[1] During the past twenty-five years many of these lawyers have striven, according to their interpretation of the present relationship between national states, to ' strengthen ' or to ' set up ' international law. There are those who believe that an international system of law has already been created, and that it is merely weak with the weakness of infancy. For them it only requires tender handling, while it gradually assumes the power and majesty of a fiat which is operative, of law which is enforceable. These writers point to the mass of written legislation which exists, to the ' settlements ' which have been effected between states through the courts. A few years ago they could point also to a growing habit of submission of ' important ' matters to international jurisdiction. But these same lawyers knew that the League of Nations was so constituted that it was a matter of dispute how far it could legally proceed against one single isolated aggressor against its Covenant, let alone adjudicate between rival groups. They knew that the voting upon all disputes submitted to the League would be by men who represented the views and interests of the national governments of the ' Powers ' (and in particular of the ' Great Powers ') at the time of voting. They knew too that the machinery which provided for peaceful revision of unjust treaties—upon the assumed validity of which both League and Court would in the meantime have to base their ' justice '—was negligible to a degree which would always make that First Covenant of the League of Nations the enemy not of one hypothetical aggressor against a peaceful and contented world but of all the states which thought themselves unjustly treated in the world as it lay exhausted after its equal contest of 1914–1918.

The Permanent Court of International Justice was little better grounded than the League of Nations itself. It was formed to give justice with the assistance of the following guides : (1) international conventions (including treaties); (2) international custom, ' as evidence of a general practice accepted as law '; (3) the general principles of law recognized by civilized nations; (4) judicial decisions and the teachings of publicists, as subsidiary means for determining the law; and (5) if the parties agreed, decisions *ex aequo et bono*.[2] What is wrong here is the

---

[1] See, Lauterpacht, H., *Function of Law in the International Community* ; e.g. Keeton and Schwazenberger, *Making International Law Work* (Peace Book Co., 1939) and Schwazenberger, *Power Politics* (Cape, 1941).   [2] Brierly, loc. cit. p. 217.

order. Surely the last should be first ? What do in fact come
first are all those treaties which represent not present justice, but
the force of past conquest and the pressures of unequal national
power. One instance will suffice. The chief question before the
Court in the twenty years between the first and second Great
Wars was whether Austria should have an economic union with
the Germany of the Versailles Treaty. As is well known, both
governments then desired and requested that union, Austria
badly needed it, and there was not even a serious minority
opposition to it in either of the countries primarily concerned.
The Court decided, although by a majority of one vote out of
fifteen, against this ' Anschluss '. In so doing it acted by the
light of the first of its guiding principles, in this case the specific
prohibition of the Treaty of St. Germain imposed upon Austria
by force of arms a few years before. The case was flagrant, but
the decision well-nigh inevitable. That was the ' law '. Behind
it lay the force of the Allied Powers ! In the whole history of this
court there is not recorded a single decision which coerced a
government against its will in a matter in which it could have
resisted in the event of the non-existence of the Court.

But despite its inequitable law for weak states and its in-
effectual restraints for strong states the International Court found
that the governments of states brought up to believe in their
vital ' sovereignty ' still approached with great caution even the
remote and potential limitations of that sovereignty which the
Court appeared to threaten. This was well shown by the reluctance of governments to sign the ' Optional Clause ' which *morally*
committed them to accept the decision of the Court upon all
matters of obligation under existing ' International Law'. The
British Government withheld its signature from this clause until
1929. Then it made reservations which included a demand to
be allowed to suspend the proceedings in court for a year or more
in matters which could meanwhile be submitted to the Council
of the League at Geneva. Upon the latter body Great Britain
reckoned in those days to command the majority required for
votes of procedure, and could certainly prevent the unanimity
decision which would be required against her to put her in the
wrong. Binding a nation voluntarily is like binding a man. In
the end it will tend to shrink back unless you show it that in
reality it is not bound at all. It has been thus with all obligations
of importance in connexion with the so-called ' International
Legislation ' of which there has been such a spate in the last
quarter of a century. It has been thus *a fortiori* with this fundamental matter of the transfer of sovereignty which our three type
philosophers of Chapter I rightly agreed to be the starting point
of any new community.

This is the cause of the present dilemma of our International
Lawyers. They have had to choose whether they will talk as if

matters only needed ' strengthening '; whether they will go on making ' rules for the guidance of conduct ' in the hope that ultimately states will be beguiled into submitting themselves to law, by gradualness and through an increasing pressure of public opinion ; or whether it is not better frankly to admit that *the step which will create the first supernational law, namely the transfer from the disputants of the force to withstand a judgment, has never been taken.*

To admit frankly that ' International Law ' is not law at all becomes more difficult as time goes on. For with every year the imposture grows. It is already an iniquity far beyond any that came under the lash of Bentham. Mankind is struggling critically, and at times almost without hope, to seize order for his world out of the chaos of things as they are. We strive to straighten and are forced to break. And all that our clever people seem able to do is to egg us on, to find more and more ' reasons ' for more and more destruction, each of us attacking his opposite number across the frontier, like marked men at a football game. In the midst of our travail stands a court with bewigged judges sitting on a bench. And below them could sit juries of honest men ! Is there a law for them to interpret ? Can they arrest, stay execution, convict, arrange, smooth over, punish—first by the justice of a rule as simple as Bentham's ' greatest happiness of the greatest number ' and then by codes of lawful regulation between sixty states as between sixty individuals or sixty corporations ? If these judges and advocates and interpreters have no law which is honest and effective and can be enforced, what are they doing there ? It can only be to pretend ! And pretence is bad for the reputation of law ! To whom are they pretending ? Have we been deceived with mock courts, in response to our demand that peaceful settlement should replace war from 1919 onwards ? Was it the public of the world they were deluding through those long saddening 'twenties and through those 'thirties in which the sands ran out ? No, to a large extent it was themselves. In 1919 certain statesmen almost certainly said that care must be taken not to let the lawyers run away with national sovereignty. But these statesmen probably added, and believed, that ' public opinion ' would never stand such a thing, that this and that reaction would come from this and that Dominion, and that ' after all one could not trust the French '. These men felt themselves to have an unenlightened public behind them, awkward opposition at their side, and unscrupulous antagonists in front of them. The truth was that they were not *themselves* free enough of prejudice to rally the first, convince the second, and understand the third. Then came the lawyers themselves. There is one international lawyer of high repute whose name is connected with both the drafting and the interpretation of that ' international law ' which did nothing but confuse and betray

us between 1920 and 1940. His attitude has always suggested
that he could draft the requisites of a World Order to-morrow,
but that clear and forward thinkers like himself have always had
to restrain themselves and provide something less (much less)
because of the mass of men who are so far behind them in international sentiment. ' It would have been impossible ', thinks this
learned man to-day, ' in the conditions of 1919 to suggest the
merging of national sovereignty in a higher power '. My own
memory of middle- and lower-class England at that time is that
everybody understood President Wilson and the League of
Nations to imply just that and nothing else, though no leading
statesman in the event did venture to suggest it. This lawyer
had lived through a period of peace in which hundreds of under-
graduates at the Oxford Union pledged themselves never to fight
again in a national cause (1933), in which one French government
proposed a United States of Europe (Briand, 1930), and another
the substitution of an international police force for national
armies (Tardieu, 1932), in which a British movement to institute
both international force and a real tribunal of supernational
justice struggled from obscurity to the point of securing the
support of over a hundred members of Parliament.[1] But in
contact with all this, this lawyer's attitude was to emphasize all
the difficulties of such adventures, and on one occasion angrily
to charge us not to blame the lawyers because nothing had been
done. I believe that in 1939 this same authority favoured revision
of the present League Covenant, not by improving its power of
doing justice and placing force behind that power, but by deleting
' obligatory sanctions ' altogether, ' because experience has shown
that states will not fulfil an obligation to go to war for a cause in
which their own interests are not involved '. For him then, that
poor and limping League had gone too far ! Through it men
had certainly promised more than it was in their power to perform. And thereby they had created an illusion of security. The
question whether we are to draw back from promising more than
we can perform unaided, or go forward to seeing that our promises
are made effective, this lawyer answers by choosing the former.
If such a choice had been made consistently by his predecessors
we would have no contract law in the world to-day.

The simple truth is that this distinguished lawyer, whose
views I hope I have faithfully reproduced, does not really *want*
his own nation held to promises which may limit its sovereign
freedom. Though he probably does not realize it, it is not others
so much as he himself who is afraid of and opposed to the surrender of British sovereignty save under conditions which would
exclude a large part, perhaps the predominant part, of the power
of the world from joining with it in community and law. The

[1] The New Commonwealth Society, founded in 1932, with branches
abroad including one in Germany until just prior to the War of 1939.

world is full of such people, who speak and think of themselves as being in the forefront of a movement when emotionally they are skidding along at the back, holding on to its coat-tails. It is by virtue of such experiences as this that many causes—and not least the great one of World Order—must pray to be delivered from their friends.

Present ' International Law ' is illusory. Inspired by ' pious aspirations ', it consists of *promises which in the very nature of man cannot be kept.* Let us now examine the place of promise-making and promise-keeping in human relationships. Under what conditions are promises kept ? When can we rely upon them ?

III. THE VALUE OF PROMISE IN HUMAN RELATIONS

1. *The purpose of a promise.*—(1) ' Promises are made to be broken.' (2) ' What need we any spur but our own cause to prick us to redress ? '—The purpose of a promise is to perpetuate an emotion. ' I'll be there ! ' is either a forecast of fact, in which case it needs no emphasis, or it indicates resolution and implies : ' I wish *now* to be there *then.* I may not wish so enough when the time comes. I will therefore call in the aid of my self-respect and the respect others have for my constancy and reliability by so affirming my present intention that I shall find that intention implemented when the time for execution comes, with its other stimuli and its other feelings.' An alarm clock has much the same effect.

2. *The relationship of promise to law.*—Pound in his *Introduction to the philosophy of law* says that jurists have come to accept that ' the whole course of legal history has been one of wider recognition and more effective enforcement of promises '.[1] Maine also held that primitive communities showed less respect for their word than modern ones : ' No trustworthy primitive record can be read without perceiving that the habit of mind which induces us to make good a promise is as yet imperfectly developed and that acts of flagrant perfidy are often mentioned without blame and sometimes described with approbation '.[2] Let us then consider what makes us keep a promise that we do not wholeheartedly wish to keep at the time of keeping. We keep such promises because of a compulsion, or ' sanction ', either external or internal. When they are honoured without duress such promises are exhibitions of self-control at the time of keeping, reinforced by decisions taken beforehand in anticipation of contrary inclination. These ordinary promises, voluntarily kept against inclination, stand halfway between a spontaneous

[1] Pound, *An Introduction to the Philosophy of Law*, p. 266. (Yale University Press. 1921.)
[2] Maine, *Ancient Law*, p. 184. (Everyman, No. 734.)

exhibition of social (duty the result of a ruling impulse of social instinct) and the freely contracted but externally enforceable promises which I have described as ideal law. Both the promises which we keep and the promises which we are made to keep are manifestations of self-control. In both the rule of a contrary self-assertive impulse is anticipated and excluded. But the promise voluntarily made and voluntarily kept creates conditions which will *morally* oblige us to sacrifice our self-assertive instinct to our social instinct at a time when the remaining balance of our inclination is otherwise : while in the ideal rule of law our resolution has been *put into commission of execution by others*. Promises freely kept only differ from laws in that they are enforced morally rather than materially, from within rather than from without. All true laws are enforceable to the extent that they carry an effective punishment for their breach. A study of promise forces us to recognize that purely ' moral ' obligations where they are enforceable in this sense deserve the title of ' law ', although in their enforcement the social instinct defeats the self-assertive instinct without external aid. To adopt psychological terms, in effective promise-keeping the social instinct invokes the ' super-ego ' [1] to control the ' ego ' [2] directly, instead of invoking the aid of society for the execution of its will as is the case in ideal law.

Promises are inherently unstable things. For their honouring depends, first upon an unknown and conditional ascendency of super-ego over ego, and secondly upon the fidelity with which a joint commission of super-ego and ego can judge its own cause. They imply in their very making a recognition that, but for the oath, conduct would probably follow a different course from that vowed. Self-esteem must be invoked, lent as it were from a general store of reputability to reinforce an otherwise weak point of social conduct. We do not trust to the victory of our social instincts in the situations about which we find it necessary to promise ahead. It is true that we may have become so ' conditioned ' that the super-ego will always win ; so that for us, ' a promise is a promise '. More often, however, promise-keeping falls into that wide category of self-deception of which we have already spoken so much, that of selective judgment.[3] We hold that *we* do keep promises : a promise is a promise, for us. But for *others* it is all too frequently evident that promises are made to be broken.

3. *The psychology of promise.*—The execution of a promise thus links law as for all other purposes we understand the term, with that internal imperative of moral duty to which philosophers

---

[1] ' Super-ego '=' conscience '=the product of ' need of love ' plus ' dread of society ', and built into ourselves by precept and our early experience of what we *seem* to need for safety and security in social life. (See Chapter III.)

[2] ' Ego '=our immediately selfish self.

[3] See especially Chapter V, Section 1.

have so often appealed in past ages. *Promise-making* is really an *attempt* to extend the frontier of the social instinct into the territory normally occupied by the self-assertive, aggressive instinct, to ensure that self-satisfaction through others shall rule where otherwise self-satisfaction against others would be the operative emotion. *Promise-keeping* is an *actual extension* of self-control in the interest of social obligation. And if the combined observations of Maine and Pound are correct, human societies progress *from* the need of externally enforceable law, *through* an increasing efficacy of promise-keeping, *towards* a self-control which does not even need an oath for its enforcement. Psychological analysis supports this view. When restraining law is absent the moral ideal of the kept promise is repeatedly set up by wishful and hopeful men. But the effective development of promise-keeping within a community does not precede the external control exercised by law. It follows it.

The reason for this sequence is that the force of a promise depends upon the emotion that can be brought to bear at the time of testing ; which in turn depends upon the training and efficacy of the super-ego. A man keeps his word despite himself for one of the following reasons : (1) He thinks some punishment will accrue if he breaks it. It is then virtually an externally enforced law which he keeps. (2) He fears the loss of the regard of others which he will experience if he breaks it. The force of that emotion depends upon how closely he feels bound to those others in community. (3) He fears the loss of self-esteem he will suffer. That means that he has been educated to be a ' man of his word ', a state unlikely to be achieved unless he has been trained in a stable domestic household. Promise-keeping, like truth-telling, is learnt by precept and example, and most often the examples are drawn from the surrounding stability of a law-abiding society. All these internal ' sanctions ' are lessened where men (1) are not bound by authority ; or (2) are not knit together in community ; or (3) have not been educated in responsibility in a disciplined and stable setting. A society which lacks these requisites does not command the loyalty or arouse the self-respect of its members to attain the moral heights of the kept promise.

4. *The enforcement of promises.*—A promise is commonly judged by at least two parties ; and the natural discrepancies of their judgment has necessitated the entry of impartial law as a third party. The donor of the promise may utilize form and ceremony to implement his present intention to perform : the recipient is reassured by such evidence of intention, and also he desires to implement the actual promise-keeping.

Where primitive law did enforce promises, it looked (says Maine) to the correctitude of the ceremonial with which the promise was made as an indication for its enforcement. It is probable that in so doing the ancient law was in part at least

seeking evidence of serious intention which had been seriously
accepted and understood between the parties. Present-day
ceremonies such as oath-taking and the making of affidavits have
precisely the same object, namely to secure the good faith, calm
judgment and due sense of respect for the solemnity of the
occasion which are necessary to a man's making reliable state-
ments, or promises which he intends to keep. Such forms still
assist in fortifying the super-ego. It is only where evidence of
correctness of ceremony is allowed to outweigh evidence against
the freedom and spontaneity of a promise that law exhibits an
attachment to magic which is both primitive and dangerous.

Religion was early invoked to raise the influence of the super-
ego over the ego in promise-keeping. Pound [1] recounts that the
Romans recognized the danger to society of an ' impious oath-
breaker ' who could impose upon others because he lacked the
religious conscience of his fellows. On the whole, European
Continental Law continued to compel people to honour duly
made promises, following Grotius' doctrine of ' the inherent
moral force of a promise made as such '. But there have been
exceptions to this view. Fichte emphasized expectation of fulfilment by the recipient as evidence of the validity of the contract.
English law separated reasonable from unreasonable promises,
and looked for intention to perform : e.g. it was thought unreasonable to enforce obviously ' ostentatious ' and boastful
promises. Pound himself suggests that the law ought to enforce
' those promises which a reasonable man in the position of the
promisee would believe to have been made deliberately with
intent to assume a binding relation '.[2] Psychologically this last
view appears to indicate the proper relationship between promise
and law. When a man makes a promise, unless he does so
fraudulently, he indicates a present intention to the performance
of which he wishes to be held at some future time. If he invokes
the aid of legal forms in doing this, he may be said to have made
a law for himself and to have put the execution of that law into
the hands of the general machinery of law, with the acquiescence
of the receiver of the promise. Since ' talk is cheap ', it seems
reasonable that the deliberate nature of the action under the
social impulse should be required to be established. Here is the
place for those forms and ceremonies upon which Maine's primitive men set such store.[3] As for the promisee, if he has acted
on his expectation of fulfilment, that action should not entail a
liability upon the promisor unless it can be shown to be reasonable
in the light of the intention expressed or implied by the latter.
Promisor and promisee each has his own notion of the obligation

---

[1] Pound, loc. cit. pp. 242 et seq.
[2] Ibid. p. 282.
[3] Perhaps, too, we may offer this analysis as the psychological explanation
of legal hesitancy to enforce *nuda pacta* for which Roscoe Pound (loc. cit.
p. 279) asks ?

incurred, and where these diverge an external party should resolve the conflict. But the man who has bound himself would appear to have the right to the most liberal interpretation reasonable upon his self-imposed self-control. The first duty of the law, if by his formal promise he has commissioned it to act for him, is to interpret his honest intention at the time of promising. Only if this has been expressed in such a way as to deceive a reasonable promisee would a consideration of the latter's actual expectation seem to arise.

5. *The place of promise-keeping in social development.*—We have seen that a promise becomes effective as an unaided means of self-control only when two conditions are fulfilled : (1) the intention of service when the promise is made ; and (2) the successful reinstatement of that intention when the promise is required to be fulfilled. The former requires the existence of some degree of social community ; the latter demands a ' super-ego ' organized by training in loyalty and self-respect to overcome varying resistances in the self-assertive ego. It is probable that the higher demands upon this self-control can only be met by education within a stable and law-abiding society. Even then, a super-ego effective by training in one community will become ineffective in a different setting in which imperative ' sanctions ' internal and external are lacking. A man who is upright in Birmingham may steal (if he can) in Leeds.

The normal order of development in the control of man's aggressive and forswearing self would appear to be : (1) Control originating from *outside* himself combining with external cultivation of his social instincts—as in the education of infancy and ' tyrannous ' and autocratic forms of political control. This is the first phase of law. (2) Control originating from *within* (i.e. self-control), but operating through agreed laws executed by society from outside. This is the second phase of law—that of self-government by extended self-control. (3) The approach to man's ideal of direct self-control—the phase in which law may be reduced towards becoming a mere regulator of custom. *It is only in this last and ideal phase that men's promises begin to represent a state of objective reliability, in which law need not be invoked for their support.*

6. *The place of promise-making in social development.*— Though it is the last mechanism of contract upon which to rely in a community which is not knit together by common feeling, common loyalties and common laws, *promise-making is the readiest form of contract to be undertaken*! We have just found that, in general, for a promise to be reliable when its honouring is left to the maker, an ideal state of self-knowledge, social community, and mutual confidence between the parties is requisite. Such a state may emerge among relatives and between personal friends after long periods of trial and error. No larger community

appears ever to have achieved the government of itself exclusively by promise and direct self-control. Yet *each individual tends to believe his own word to be reliable.* As with aggressiveness, the fault appears to be only in others. Even the alarm clock is often purchased only as the fruit of repeated disillusionment ! *The enforcement of promise by legal means fills the whole wide gap in social development between the ready promise-maker and the reliable promise-keeper.*

Men are usually dimly aware that their promises may lead to awkward predicaments, without being aware that they will wish to break them. That is why we tend to give our word with instinctive caution over detail, but much more readily over general matters. For the most part, the more readily general promises are preferred to specific guarantees, the less of community really exists between the parties, and the less are those promises to be relied upon in an altered emotional setting. It is the same with the voluntary submission of promises to legal means of enforcement. Unless he be a rogue (which most men are not) a man gives his word because he believes he will keep it. But if promisor and promisee do not trust each other sufficiently to place the execution of their promise in the hands of a third party, they really do not trust *themselves* not to want to make use of a ' unilateral interpretation ' of their treaty. And this, when seen from outside, means to break it.

7. *Promise in the world community.*—Our international life of this century has shown pre-eminently the evidence of weakness of community set out above. It was possible to promise general disarmament where it was impossible to implement any one of many available plans for a reasonable reduction of war effectives. It was possible to renounce war as a means of national policy when it was impossible to make appropriate treaties with any of our likely enemies. And, with the exception of the disarmament proposal which came from France in 1932,[1] no European govern-

---

[1] The ' Tardieu Plan ' which proposed the replacement of present national armies and navies by small ' frontier ' forces and the creation of an international military, naval, and air force under the control of the League of Nations. The French Government pointed out that the Disarmament Conference offered ' the best opportunity that has ever occurred to make a definite choice between a League of Nations possessing executive authority and a League of Nations paralysed by the uncompromising attitude of national sovereignty ' (Disarmament Conference Document, No. 56). In deference to criticism the French later proposed to limit this plan to Europe, but to include in it a civil international Air-transport Union (so that no nation should be able to convert its civilian aeroplanes for military purposes), the abolition of all bombing, and an international air force of specialized and powerful units set up and maintained by the League of Nations (Disarmament Conference Document, No. 146). These proposals received scant consideration from the British Delegation under Sir J. Simon and were subsequently dropped. It should be noted by students of the subsequent history of France that this attempt to escape in 1932 from the limitations and the implications of national sovereignty was endorsed by the French Chamber of Deputies by 425 votes to 25. (Toynbee, *Survey of International Affairs*, 1932, p. 274, from which

ment has shown any readiness to leave the ultimate interpretation of its promises in the hands of a third party.

In spite of the fact that promise-making is facile and promise-keeping requires external enforcement unless the community be both a mature and an ideal one, we find that the ' International Law ' of our budding world-community employs promise without external enforcement as its first and only method of guaranteeing contract. An attempt has thus been made to found international law upon the shifting sands of self-honoured obligation upon which no law has ever stood in the history of man. We know from our present studies that no law could so stand, and any objective investigation of human conduct will confirm that, equally for individuals and for groups, *because of the altered view-point which comes with an altered emotion, the cry of ' circumstances alter cases ' would ultimately arise from one party to every con-tract, unless he were educated to place upon his ' super-ego ' that strain which, in the absence of a supporting loyalty to a close community, the ' super-ego ' is unable to sustain.* The alternative possibility, that the initial emotion will never change, postulates a community very much at variance with the present state of the world.

How came it then that national statesmen and international lawyers could not see that, unless you have built your community, established your loyalties and exhibited your strength through your law for long years, promises are indeed made to be broken ? Actually many statesmen were aware of this fact, as far as it concerned other people. They argued as we argue in private life : ' Promises are made to be broken—by others. A promise is a promise—for me '. The problem was then quite honestly seen as ' how to bind the other man, because it is he who needs binding '. It was put to me in these terms by a prominent British politician in about 1931, as evidence that the League of Nations and the Locarno Pact offered such an adequate inter-national guarantee of the frontiers of France that it was unreason-able for French statesmen to seek for further protection. That was the British view, because the guarantee depended upon a British promise. Throughout the world, for one Machiavelli there are a hundred statesmen who would honestly defend their own country's treaty history as impeccable, at least during their own period of office, though their detailed defence would often

the above references are taken.) But here it is appropriate to point out that though ready to forgo national sovereignty to attain a greater security, the French mind was not accessible to the interpretation of foreigners that the proposed international force would be liable to be used only to maintain the *status quo* in Europe. For the French trusted themselves to be just where the power lay with them, and thus required frequent reminders that, to Powers less favoured than they then were, an international force required a stronger guarantee of impartiality of administration than was offered in their proposals. The British Delegation to the same Conference was equally inaccessible to French dissatisfaction with a security that depended upon the word of Britain.

have to rely upon the spirit coming before the letter, and circumstances legitimately altering cases. I fancy such politicians to be far more numerous too than those whom Carr[1] has recently described as the ' utopians ' or the ' metaphysicians of Geneva ', whose wishful thinking made them mistake textual for actually enforceable prohibitions. Behind the honest conviction of Lord Cecil that the executive instrument of the League of Nations would be ' not force but public opinion ' were there not arrayed the multitude of politicians and officials of all nationalities who, fully aware that the Covenant was only morally binding, anticipated the ' just ' use of their own forces in its support, but more than doubted the reliability of their neighbours' promises ? It was by means of such thoughts that statesmen who tried to turn a unilateral victory into a world security system could honestly believe that, for real security, power should remain with themselves and their allies—a view which betokened a naïveté difficult for outsiders in their turn to accept as honest.

IV. ATTEMPTS TO RECONCILE ' SOVEREIGNTY ' WITH ' LAW '

1. ' Fundamental rights ' and (provisional) ' consent '.—Two English authorities on ' International Law ', Lauterpacht and Brierly, both deplore the claims to national sovereignty which led to the attempt to found a system of international relations upon contracts which are supported, not by the external sanction of law but by moral obligation alone.

Lauterpacht[2] attacks the designation of a category of ' non-justiciable disputes ' in international law. By this doctrine ' states claim to determine what shall be for the future the content of international law by which they are bound, and also to determine what is the content of existing international law in a given case.' He describes international law as ' lagging behind morals to an extent unknown to the law obtaining within the state ', and warns us of the need to revise the present list of guiding principles for international law (see p. 189) before we attempt to place force behind that law. ' The main source of conditions calling for change is the obsolete or unjust rights of individual states grounded in contractual agreements of indefinite duration based on force.' In holding such treaties legally valid do we not come very near to Maine's primitive man, for whom, once the forms had been complied with, signatures under duress or deception were held enforceable ?

Brierly[3] also holds that the theory of sovereignty should never have been applied to the relationship between state and state,

---

[1] E. H. Carr, The Twenty Years Crisis, 1919–1939, p. 41. (Macmillan. 1939.)
[2] H. Lauterpacht, The Function of Law in the International Community. (Clarendon Press. 1933.)   [3] J. L. Brierly, loc. cit. pp. 39 et seq.

because it is ' inconsistent with the subjection of states to any kind of law '. But he describes some of the efforts which have been made to combine in theory the sovereignty of states with their submission to law. There is, first, a doctrine of ' *fundamental rights of states* '. (to ' self-preservation ', ' independence ', ' equality ' etc.), which claims analogy with Locke's doctrine of the natural rights of man. This theory evidently forgets that, according to Locke, any right claimed for the state should be in the name and for the sake of its citizens, whose collected individual rights to a peaceful life must take precedence over any claims by which arbitrary and changing rulers demand freedom to tyrannize their subjects in the name of the state. There is also a ' positivist ' doctrine that international law is the sum of rules by which states have *consented to be bound*. Implied consent is included. There will be no great objection to a legal assumption that states have consented to be bound, when in fact they *have* been bound to international law. Such a doctrine might become a useful legal ' fiction '. More pertinent to our present reality is the other side of this doctrine, a modern German view deriving from the ' autolimitation of sovereignty ' of Hegel. This regards so-called ' international law ' as ' external public law ' (*ausseres Staatsrecht*).[1] It binds the state only *as long as* it consents to be bound. The obligation does not outlast the desire. If it were made to do so we should be able to derive from ' autolimitation ' the legally enforceable promise which we can regard as good law.[2] Such an autolimitation of state sovereignty which allows a nation to bind itself may yet be made the starting-point of a world system of law. Meanwhile, for all who regard a co-operative grounding of law as the only grounding that law can have which is compatible with the dignity and aspirations of adult man to-day, to absolve either man or state from the moral and legal obligation attached to effective promise-making and promise-keeping is to leave that man or state subject to no other law than that of mistrustful tyranny. For if a man claims to stand above the obligations attached to his contracts, he must either incur the resentful subservience or suffer the tyrannous discipline of his fellows. This is the law of the jungle. Law can indeed be given to others by a sovereign who stands himself—in name—above all restraint and obligation. But such an one can never participate in law : he must rule alone or be crushed. We must recognize and profit by the great law-giver when he arises and is able within a certain realm of power to dispense a sovereign law. But the experience of history suggests that, since normal men do co-operate, the lonely tyrant is more likely in the end to achieve the second of his alternative destinies. In either event, it is for a state as for a man. It cannot at one and the same time free itself of its obligations and be bound by law.

[1] Jellineh, Kaufmann.   [2] cf. Triepel, see Lauterpacht, loc. cit. pp. 409–415.

2. *The view of Brierly.*—Brierly's own view is that, though
it falls far short of present international requirements, ' International Law ' does not raise ' any peculiar problem ' i.e. as
distinct from law in other fields. He considers that the obligation to obey is the same as in municipal law, and further, that
the subjection of the states of the world to law, though imperfect,
is ' *real as far as it goes* '. The problem of extending it is ' *one of
great practical difficulty, but not one of intrinsic impossibility* '.[1] He
holds it ' confusing and pedantic ' to classify international law
as a branch of ethics rather than of law proper : for its difference
from national law is ' *one of the stage of development which has
been reached ; international law is law at an earlier stage than the
law of a well-ordered modern state* '.[2] He claims that violations
of international law are ' *extremely rare* '.[3] He describes the
' *defects* ' of international law—its small range, uncertainty of
rules and slow development—as ' *merely reflecting the weakness of
the international social consciousness* ' in weak institutions, and
cites as examples of these the absence of a legislature and the
absence of an executive power to enforce the law. On the other
hand ' *international society is not, except in the matter of its law . . .
at the primitive stage* '.[4]

The argument is that somehow or other international law and
international social consciousness are lagging behind the development of the international society. Earlier in his book *The Law
of Nations* Brierly has described the interdependence of law and
community as follows : ' *Law exists only in a society, and a society
cannot exist without a system of law* '.[5] That looks as if both law
and society develop together, as of course they do. But he also
speaks of the ' *common moral and cultural standards* ' and the
' *social consciousness* ' which ' *afford some basis for law* ', and ' *the
sentiments of international community upon which the strength of
international law depends* ',[6] which looks as if he puts the established community before the *stable* institution of law. I take
his whole implication to be that law grows up into a well-ordered
and well-enforced condition in the protective medium of a stable
community. From his survey of the international field one
gathers that his order of anticipated social development therein
is as follows : (1) international ' *society* ' (' not now at the primitive stage '); (2) *awareness of community* (' social consciousness ');
(3) *advance of law under the protective cover afforded by the society
and its social consciousness*. If I read Brierly aright, the present
defect is held by him to be that ' social consciousness ' lacks
realization of the actual state of development of ' international
society '. And because of this there are ' great practical difficulties ' in the extension of international law.

[1] J. L. Brierly, loc. cit. p. 45.   [2] Ibid. p. 59.   [3] Ibid. p. 60.
[4] Ibid. p. 61.   [5] Ibid. p. 34.   [6] Ibid. p. 35.

V. HOW FAR CAN A COMMUNITY PRECEDE ITS LAWS ?

1. *The law of order and the use of ' Equity.'*—We must take this question as far as we can.

I judge Professor Brierly to hold that a community, having become aware of itself as such, makes its law, which then becomes better and better enforced. But surely there is much evidence, historical as well as psychological, of a sequence quite other than this ! Men had to associate, and so needed law. But when those early laws came to men, were they not either given by a tyrant, or at best acquired in a Hobbesian determination to achieve elementary law and order at any cost ? Is it not the strongly enforced law of order which makes possible the development of all the subtleties of community ? It seems to me that what is slowly raising the ill-kept promise of primitive man to a self-controlled, law-making participation in his organized society is the training in orderly and responsible life which only a law-abiding community can provide. Men can come together in an association, or the beginnings of a community, to initiate (or to receive) that fundamental law which is the vital skeleton of law and order, namely *the abnegation (or the abrogation) of individual sovereignty among the participating members.* From that abrogation both community and further law can wax and flower. But if you wait for community to solidify and law to develop in the absence of a crucial sequestration of force beyond the reach of the subjects of the law themselves, then you wait in vain ! When Brierly regards the strength of a community as preceding the strength of its laws, he fails to discriminate between the development of elaborate law and the institution of effective law, between the complex and subtle law which can only be built up in a well-ordered community and the fundamental law of order—the control of aggressiveness—without which a community can have no established life, cannot come into being with a life which will endure the first gust of prejudice and passion. Brierly thinks of the new community growing into order, whereas it must be given an order in which to grow. That initial order the international community has not yet got. Brierly's ' great difficulty of extending international law ' is really one of establishing it ; and the ' stage ' at which it lags behind national law is that stage, hardly to be claimed by lawyers as advanced, where the litigants interpret the law in their own way, and successfully reserve the right to resort to fisticuffs whenever they judge it to be expedient to do so. Neither men nor nations can establish a political community whilst retaining the discipline of their own aggressiveness each in his own hands. Jellinek's ' autolimitation of sovereignty ', like Hobbes' ' state of nature ', must inevitably lapse into the state of war because of the disruptive partiality of human judgment under the unleashed influence and misapprehensions of the aggressive self. Under such influences men withdraw from or even attack the community which they had intended to establish. Only if its members have found, or are given, a law which will hold them *against themselves* can a political community, whether national or international, exist.

To hold that municipal law has ever grown from custom to binding rule within the shelter of established communities, unbound by an iron law of order, appears to me to be a fallacious reading of history. Any expectation that international law will develop thus from custom through community to binding rule certainly has the strongest psychological presumptions to rebut it. *It is law that selects and stabilizes the desirable custom ; not custom that makes the law.*

The error of confusing the elaborate regulative law which grows within an established community with the fundamental law which establishes a community has naturally led to grave misinterpretations of the initial legal requirements of the world community at its coming inception. ' Obligatory arbitration ', writes a Professor of International Relations, ' of claims not based on legal right (meaning on existing written law) is rarely enforced in civilized states, and *least of all in those which enjoy the longest record of domestic peace* '. To attempt such arbitration in the international sphere would be to ' dissolve politics into law . . . propounding a solution which nobody regards as either feasible or desirable *in our far more highly organized national communities* '.[1] My italics display the fallacy. Do we need and do we find the more determined, effective, and comprehensive enforcement of the law of order in stable communities enjoying the longest records of domestic peace, or in a newly welded community, ill to discipline, ready to resort to civil strife or to relapse into violent anarchy ? To Mr. Hoover's observation that Americans would not tolerate such suppression of liberty as he found in Germany, Herr Hitler is credited with the reply that Germany could not *yet* afford the luxury of such liberty as America enjoyed.

So much for order : its effective enforcement is an essential characteristic of the life of a community which is still seeking its initial stability. What of legal ' Equity ', of judgment apart from and overriding written codes ? Another Professor of International Relations writes of the proposal that the principle of ' Equity ' should take precedence over all other international law : ' Do we expect to achieve *what would amount to an improvement, theoretically, upon the sort of thing that happens in the domestic sphere* ? '[2] Professor Manning may hold, though he does not here assert, that true ' Equity ' has never yet been

[1] E. H. Carr, loc. cit. p. 260.
[2] C. A. W. Manning, in *Anarchy or World Order*, p. 171. (Allen & Unwin. 1936.)

enjoyed even by domestic law. But, however ineffective it may have been in practice, theoretically ' Equity '—in the shape of courts empowered to give binding decisions directed by principles of justice ' which all men can be expected to consider just '— has been a common and characteristic feature of the earlier phases of domestic law. There is now no technical appeal to ' Equity ' in English law. But the medieval Lord Chancellor of England was empowered to remedy injustice by giving such decisions in default of the adequacy of the code laws. Medieval England inherited the principle of ' Equity ' from the Romans, and Continental Europe still understands the principle in the Roman sense of *ex aequo et bono*. It is used in practice by the judicial administrators of the British Crown Colonies to-day. In short, the principle of Equity has been an important historical ingredient of laws for primitive and new communities, while an iron law of order has been a condition of their very creation. Both are relaxed, not strengthened, as community and complexity of life develop. And the fact that medieval Equity law was not in its time an all-providing source of justice is surely a reason, not for the abandonment of the cause of international Equity, but for making that legal instrument an improvement upon the sort of thing that *used* to happen in the domestic sphere.

As the international community solidifies, International Equity decisions will no doubt ultimately become codified or absorbed into a body of statutory law, just as English Equity law was absorbed into the general body of English law many years ago. But while it is eminently necessary that codes should be drawn upon and principles of international justice laid down with increasing confidence in the light of increasing experience, the first historic requirement of International Law is the universal use of law to preserve order and peace by standards of justice which are everywhere acceptable. That is what is meant by the ' enthronement of Equity '. Its essential purpose is to perform precisely the task which Professor Carr upbraids its supporters for attempting, namely to ' dissolve politics (i.e. political power) into law '. And when Professor Carr lists conscription, the ' Means Test ', the legal status of trade unions and the nationalization of mines as matters which are now settled within the nation not by Equity courts but by ' procedure which allows for the intrusion of power ' (by threats and bargaining) it should be noted that he is dealing with a community so well established that it can have large problems of difference of opinion which nevertheless do not threaten the internal peace. If civil war were threatened by any of these differences the neutral body of the community would be only too glad of a court to which they could be taken. For few people can consider the alternative method of settlement by ' power politics '—which was used, e.g. in the British General Strike of 1926—as being either very creditable to the state or a very safe experiment for repetition. The ' liberty ' which allows power politics within the community is indeed a luxury which only firmly established communities can permit themselves. Settlement by power politics which can lead to physical strife is a luxury which no community can afford.

To advocate the recognition that national power politics is the present regulator of international relationship is salutary. This Professor Carr does in his admirable and penetrating analysis of the international relations of the past twenty years. But when he concludes his exposure by advising us that the power of forcing favourable decisions must continue to rest with the individual members of the world community he is advising our acquiescence in a continuation of world anarchy. And when he attempts to sweeten his medicine by suggesting that the men who control nations are capable of avoiding war by recognizing and withdrawing before superior power in other nations, he has fallen a natural victim to the psychological error we are here most concerned to combat. Such a just appraisal of a situation of conflicting interest and passion *from within* is just the very thing that it is impossible for human nature to attain. In canvassing such a solution this author has exposed and rejected other people's ' idealisms ' of feeling and sentiment, but has then substituted his own intellectual ' utopianism '. We can see where the other man ought to retire, seldom or never where we ourselves should. Historically, we can be wise and just in our appraisals of forces and sometimes of merits. To ask us to do so contemporaneously, and with forces and claims, virtues and vices which we share as parties to the dispute is to ask the impossible of the human mind.[1]

We cannot let our world community proceed under the guidance of Professor Carr's supreme *laisser-faire*. Nor can we trust to Professor Brierly's future development of international law from custom. The customs of present ' International Law ' are only adhered to as part of the courtesies of those interludes of peace, when armies are retrained, weapons are resharpened— and men mean well. To expect those ' customs ' gradually to become binding law is to hope for the very self-control that we find so conspicuously absent in all immature communities. Such

[1] Nor indeed can any political negotiation safely be conducted by the light of Professor Carr's precept—which so many statesmen have hopefully followed, from the dawn of history to the Munich Agreement of 1938—of attempting to remedy dissatisfactions by ' peaceful negotiations preceded no doubt in the first instance by threats of force '. (Carr, loc. cit. p. 272.) Of threatened force we may list three alternative outcomes : (1) the threat of force is sufficient : then the opponent is extremely weak ; (2) the threatened force is bluff : then the bluff is called ; (3) the threatened force is serious : then the enemy's ' misjudgment ' (as it will be held) of his own power requires that force to be used, e.g. August 1939, Sir Neville Henderson *loquitur* : ' Herr Hitler said he realized that we were not bluffing and he assured me that neither was he bluffing '. Both were serious. Each party might have held himself to be engaged in peaceful negotiation (preceded by the threat of force).

errors of thought may well come from the ideals of modern
' Democracy '. The ideal assumption of Locke and Rousseau
that men started their communities with self-government we
know to have no historical justification : on the contrary, though
political institutions and social development may be slowly
tending in that direction, no large numbers of men living together
have ever yet achieved real collective self-government. We may
hope that this will come in the future. If it does so it will only
be by dint of long education and self-discipline, a mature product
of security, confidence, and devotion. Communities are *started*
by the *surrender* of self-government. We have been trying to
start our international society at the last stage in the ideal development of a community, that stage at which it has passed, by
education and the mutual confidence which is inculcated through
long periods of coercive law, to the point when each member
keeps his own promises and trusts the others to keep theirs.
That is a stage never yet reached by mankind in his smaller
communities. The world community can never be so founded.[1]

But while we must not expect international law to follow this
idealized and erroneous conception of early municipal law, need
it follow the development of that law at all ? May we not in fact
find ' peculiarities of obligation ' for this system of law, so that it
will not need to be developed by trial and error through varying
phases of community life which correspond to the growth of
municipal law from the dark forests of our primordial ancestors ?
Can we not start anew, with all the light at our command in this
twentieth Christian century ? Do we know nothing of man's
needs of law which will give us a short cut to general world-wide
law ?

2. *The validity of an analogy.*—Individual psychology has
taught us that if the community be one of individuals (such as
we find *within* the nation state) there normally exists in each one
of those individuals an effective preponderance of co-operative
social will to enable law to be grounded upon what I have called
extended self-control (Chapter V, p. 168). The co-operative social
instincts of the members of the community are given an executive
machinery against the instability of the social instinct of each
individual in the face of misjudgment and the crises of passionate
individualism. I have held that the accessibility of all normal
minds to this process of prejudicial judgment and self-righteous
rage will disrupt any society which is not ruled by law. *Do these
psychological principles and does this analysis of the function of law
in a co-operative society hold when the units of the community are
not men but nations ?*

---

[1] The imposition of self-sacrificing ' Sanctions ' in a cause not one's own
is an example of promise-keeping in its highest form. It attempts an extension of
the ' hue and cry ' which surely never worked successfully except in conditions
of the frankest and most pressing common danger.

It has been said that in as far as men personify foreign countries in their minds and in as far as states do act as individuals, there is a great difference between the attitude of an individual to his society of millions of unknown compatriots and that of a national state to its total community of sixty neighbours the past conducts of most of whom are very well known to it. Our knowledge of the mental processes involved enables us to dispose of this argument briefly, as follows. The attitude of most men to the *unknown* and *unfantasized* is one of benevolent but enquiring neutrality. Strangers about whom nothing evil is known or suspected generally excite a preponderance of social instinct in others. Every traveller in time of peace or in wild regions with inhabitants unprejudiced against him will confirm that fact, provided he does not bring with him provocative prejudices of his own and arrive, like some nineteenth-century Englishmen in Asia, armed to the teeth and truculent to boot.[1] Our emotional problems are with the *known*, and especially as we become more civilized, with the *imagined*.[2] The fewer and the nearer the units and the more our dealings with them the greater the knowledge and also the false knowledge—the prejudice —between us. A society of sixty with a committee of ten requires external control by the full and the identical process of law which we have analysed, whether each unit is an individual or a hundred million individuals, *provided the unit is seen as a unit*. The processes by which we misapprehend and quarrel with each other are then able to operate fully. They are those already familiar ones of psychological ' *identification* ' and ' *projection* '. Directly we come to regard a complex thing as an integer, be it a man's mind or a nation's ' persona ', our unconscious mind can begin to search the past for a suitable identification. Once that unit becomes endowed with a personality, the identification has become active and influential. The process of our distortion is then similar, whether we are contemplating an individual or a nation. ' That *bad man* A. on the committee ? ' What nonsense it is ! The true analysis is : ' Those seemingly bad responses which are exhibited by A. when we meet him on that committee ', or, better : ' That unfavourable exchange which occurs between A. and myself under those particular conditions.' For A. has *his* unconscious fantasy-identification of *you*, remember, as that repressive father, or that exasperatingly clever younger brother, a deadly rival whose thrust must always and instantly be parried, or a malignant Nemesis brooding over his inevitable undoing. Among the nations, there is little in our knowledge and imagined knowledge of France, Italy, Germany, America, Ireland, or India to prevent, and there is everything that uncertainty, strangeness of temperament, threat to life, confused hope of

[1] See e.g. Kinglake's *Eothen*. (Everyman, No. 337.)
[2] See Chapter V, pp. 155 to 165, on the formation of prejudice.

brotherhood, apparent black ingratitude and endless misunderstanding can give to aid our unconscious and primitive minds in making of those countries such identifications as prevent all community relationship based upon predominating co-operative impulses. In whichever sphere it be, once those unfavourable unconscious identifications have occurred, we falsify our intellectual judgments of each other so as to require the externally imposed law of a strong chairman, with behind him the force of further ' sanctions ' if our committee life becomes ' intolerable '. With loss of trust and rising suspicions come unconscious desires to triumph over our evil adversary. This aggressiveness is usually unwelcome to our conscious minds. Half to justify whatever steps against him we may take, half to blacken him further, we *project* our own aggressive impulses on to him. He does the same to us. And while we ' wilfully and gratuitously ' attack him, he ' coldly and malignantly ' encircles us. But it is only in fantasy, provided there be externally administered law between us. He may really be a worse man than we are, or he may be a better. We are not to judge that. The onlooker, strangely blind to merits, may say merely that ' those two are always scrapping with each other '. Let us hope the chairman will be just !

In the mental mechanisms which require externally enforced law the analogy between group and individual units appears to me to be completely valid. The requisites of (1) *personification* and distortion by *identification* of our opponents with infantile or primitive fantasy figures of our unconscious minds, combining with (2) (*unconscious*) *falsification of our own aggressiveness* and its *projection* upon our opponents, leads to a divergence of our judgment from his in precisely similar ways in each case. The more we are dealing with opponents whom we think we know, the more readily does fantasy-distortion build up prejudice. The less the complexes are considered as units and as known, the less will distorting identification operate. If ' 70 million Huns ' (equals x) opposing ' 200 million fighters in the cause of freedom ' (equals y) become reduced to 70 million persons whose relationship with 200 million other persons badly needs straightening out, the identifications of Good and Evil become lessened, prejudice is lessened, the need of regulative judgment and force external to x and y becomes less urgent and the conflict between units who ' know ' each other is diminished towards the more normal basic relationship of individuals in society, enquiring and benevolent. The self-interest of individuals will see that it never reaches the utopia of a law-free community however.

Where the world community of states does appear to offer a special problem is not in their limited number, their personifications or their ' knowledge ' of each other as entities, but in the sources of the collective force which must be placed behind the new Law of Nations. For here it may seem that the very ideal of co-operative law—that of mutual- or extended self-control— may be the only form of law which is available. For at least as long as the present nation state units survive, those sixty units must provide the total force which is to keep each and all of them in order. And, at the time of writing, half a dozen of them possess nine-tenths of that force. An adequate machinery of super-national law will have to draw directly upon the power provided by the co-operative social instincts of the millions of men with whose welfare and organization it is concerned. We shall see, however, that such a present distribution of force as exists among the *states* of the world does not preclude the *initial* submission of those states to supernational authority (Chapter VIII).

But another and important doubt has been thrown upon the psychological analogy between individuals and groups. It is a doubt whether *the effective general preponderance of the social instinct over the self-assertive instinct* which we believe we have established as a general axiom for the individual *is at all applicable to groups*. ' Associate one hundred often unselfish individuals in a trade union : will there result an often unselfish trade union ? . . . Likewise, who would look for altruism in a democracy ? '[1] Here we are dealing, not with fantasies which portray a group as a unit and so cause us to react to it as to an individual, but with the actions of an executive of a group in relation to the sentiments of its component members. The organization of the executive may of course be such that it is vested in the selfish elements of a community. But what of the sentiments of its component members ? If a given group never acts and never feels unselfishly *vis-à-vis* other groups, the reason is that the feeling-thought effective to such actions is never directed by the social co-operative instinct but always by the aggressive self-assertive instinct. Setting aside the question of an evil oligarchy in charge of the direction of the group, it is quite possible for this preponderance of aggressive assertion to apply universally throughout the membership. A society can exist for aggressive and competitive purposes only, and its members will then reserve their co-opera-tive impulses for service *to* their group (and elsewhere) and discharge nothing but aggressive assertiveness outwards upon their rivals.

The determining factor here is the loyalty of the individual, and to that subject we shall return in the next chapter. *A man shows his co-operative self to his own community, to which he is loyal, and his aggressive self to ' those not of it '.* When the units of a community are themselves groups, what matters is the loyalty of their directorates. (If their government be democratic that should reflect the preponderant attitude among the individual members of the group.) *Groups will never act unselfishly unless*

[1] C. A. W. Manning, loc. cit. p. 160.

their directorates are loyal to the larger community in which they are acting. The absence of such loyalties has been the curse of international relations. There is no reason why they should not be created. Once the directorates of our groups are loyal to an idea or an institution—*and while they are loyal to it*—they will exhibit the unselfishness necessary to enshrine that idea or to secure that institution. There is nothing false in our analogy. For we are still dealing with our original problem of utilizing the preponderant social instincts of man in his own interest. Arouse the devotion of the trade unionist and his leaders to ' International Labour ', or it may be to National Government, and your trade union will soon exhibit unselfishness in its conduct.

But the analogy with individual psychology holds for a further step. Because of the periodic ascendency of the self-assertive instinct which occurs in men and in groups alike, *their loyalty alone will not continue to secure the new community.*[1] To say, as its Under Secretary-General once said of the League of Nations, that ' the Covenant will prove a highly effective basis for International Public Order if only its provisions are loyally carried out '[2] is to ignore the inevitable result of this fluctuation of human passion, and beg the question the true answer to which escaped Lord Cecil when he built his hopes of the League on the maintained force of public opinion. For a new community whose members have old loyalties and interests which will occasion conflicting and mutually aggressive emotions among them, neither the new opinion nor the new loyalty will survive the distortions produced by prejudice and counter-loyalty, unless the necessary fact-finding and force-directing machinery is created out of that new loyalty and that new public opinion and is then protected against its subsequent destruction by its own parents. In all matters of promise and loyalty Philip sober has to forge the gyves for Philip drunk. *The League of Nations has so far failed because its First Covenant did not provide the requisite machinery for utilizing the loyalty of its members by taking the execution of their promises out of their own hands.*

The world may never become that ideal community which can replace law by promise in its self-regulation. At present the world community is still unborn. It can be born only by a transfer of loyalty and an exhibition of power. We shall find that for most men the loyalty waits upon the power. The Judges of a World Court which is given the responsibility, the honour, and the satisfaction of administering a law which is enforceable will soon be loyally attached to the *civitas maxima*, and thus able to fulfil

---

[1] The mechanisms of personification, identification, and fantasy-distortion dominate the minds of individuals as members of a group not *less* but—by the operation of the factors of repetition, identification, and mimicry which go to form a consensus of opinion or a group ' sentiment '—*more* than among individuals *vis-à-vis* each other.

[2] F. P. Walters in *Anarchy or World Order*, p. 4. (1936.)

their function of maintaining justice within it. The principle is of the widest application. *When we place world force behind justice we shall create the loyalty of a world community.*

4. *Order by abrogation, community by abnegation of sovereignty.*—In summary of the position reached in this chapter we may first recapitulate the expectable order of development of law in a social community. *First,* the institution of *fundamental law and order* by a compulsory renunciation of disintegrating individual aggressiveness, a renunciation imposed upon a society from without, or arising from within by such an act as that by which Hobbes imagined the first order to have been wrested from man's violent and unstable state of ' nature '. *Second,* an elaboration of community life and law within the shelter created by that initial renunciation of self-judgment and self-help. *Finally,* the relaxation of external legal sanctions and their replacement by the products of social education and the fuller flowering of the social instinct—a progress towards self-control and the moral heights of kept promises, justice to enemies, and all those virtues which partial man believes to be present from the very start—in himself.

International society is still in the chaotic ' state of nature ' prior to the institution of fundamental law. Here and there have appeared evidences of the beginnings of a sense of community, leanings towards association, and an awareness of the issues involved, which may mean that a nascent world community may soon choose either to set up or to accept those fundamentals of law and order in which a real and war-freed Greater Society may thrive. The world has a choice of starts : for it has not yet started. Abrogation of sovereignty lies at the root of social order and abrogation of national sovereignty there must be. That can come to the world community by either of the two ways in which it has come to our earlier communities—as abrogation from without, or as abnegation from within. And while *abrogation of sovereignty lies at the root of social organization, abnegation of sovereignty is the basis of an organized self-governing community.*

Finally, there exist in the world to-day factors which give us an opportunity for the institution and development of International Law which can render it unique and ready to our hands. It need not pass through the prolonged processes of forging and testing which their pragmatic development has made it necessary for our lesser laws to undergo before it.

PART III

VII

THE EMOTION OF LOYALTY

1. *Loyalty in its simplest form.*—Loyalty is an emotional expression of the social instinct. It is a fluctuating emotion ; for the social instinct of man, though usually in a state of ascendency over the self-assertive instinct, is in no man always so. But it is a very strong emotion, capable at times of excluding the operation of that love of self which supports the self-protective instinct. ' Greater love hath no man than this, that a man lay down his life for his friends.'

We know how the social instinct is strengthened by conscience, that combination of dread of society and fear of loss of love which operates against self-assertive and personal aggressive impulses when these are not approved by that society which the social instinct serves. Here we must not forget how early are the first concepts of what essential society is—those forgotten imaginings of infancy about what will please our parents and nurses, those notions of what we must do and what we need not do to win and retain their love and approval. These concepts have gone far to form the groundwork of our consciences and the conception of society, its whole and its parts, which we build up in after life. To-day, as then, we need others for our enjoyment, for their approval, for our external security, for security against our own passions, and in the words of a patient of mine who was much worried by his concomitant hatred of others ' so that we shall not be left to die alone '.—Let us now study the roots of the emotion of our loyalty to others. Let us find out as far as we can its essence. For its control is the beginning and the end of all society, great or small. We will first take loyalty as it seems to us, warm and strong as love itself. Next, we will consider whence that emotion springs, what its real meaning is, for us and for others like us. Finally, what changes in the manifestations of this passion are required for the good of mankind as a whole and of ourselves in particular ?

To us as we experience it loyalty is an emotion of the highest order—an awareness of a bond to others or to an idea, to something larger than ourselves, often to ' something afar ', a bond to be honoured, and which we delight to honour. At its strongest loyalty is more even than that : it is an obligation which we *must fulfil.* For all our joy depends upon being found worthy, upon

213

15

winning that ' Well done ! ' which comes to us from lips human
or it may be Divine, and upon escaping that alternative curse
which follows a great denial, to have been weighed in the balance
and found wanting.—I heard a distinguished general, speaking
professionally, say ' Man is a queer animal ! If you train him a
bit, and lead him well, he will nearly always fight, if necessary
until he is killed.' Of those adequately trained and well-led
platoons and batteries which were deploying before the mind's
eye of that experienced commander, each man was probably
feeling : ' With such a commander, and such comrades, it is
better to die than to turn back ! '

This is very near the simplest form of loyalty, the form that
seems to point to the biological significance of the emotion.
' This is my group ; this my allotted station. Here let us act
as one, and living or dying we shall be glorious. To break from
such a harmony spells failure and degradation.' A thought of
gregarious animals or insects whose strength is in their numbers,
and of the readiness for individual sacrifice which they always
show, gives biological justification for an emotion which, at its
simplest, inspires man (also a gregarious animal) to a very pure
instinctive expression of maximum feeling, accompanied by the
very minimum of intellectualization possible. Man has an ample
racial history to support him in such instinctive reactions. As
Freud put it, he has been ' forced into co-operation ' from the
start of his history. He had his own property to safeguard ; but
the household gods were shared with brothers, and the collection
of huts or farms crystallized into a village, with a pride that needs
must be communal to be effective. He had his own land to
cultivate perhaps ; but for tools, and harvest, and exchange he
needed his neighbours. Or he slaved with others for a master,
and built up his community-feeling thus. From the first, the
taming of nature—flood, storm, fire, and frost—required colla-
boration. He could not even fell a tree alone. Common acts
have always brought common sympathies to those who have
striven, won, or suffered together. Acts necessarily common
bring automatic co-operation, and often, as with the honey-bees,
a devotion in crisis which takes no thought of personal life or
security.

Materially speaking, men combined in communities for two
essential purposes, to defend, and to acquire—to protect themselves and each other against the less kindly aspects of nature,
and to win greater power and comfort and happiness from nature.
It was the second of these functions which early brought human
communities into conflict.—A tribe colonizes a valley. At first
the valley bed offers plenty of food and material for shelter.
Then, with growing numbers and expanding ambitions, the
sides and crests are settled, till, finally, in the high uplands beyond,
splendid new pastures are discovered. But in those pastures

are strange settlers, speaking a foreign tongue, worshipping strange gods ; men who have never helped to put out our fires or stem our floods. We owe so much to each other. What do we owe to them ?—The early loyalties of mankind soon bound him into little groups with common interests, common experiences, and, in consequence, common sentiments directed not only to the common defence from and war on nature, but developing similar motives in regard to other human units. Human loyalty and human strife came to this world together, when the first co-operations of necessity began. And no economic or political organizations of history have checked man's passionate devotion to his ' ain folk '—his little group.

2. *Accumulating loyalties.*—The primitive loyalties of groupings of men concerned with food and shelter, or with territory and pride, developed ; and to them were added others, particularly those concerned with behaviour and belief. Common needs of life ; common customs kept ; a common language spoken ; a common religion held ; these in their turn bound men together. And always potentially against other men. To-day we have loyalties of strength and tenacity built upon the various groups which excited the loyalties of the past. We have the sovereign state, a political and administrative unit, built up from smaller states or cities which have wholly or partly lost their identities in the building. We have racial, cultural, and language units, such as the English-speaking or Germanic, which do not necessarily coincide with sovereign states. We have religious units, such as that of the Roman Catholic Church, demanding and receiving loyalties which cut across those of nation, language, and race. Another unit of loyalty, that of economic or political ' class ', still cuts right across the strong unit of the national state, though hitherto it has almost invariably proved weaker in its appeal than have those geographical and cultural loyalties of men living together in a territory which on the whole serve or are made to serve the state. In addition there are loyalties technical, professional, artistic—a host of loyalties as manifold as are our diverse activities, calling us all this way and that.

3. *Loyalty and power.*—It is not of course surprising that a very strong loyalty is biologically attached to the unit of defence in danger. It is true that in the past countless lives have been sacrificed in defence of religion or religious ideals. And many will doubtless be so sacrificed in the future. But for some time now the military services of the nation-states and the nation-states themselves have represented the only focus of loyalty which frequently demands risk and loss of life from its members. These nation-states, these ' Powers ', represent the latest stage of enlargement of the units of power to which men have become attached. Also they are so organized as to command and control his service. We may imagine that many men have always been

greatly attracted by each new enlargement of these units of power and ' security '. On the whole each enlargement represented a greater ' freedom ', actual or imagined, and a (largely imagined) participation in a greater power. For the Swiss peasant in his hut high on an alpine slope it was a wonderful thing to know that a commune had been formed in the valley, to look down upon the cluster of roofs and upon his fine new church, and to feel that now there was all that behind him when the wolves came over the pass, or the snows engulfed his home. For a farmer to turn from his plough in the evening and look across at the great walls of his new-built fortified city, which would defend him and which he would defend to the death against the marauder from across the river ; for England to have one monarchy instead of·seven ; these were stupendous advances each in its time. Then came the great achievements of the new units. As the commune grew to a prosperous town, as the medieval city wall darkened with age, and heroic history was enacted within its gates, as the new state went forth and conquered and was honoured and brought pride and comfort to its people, so did the loyalties ripen and strengthen. Until the time came for the conversion of each—often with force and not seldom with a measure of humiliation for somebody—into something larger and more prosperous still. And the commune become lost in a canton, the city in a state, the state perhaps in a nation.

To-day for most of us the nation-state is still the largest, as it is the most recent, political unit. Two of the greatest nations of Europe have been formed since the middle of last century ; a number of nations were created less than twenty-five years ago. The older nations of the world look, or imagine they look, to brilliant records of one, two, or three centuries of ' almost unbroken progress ' in material welfare and in social enlightenment and freedom. The nations that have undergone reverses of fortune feel that they have suffered temporary rebuffs, as heroic units which have great futures of expansion and prosperity before them. On the whole the nations have felt proud of their achievements and have attributed much of their well-being to their nationhood.

4. *Intellectualized loyalties.*—At first sight the elaborated loyalties of the modern world show us little of the underlying instinct of gregarious primitive man, which argues simply : ' This is my group. I must fight for it.' Such underlying sentiments are present, but they are intellectualized or ' rationalized '. Much of the intellectualization bears a clear stigma of its emotional origin, in its fluctuations with the demands of the instinct from which it is derived, finding reasons for loyalty in times of danger and warfare of which it would and does deny the validity in times of peace. Intellectualized loyalties are very important matters. Although the simple peasant or uneducated artisan will fight

when led to the presence of his enemy, he will not develop great enthusiasm over abstract causes or derive great elation from intellectual concepts of absent foes. The plain man's strength is for *tactics*, for action in the presence of an enemy. Gather him up with others, train him, show him his ' enemy ' face to face, and he will fight him. *Strategy*, the manœuvrings of warfare in the absence of the enemy, and its predecessor, high politics, are not for him. It is to those who can intellectualize their partisan feelings, who can extract from a simple passion to suffer or to destroy an intoxicating essence, an ideal of sacrifice or victory and *an intellectual conception of what that ideal is*, that societies must ever look to maintain the element of crusade without which the clash of loyalties on a large scale would probably seldom occur and perhaps would never be maintained.[1] A loyalty which demands a supreme sacrifice demands at the same time a high intoxication. The simple man can reach the requisite elation of spirit in the physical presence of his enemy, i.e. when he is attacked by him, or is himself ' well led ' to the attack. But the ' intellectual ' man or woman is spurred to bring a war about or to continue a war to further battles by a partisan evaluation of a thousand doubtful and erroneous facts, by contemplation of all that is believed to be good in one nation or alliance or ideal or 'ology, and of all that is alleged against another ; until, with the aid of a consensus of written and spoken opinion, certain fixed and unshakable ideas are established in many minds, ideas which, if they can be implemented, are inimical to peace. How many thousands of upper and middle class housewives and mothers of any belligerent, as kindly at bottom as their unthinking and charitable charwomen, lose their peace of mind throughout the long lean years of our modern wars by contemplation of the horrible acts of their enemy, the nobleness of their friends, the necessity of sacrifice and the rightness of a cause which makes slaughter virtuous ? Beneath such thoughts lie certain elemental fantasies which are necessary in order to reconcile murder and starvation with blameless sacrifice. The justification for violence is achieved by the grim and continuous perpetuation in sensitive minds of a fantasy which the mind of the simple soldier reserves for the battlefield itself.

The emotion of loyalty is closely linked with the blinding prejudice towards partisan causes of which we have written earlier. The initial identifications with good and evil are the products of desires for union, security, and power. Once these are made, the mind unconsciously desires to be misinformed. For accurate information upon the distribution of virtue between

[1] William McDougall and influential social psychologists who follow him prefer the term ' sentiment ' whenever a conscious intellectual process, at work upon an emotion, elaborates an idea. For them loyalty has here become such a ' sentiment '. (See e.g. McDougall's *Social Psychology*, Chapters V to IX. (7th edition. Methuen. 1913.)

any two antagonistic groups, each millions strong, would obviously diminish the justification which the intellec* seeks for the instinctive leanings of the mind. In the modern world, as in earlier worlds, the requisite misinformation is easily come by. Compare, for instance, the catalogues of the facts causing the present state of affairs in Europe (whatever it be at the time of reading) which one would receive from an honest but ordinarily informed Italian, Frenchman, German, or Englishman.[1]

These are the manifestations of loyalty which we see operating around us. Deeply rooted biologically in the ' instinct of the herd ', as Trotter called it, we may find them (1) as simple unadorned urges to service and sacrifice; (2) intellectually synthesized into more elaborate ideas and ideals (the ' sentiments ' of ·McDougall); or (3) rationalized by perversities of reason as strong as any which can support the partisanship of an individual for his own cause. Let us now examine loyalty psychologically, and try to discover its function in the life of the individual, and also its significance for human society, where it aids and where it hinders the good life of mankind.

II. LOYALTY AND THE OBSESSIONAL CHARACTER

1. *An uncertain borderline.*—In Chapters III and IV we drew especial attention to a type of mind which psychologists class as the ' obsessional ' or ' aggressive-obsessional '. In such minds the general ascendency of the instincts of self-satisfaction through others over the contrary instinct of self against others may in practice be as complete as in normal men.[2] But in them that ascendency of social instinct is only attained by a restriction of the direct expression of aggressiveness so severe as to occasion mental stress, and in some of them to precipitate neurotic symptoms. In these people an abnormal challenge on the part of the aggressive instinct has led to its abnormal and painful repression. The obsessional character has built a formidable conscience out of his notion of what society requires of him;

---

[1] The effect of governmental censorship of news upon the misinformation of the public is difficult to estimate. Governmental censorship is a machinery which is much more effective in arousing hatred by the constant selection for emphasis of news unfavourable to the moral reputation of its enemies than in actually suppressing important factual information. For the most part the latter has soon to be admitted, directly or by inference, or else it leaks out. An early and constant result of censorship is a heightened criticism and scepticism about published news, and an increased sensitivity to any contrary rumour or intelligence. During the twenty-seven years between 1914 and 1941, the English and French peoples have had about six years of censorship, the Germans eleven, the Italians a much longer period. But Governmental censorship is not the only distorting partisanship that influences the press ; e.g. I obtained a clearer and more objective account of the British economic crisis of 1931 in a penny Italian evening newspaper than in the corresponding (uncensored) files of the British daily press.

[2] See Lessons of case material, Chapter IV, p. 150.

and with this he forcibly represses his conflicting assertions of self. That is agreed to by all psychoanalytical observers. About 'normal' characters no such agreement exists. The obsessional neurotic character shades off to merge with those of the rest of mankind in a manner suggesting difference of degree rather than of kind. On the other hand psychoanalysis has revealed a field of mental process which does differentiate the men and women of well-marked obsessional character from the normal, namely the peculiarities of their fantasy life. This qualitative separation, combined with the general shading of character from obsessive to normal to which I have just referred, suggests that it is to the nature and strength of their fantasies that we must look for the distinctive features of the 'obsessional' as opposed to other character types.

We may recall that Freud attempted to solve the baffling question of how far the underlying aggressiveness of the obsessional character is shared by normal people by foisting the discoverable mental mechanisms of the former in toto upon the latter.[1] That he did this through the introspective powers of the aggressive-obsessional character itself is inferentially established by the psychoanalytical notes of my patient Mr. C.[2] To this character-type Freud himself belonged ; and so he mistook it for the normal. In contrast with Freud, Ian Suttie, starting with a different set of fantasies about life, established his normal by inverting Freud's conclusions, to derive the obsesssional character from undue thwarting in early life, and to replace Freud's 'primary hate' by a 'primary love'.[3] The truth will probably be found to lie between the extremes of doctrine, and to this our present available evidence points. We have not all suffered such fantasy distortions as I have recorded of Cases A., B., and C. of my series. The aggressive-obsessional character is, however, widespread in modern civilized life. And we have all of us repressed some aggressive lust in fear of the 'loss of love' either of 'society' or of an ideal antitype of distant parents and guardians of our infancy.

There can be no doubt, however, that there is truth in Freud's description of the heightened rage which can occur in an individual when the restraining influence which society exercises over his aggressiveness through his conscience is replaced by the edict of war. In a striking passage which I have already quoted [4] Glover develops Freud's picture of the outward surge of sadism which comes from the individual when he thus not only becomes conscience-free to hate and destroy, but receives a benediction in destruction from the one authority which can normally restrain

[1] See Chapter III, pp. 78 et seq.
[2] See Chapter IV, pp. 135 et seq.
[3] Chapter III, p. 98.
[4] In a footnote to p. 97 of Chapter III.

him, his society—or rather the conception of it which his social conscience has formed. When Freud and Glover describe this as happening to ' an ordinary person not actively warlike but not actively peace-loving ', how far are they still confusing the behaviour of normal people with that of a particular character type ? In order to answer this question we must study the aggressive-obsessional character in somewhat greater detail.

2. *The ' obsessional' in everyday life.*—We will briefly describe the aggressive-obsessional individual as we find him living his social life in our midst. (1) Such men and women have *surface characteristics* which are frankly obsessional, but their undue aggressiveness may be well or thinly disguised. The obsessional is conscientious to a degree which puts his neighbours to shame. All that he undertakes for others is performed to the limit of his capacity. To those who know him well or observe him closely, it is apparent that, in addition to what is required of him by others, he gives himself numerous tasks, following a rigid personal routine or code, and he often seems to do this in penance for whatever pleasures he allows himself. These tasks also he performs with meticulous care and scrupulousness. Each act must be well done, not only or necessarily in the eyes of others, but to satisfy an inner standard which often surpasses anything others would ask or expect. Indeed, the obsessional amazes his associates by his tireless performance of unending duties, and often annoys them by his apparently unnecessary precautions, repetitions, safeguards, anticipations, and efforts, the disproportionate share of work which he demands in collaborative undertakings, frequently with a tacit implication that his standards are indeed higher than others can be expected to reach. Hidden behind this over-scrupulous and never satisfied conscientiousness is a readiness to suspect aggressiveness or blame—a trait which is often paradoxically exhibited in conjunction with a certain imperviousness to criticism. Such a man will pursue a course of action in defiance of strong criticism, yet touchily assume that he is suspected of selfishness or slackness or voluptuousness, where such a construction could hardly be put upon events by a reasonable mind. When the obsessional characteristics reach ' abnormal ' levels their possessor is found to be performing absurd rituals, of cleanliness and orderliness perhaps, or of precaution against imagined danger, or else, as a ' phobic ', he ' has to ' avoid this, that, or the other situation (of exposure, constraint, etc.). His attitude will then be considered superstitious or fantastic. He will try to find reasons for his fears, taboos, or obsessions. More often than not, he cannot do so, and is himself more aware than anyone else that he is hag-ridden by motives to which reason is a stranger. (2) *The undercurrent of aggressiveness* is seldom so far hidden as to make an obsessional personality ' easy to get on with '. Often they are dictatorial and overbearing. Not only

they themselves, but others—particularly those they may have
to control or educate—must be made either to keep or to respect
the standards which they have set for themselves. But often
again, and particularly if they are in subordinate positions, the
difficulty which others find in their company is a different one.
The obsessional may be kind and considerate, may become loaded
with unjustifiable duties through the laziness or acquiescence of
others, performing them all in exchange for scant recognition,
as long as his personal contacts are upon a very superficial plane
emotionally. But, while with colleagues they are the invaluable
servants, the painstaking and self-sacrificing collaborators, with
friends they exact a heavy emotional tribute of one kind or
another. It may be that they demand a constantly reaffirmed
recognition of their services, or else those services can only give
satisfaction to their performer if the recipient allows himself to
be 'put in the wrong by them'. 'See', they seem to insist,
'how I do all this for an ungrateful and unloving friend.' But
close the relationship further still, so that the object of attention
is a close relative or a loved one. Then usually there becomes
apparent another side to all the kind acts, the unremitting toil
and service and love. In between the performance of rituals of
self-abnegation or even in their very performance itself, appear
the wounding jibes, the desire to thwart, the symbolic degradation
of the 'loved' one which introduces the clue, so conclusively to
be followed out in psychoanalysis, that the kindnesses, the efforts,
and the sacrifice are complementary to unkind, neglectful or hurt-
ful impulses, forming a sort of concurrent penance for powerful
aggressive discharges which accompany love and lace it with
hatred. (3) *Aggressiveness*, ' *primary* ' *and* ' *reactionary* ', is inextricably interwoven in the obsessional character. The very
sensitivity to criticism and the sharp retort to imagined insult,
the imaginings of malice received which lead directly to malice
shown, the inexplicable quarrelsomeness and violent temper, are
reactions to ' the aggressiveness of others ' which appears so
striking a feature of life to the obsessional when his own aggressiveness is thus easily awakened. The aggressiveness which is
called ' primary ' is already in him, or unduly ready to be excited
in him, desiring and demanding its release whenever suitable
emotional objects offer themselves. (4) The *emotional tension* of
such characters is high. If they are never pressed by their
obsessions to seek medical relief, they inevitably find life strenuous
and difficult. For in all of them there exists a relationship between
hatred and love which is at once intimate, inescapable, and fatal
to their peace of mind. Where they love, where they seek approbation and response most, there there is tension. *The tension*
proves to be due to the closeness of the association (*unwelcome to the*
conscience and inimical to happiness) *between the desire for love and*
a desire to vent rage and to injure. The series of cases quoted in

Chapter IV, Section III, demonstrates the type of association which is formed. (5) *Infantile origins or occasions* of this conflict of desires are traceable in all cases of aggressive-obsessional character that have been investigated by psychoanalytical means, whoever performs the analysis. Whatever be due to a misreading of actual events (e.g. of the intimate relations between the parents of the observing child, or of the relation of either of them to himself) or whatever be due alternatively to fantasies wrought in the child's mind by his own inherent feelings and convictions, the fact remains that, from the days of the earliest coming together of physical desire and spiritual love in the child's world, in the obsessional character the desire to hurt has crept into and remained firmly associated with the desires to love, to possess, and to be cherished.

We need not here revert to the peculiar forms which are taken by the fantasies of infancy. They are important to the individual only when they retain a disturbing hold upon his adult life. They are of interest to social psychology only where they seem to account for general misinterpretations of adult relationships [1] or for these type distortions of adult feeling and thought with which we are now concerned. (6) *But men and women of obsessional character dare not indulge their hatreds because of the fears to which those hatreds linked to love gave rise in early life.* It is owing to the determination at all costs not to exhibit hatreds which it is felt would alienate vital happiness, that the developing child has striven so hard to suppress his sadism and embarked upon the chain of acts which are intended as earnests of penitence, reconciliation, and amends, and which become the obsessions of later life. Both in the obsessional 'neurotic' and the symptom-free obsessional character *sadism is repressed by conscience in fear of consequences, and replaced by these restitutionary and compulsive efforts and achievements of social merit.*

Now, it is because we do not know where to draw the line between individuals of obsessional character and normal men and women, and because we do not know to what extent the combinations of social effort, love, and repressed hate which characterize the former are at work in the latter, that we must be content to think of society as containing an unknown proportion of people who have varying degrees of aggressiveness which either cannot utilize or cannot be content with the occasional outlets sufficient for the aggressiveness of freer minds. Hatred and aggressiveness are present, often deeply repressed, sometimes very near their full consciousness, but constantly upsetting their equanimity and making them hurt their friends and particularly their loved ones. They have to repress these impulses as well as they can, because they are deeply felt to be dangerous. Also they have to work doubly hard in restitutionary service to

[1] See Chapter V, p. 156.

their loved ones. Yet (7) all the time these characters of uncertain numbers in our midst and with varying degrees of compulsion driving them forward, are *unconsciously seeking legitimate vents for their aggressiveness as close to the objects of their love as they dare go.* The social conscience of the obsessional is so strong and so necessary because it is based upon peculiar fantasies. His friends and acquaintances, society itself, or some more abstract conception of a judge of right and wrong—whatever in fact his loyalty is focused upon—come to represent the father or mother of earlier times, the object whose approval is cherished, whose wrath is feared, and yet upon whom there is a compulsive urge to wreak a vengeance of hate and violence. Substitutes and symbols for the ' sublimation ' of the aggressive passions are sought. The obsessional may become athletic, and beat the members of his loved family symbolically by superhuman achievements of competitive physical effort. He may conquer by scholarship and prize. He may passionately follow a cause and if it be a persecuted cause so much the better, for in it he can both be justifiably aggressive and suffer the retribution which is a further salve to conscience. The psychological ideal would be for the loved object to sanction and yet survive its own destruction !

Here we find a contrast between the obsessional and the un-obsessional, or as I have called him the ' simple ', man. The latter finds as his enemies objects physically near, but mentally alien to him ; for him an enemy who has to be imagined is a rather unreal enemy. But though to an utter stranger he is naturally friendly, an alien type which he recognizes as such (e.g. a Latin to a Saxon of our era) is a ready object for resort to hostile prejudice and arms.[1] The obsessional man on the other hand has been anxiously observing others all his life. To him the danger comes not from a new, strange, and relatively dispassionate thing, but from familiar likenesses to loved objects. Traits of character unconsciously recognized as being (e.g.) ' like Father ' will excite that early mixture of love and hate. If the adult objects of the love and the hate can be separated, it is a great relief to the conscience. If in addition to the love being gratified upon one father (or mother) substitute, and the hatred upon another, approval can be obtained from the first of these for the emotional discharge against the second, the conscience obtains a very great, though never a complete, relief. But to the obsessional neurotic and to any society whose sentiments he dominates, the chosen object of hatred tends to be something familiar, related, *one who could be loved.*

3. *The ' obsessional ' in war-time.*—What then are the characteristics of the loyalty of an obsessional character to his community ?

[1] We may recall how Mrs. Isaacs' young children showed immediate hostility to new clothes, and greeted a strange child with the question : ' Shall we hit him ? ' (Chapter IV, p. 118.)

It is a restless emotion ; for it is near hatred. It is devoted to 'isms and 'ologies ; for with a two-sided passion the label serves as an artificial separation and makes all the difference as to which passion is allowed to emerge. It is passionately strong ; for it canalizes the pent-up energies of a character which is full of internal strife, pressed on to endless and often heroic activity by the dual needs of combative achievement and restitutional endeavour. ' I must smash and overcome ' and ' I must serve and atone ' are powerful horses of achievement when harnessed together. In the obsessional nature, too, prejudice is peculiarly blind. A character similar to himself is attacked without a spark of comprehension or sympathy for motives very close to his own. A mind that feels a demand and seeks a justification by shibboleth and symbol for the artificial separation of its loving and its hating is not going to say, with a bombed working woman about the bombers—' They can't help it. They've got to do it—just like our people.' Rather does that mind seek every possible support for a division which will maintain their difficult separation between love and hate, a division, that is, into black and white, such as is epitomized by the exclamation ' *They* are beasts ! *Our* men are splendid ! '

For the obsessionals among us loyalty *to* a cause is passionate with the blind passion which says : ' Here I *can* love and *must* serve '. And loyalty *against* a common enemy of the group is equally passionate. For there the mind can say : ' Here I can *hate and serve* in one '. The obsessional hates his enemies. He hates them with the freed hatred to which he dared not expose his friends. He hates them with the condonance and encouragement, so he feels, of his conscience-keeper, Society. If those enemies are near him in temperament or ought to have been his friends, he hates them with the added fury of his compulsory links between love and hate.

With all this mental equipment it is easy to suggest the part that the obsessional character can play in warfare. Does he play it ? He tends to. But there is such an instability of motive, such an absence of logic in the unconscious minds of these people, that endless cross currents of loyalty and its counterpart of sabotage are possible, and occur. Many of them altogether refuse to take part in the patriotism of the masses around them. The keeper of their conscience is not the power unit of their society, but an ideal or fantasy which is independent of, and may run counter to the normal reactions of their power group. Among the obsessional neurotics who have attended for medical treatment there is a great diversity of reaction in warfare. Of my small series (Chapter IV, Section III), Mr. C. might have been very aggressive and bitter to his country's enemies had he not completed his analysis. As it was, he declared his hatred to be ' nil ', except against such as ' withheld softening influences from the young ' whilst ' fostering barbaric instincts '. He has already been mentioned for his emergency efficiency in civil defence. Mr. A. had joined the Naval Reserve prior to the war, and wrote cheerfully and contentedly from his battleship after its outbreak. He might, I think, be in danger of committing sadistic acts under provocation. The journalist (Case VIII) ' wanted and did not want ' to be killed, to be overcome, to fight for ' humanity ' and to be on the winning side. He was very incompletely analysed. The clerk (Case VI) was a straightforward patriot, anxious to serve his society, and, largely freed as he was from his earlier fears of cowardice, would very likely have done so with military distinction if the Church had not claimed him first. On the whole it is among the unanalysed obsessionals and those who do not produce symptoms sufficient to demand the doctor that we may expect to find the combination of passionate national loyalty and ferocious and convinced hatred of national enemies in war-time. For in them the ban which fear of consequences places upon aggressiveness is less general and less severe than in those who are made ill by their repressions.

We now reach again the point of our divergence from the doctrine of Freud. Freud *believed* in fundamental human aggressiveness. Consequently its ready discoverability in the obsessional neurotic signified for him, not an abnormal trait of aggressiveness in them, but merely a less adequate repression of aggressiveness than that of character types in which its manifestations were conditional or absent. The rich and strange fantasy life of the obsessional he accepted as typical for all men. To this subjective evaluation Freud conjoined another. He erected his Libido Theory of emotion collecting under tension and then awaiting opportunities of effective discharge, rather than subscribe to a theory grounded upon the physiological facts of conditioned reflexes responding to stimulation. The product of these feeling-thoughts demanded that, if the obsessional could be shown to repress much aggressiveness in order to attain an incomplete and unstable subservience of self to society, the more stable social conduct of normal men must involve a yet more severe repression of an aggressive emotion which was dangerous and accumulating and which positively demanded a channel for its periodic catharsis. This conception Freud applied *a fortiori* to the ' élite ' who formed and led new societies : but the mechanism was made to account in general for those ' vile propensities ' of group warfare which must ever and anon descend upon man, and increasingly so as he mysteriously approaches a social organization embracing humanity.[1]

Instead of this picture we may present our social norm, who does not usually exhibit aggressive problems because he is not usually hampered by them. It is the man with the heightened

[1] See Chapter III, pp. 92, 93, 96.

and abnormal infantile fantasies who is troubled in his intimate social life and who, armed with the weapons of identification and projection, sallies forth into his wider political society ' looking for trouble ' there. He finds it, alas, in whatever society he may live, in contemplation of the evils of others and the need for a heroic crusade against them. And he returns with his discovery to awaken his fellows. He is, in fact, very nearly one of Freud's ' élite ', who attempt to create an ideal society, to live together ' without domination ', but who suffer ' terrible burdens of repression ', have to ' fight Nature . . . forfeit happiness through their growing (unconscious) sense of guilt ' and who at last become aware with pain that ' men are not gentle friendly creatures '. *It is the obsessionals who lead us into aggressiveness, though they know not what they do.*

War, when it comes, may have a greater distorting effect upon a ' normal ' than upon an aggressive obsessional character. For, stimulated repeatedly by the causes of rage which have aroused his ancestors for thousands of years—attack, threat, account of cruelty, risk of life to himself or his loved ones—the balance of restraint of the normal man can be fatally upset. The rage that then surges out has not been pent up, was not there before, need never have come there. But goad him sufficiently and it will come, often, as we shall see, with manifestations closely resembling those of the obsessional character itself.

III. THE DISCIPLINE OF LOYALTY AND THE CONTROL OF AGGRESSIVENESS

When we come to the question of the control of loyalty, there are a number of properties of this emotion which derive from what we have said, but which need clarification and emphasis.

1. *The transferability of loyalty.*—I have described loyalty as a fluctuating emotion ; for it depends upon the ascendancy of the social instinct, which is a general but not a constant feature of man's social life. It also varies with demand and need, and, at least in obsessional characters, with the identification of its object with an ideal prototype conceived as worthy. But in addition to being naturally fluctuating, *loyalty is essentially questing and originally object-less.* Like love it has to seek and find its object. The emotion of loyalty is a servant of man's strongest instinct, that which binds him to his fellows ; but there is nothing predetermined as to who is to receive this bountiful allegiance. In the domestic sphere a man tends to be loyal to his wife and family, his relatives and friends, just as he tends to love them. But his loyalty can be alienated from any of these, and it all too frequently is, in part or whole, so alienated. In the wider circle of our social life there is no particular object which naturally awaits our loyalty to the group. A healthy

community is determined by common interest in devotion to a common purpose. Common purposes appear and disappear. A man may lose all interest in the affairs of his village when it becomes absorbed in the neighbouring township. Many Irishmen were fanatically devoted to the British Empire in 1914, yet could view its struggles with calm neutrality in 1940. In 1915 thousands of American citizens endorsed President Wilson's apparent view of that year that there was nothing to choose in merit between the ' Central Powers ' and the ' Allies ' in Europe, and yet by 1917 felt themselves to be the mainstay of the latter's cause. It is probable that loyalties, even the mental loyalties of clever people, are determined as much by their environment as by their temperament. A man who becomes an ardent communist in present-day England might well be a saboteur of communism if he lived in present-day Russia. Loyalties, simple or complex, profoundly moving and held to the death, may be determined by a straw, an accident, as the passionate devotion of a London schoolboy to ' Cambridge ' on Boat Race afternoon may have been determined by the colour of the Cambridge favour when he went shopping on that same morning. The ordinary man has a loyalty waiting, an instinct to give devotion and self-sacrifice, if need be to suffer death itself. For whom ?

2. *The sources of aggressiveness in the group.*—What of the aggressive side of loyalty, the hostility of man to the foes of his group ? Apart from aggressive leadership and the stirrings of obsessional hatred, the aggressiveness of one group which manifests itself against another group arises essentially from simple misunderstandings. (1) Misunderstanding its human frailties because of his idealization of it, man gives unquestioning assent to an assumption that his group is always in the right. (2) Misunderstanding its own selfish, acquisitive and aggressive qualities, because it does not wish to admit, or even on the whole to possess them, the group tends to invade the interests of other groups. (3) Misunderstanding the conscious motives of other groups through prejudice and suspicion, and an instinctive awareness of some of their unconscious motives, the group meets the clumsy self-righteous claims of others with a violent resistance which in its turn awakens a ' persecution mania ' and further counter aggressiveness. Upon these rising tides of misunderstanding, thwarting, and rage, play the influences of our minorities—the frankly aggressive to wrest power, the dishonest to betray, and the obsessional to stir early hatreds to fever point by virtue of their own peculiar and deeper misunderstandings of life itself.

Group loyalty then is transferable. And the group hostility which accompanies loyalty need never occur if there existed a machinery either to enlighten the misunderstandings of the ordinary man, or for the control and dissipation of his consequent aggressiveness and that of disturbing minority influences amongst us. Our experience of the need and the place of law in the life of man tells us that we shall never succeed fully in removing mis-understanding. But *the aggressive hostilities of men are naturally as evanescent as are their loyalties.* We must therefore try to attach sufficient of the loyalty of man to a unit which can control his group—as well as his individual—aggressiveness. By giving him real material security we shall remove all real cause for group hostilities. But that is not enough. Only by abolishing power units which can cross the paths of other power units shall we detach the loyalty of normal man from a point of danger where it can breed dangerous hostility.

For the present, dealings between groups there must be. And, aware of their place in society and of the nature of their minds, we must endeavour not to be led astray by the personal and private fantasies of the dishonest, aggressive, or obsessional characters in our midst.

3. *Leadership.*—Loyalty is an emotion peculiarly susceptible to discipline and leadership. As with love, here is a strong emotion awaiting a master. But with loyalty there is far less that is pre-determined, far more that is educable than with love. Love will follow the dictates of unconscious association and reasoning and be tenacious of its choice. Loyalty also is susceptible to unreason-ing instinctive judgments of suitable objects for its allegiance : but it is more ready to adapt, it is freer because its aims and associations are vaguer. Loyal to what, indeed ? In primitive life it might have been a marauding band to support, or a village to defend. To-day there are loyalties to church, and state, and friends, and profession, to sport and art, to nature and to science. At various times in the life of a modern man a number of these loyalties will be held before him as vital ; and he will yield them affectionate allegiance. One or two, religion and sport, or pro-fession perhaps, may make demands upon health or risk of life. The sovereign state, because it is the power group of to-day, will certainly make these demands, and so call upon the peculiarly primitive biological loyalties of group defence against physical danger. But even to these units man's allegiance is variable and educable. For *his biological urge is to stand by whatever will give him security.* And upon that matter he can be variously persuaded in a remarkably short space of time. From the ' Little Father ' to Lenin did not take long in 1917. An immigrant to the Americas will become a loyal and devoted citizen of a new, complicated and confusing democracy, almost before he has learnt the language, and long before he has abandoned the customs of a far distant European home.

Groups may be created by a leader. Freud would not con-sider any group otherwise created ; and Susan Isaacs speaks of this as the common way in which a group is created among young children. The twentieth century has notable examples of the largest of existing power groups being created or recreated around the personality and in response to the call of a leader. It is the simplest way. Instead of the shared responsibility which characterizes a co-operative power group, there is a surrendered responsibility on the part of the subject. The difference may be of little moment to a simple man, in that he does not really acknowledge responsibility for state affairs in any event : nor is he acutely aware of self-surrender in a well-run tyranny. But the difference is of considerable significance to many obsessional characters, who can give themselves over to the direction and will of another in a manner of high implication to certain of their own unconscious associations. Obsessional characters provide the heralds and pursuivants of the heaven-sent leader. The simple man also looks for leadership and direction. He does so from long racial habit; and where, during the last century or so, he has become used to demanding votes and political powers, it has been largely because he has been led to do so. For though the ordinary man may be a shrewd critic of public policy as it effects him directly, and again (which is a different matter) where it errs through prejudices which he does not share, he seldom originates policy, or has matured views upon policy, or indeed cares very much about state affairs (except perhaps as sporting events) unless he sees them as touching his pocket or his life.

A leader may make and keep the loyalty of a group. In fact he seldom remains for long the leader pure and simple, though symbolically the process may seem absolute.[1] Political loyalty can however be very powerfully excited to an individual for a time. And while it lasts that loyalty can be very blind to realities and to faults. Lord Acton,[2] describing the charm that monarchy used to exert over the imagination, records that on learning of the deaths of Charles I and of Louis XVI men are reported to have died of shock. He also cites Louis XIV, who with his standing army of 450,000 and six million of his subjects dying of starvation, yet inspired the unstinted loyalty of his people and the admiration of the most illustrious men of his time.

When a leader thus awakens a personal loyalty there is probably always a large element of unconscious fantasy in the devotion shown to him. He represents infinite power, omniscience, and if necessary overwhelming aggressiveness, in the cause with which the group has identified itself. When new units for loyalty are formed, whether by leadership or by co-operation, there is also a union of prejudices, an overlapping and sharing of fantasy in the members, such as Mrs. Isaacs records when children pass from shy individualism to co-operative play.

[1] ' Few children accept a passive rôle all the time,' writes Susan Isaacs ; and ' even the oldest will occasionally agree to change rôles and become subordinate for a time '. Each man, even a ' leader ', needs both rôles, among adults as with children.

[2] Acton, *History of Freedom*, p. 48.

Obsessional characters may share their fetish symbols ; they often form a strong bond between them.

4. *Discipline.*—But whether group loyalty starts spontaneously by men coming together for mutual support in a common purpose, or is awakened at the call of a leader, loyalty will not hold a community together without discipline. It is worth recalling here how Mrs. Isaacs found discipline essential in the establishment of a stable group of young children. Without it the group broke up through individualism, distrust, and bullying, and became victimized by the ' periods of acquisitiveness and defiance, anxiety, and brooding ' which occur in individual members. We note how ' nobody gets the tricycle because nobody can give up the tricycle '. The children tend to break their agreements, partly from acquisitiveness and partly in fear that the others will do so before them. When children learn discipline, selfishness and distrust have to be overcome by external means. ' Neither child would willingly accept arbitration of a dispute until she had proved to herself that she could not gain her point by her own efforts.' Next, each fought distrustfully for equality in the sharing. For the untrained participant in a new community, justice is ' *the next best bargain after a sense of reality has removed the hope of complete possession* '. But fear of the violence of others, or of self, leads to a welcoming or at least an acquiescence in external control once it is established. As the children began to reap the advantages of an external discipline of their individualist tendencies, their enmity rapidly diminished to vanishing point, though every one of the children in the school had been hostile to the others in some degree and some form at one time or another. Here Isaacs makes a contribution in differentiating normal from abnormal characters. For she separates ' a simple aggressiveness for possession, power, and rivalry,' from ' aggressiveness with moodiness and superior and inferior feelings '. The latter may reasonably be held the forerunner of many of the obsessional reactions of adult life.

5. *The pro- and the contra- in loyalty.*—When we consider the tendency towards exclusiveness of groups and their loyalties, we find that Isaacs' children help us again. They confirm the variable but real and constant tendency to consider others as rivals. She notes that when groups are formed there tend always to be at least two such groups, whatever the number in the classroom. Hostility tends to develop between the groups in the absence of a mediatory authority, an important matter as borne out in the effective loyalties of later life, and of larger groups. Slight and unconscious as may be the normal tendency of normal man to combine hostility *against* others with his loyalty *towards* his group, yet in fact the misunderstandings of natural partisanship, combined with the pathological trends of obsessionalism at work in a community, cause its members to look as a whole

outside themselves and their group for the ' evil ' which may
threaten the ' good ' which is theirs. Among adults as with
children, there tend always to be at least two groups. The
children must play together : but they will naturally become
aggressive at times, naturally show suspicion and dislike of newcomers, pass severe and cruel strictures upon weaker brethren.
To weld their community, so that distrust within it is diminished
and aggressiveness against others is controlled, external authority
is at all times necessary. Like son, like father.

IV. AGGRESSIVENESS IN WAR-TIME

We have seen aggressiveness (1) pathologically developed and
linked with loyalty in an unstable way in the obsessional minds
among us, and (2) manifested as the inevitable reaction of normal
man to his failure to judge his own cause equitably when he is
allowed to try to do so. We have hitherto left open the question
of how far the obsessional psychological mechanisms invade the
character and determine the social reactions of the ' normal '
member of society, where in fact and whether the line between
obsessional character and normal character can be drawn. We
have adhered however to a description of the normal man, as if
he were free of that obsessional aggressiveness which is derived
from imagined threats and persecutions of infancy, with answering
rage repressed because of fear. But now let us finally face this
question : *What is a psychologically ' normal ' individual in a large
and complicated society ?*

I have described a simple man, who is loyal to his own group
almost automatically, as being free of actual or threatened aggressiveness and hostility to any other group, unless that group
threatens or appears to threaten his individual or collective
interests as he sees them. Neither the character of the people
of the Argentine nor the high policy of the Republic of Argentina
is felt to be even potentially stimulating of aggressiveness by a
Briton of this generation. But I have also said that loyalty pro
implies a readiness to loyalty contra. And if you could demonstrate a discrimination against Great Britain by the Argentine
Government, and claim it as unfair, there would spring to life in
the minds of ordinary Englishmen that wary distrust of something strange, unknown, foreign. It is something like a reasonably trusting and self-confident child who suddenly sees a strange
face, and finds it ugly.

But if you institute a five-year-long campaign of unfavourable
reference to a strange country, with a character and a regime
about which the simple man's mind starts as a blank ; if, ever
and anon, as he turns in normal healthfulness to the sporting page
of his newspaper, his eye is arrested on its way by references to
' What will Buenos Aires do next ? ' coupled with urgent and

highly authoritative references to his own country's relative peril, then, without knowing any more of the merits of the case than he did initially, he will come to 'know' very much more to the prejudice of the state selected by his leaders for him to hate. And he will gradually come to hate it.

The natural hatred of a healthy man may outlast the duration of Mr. Pickwick's annoyance with Mr. Tupman for wanting to go to the fancy-dress breakfast as a bandit in a green velvet jacket with a two-inch tail. But it is a very unstable affair, depending as it does upon the citizen being able to picture a malicious attack being made upon himself, or his family, or his country by the enemy in question. And the simpler the man, the less easy is it to inflame his imagination, in default of material for his eyes actually to witness. Nevertheless with sufficient apparently incontestable evidence, the plainest man can be convinced that his enemy is behaving brutally. He will not then consider why that is so, or whether such behaviour could be stopped. For now he does not see his enemy as being subject to the same passions as himself, but rather as something quite different from himself and all his own community. Our enemy elect becomes an incarnation of evil, as our own side emerges in guise worthy at last to demand our personal sacrifice, i.e. as the personification of good. What has now happened is not that repressed aggressiveness of an infantile obsessional origin has been 'freed', so much as that *a new and acute neurosis has been suddenly precipitated*. A neurotic is one who has stopped judging men and women as they are, and is fitting them, as 'identifications', into moulds which are the products of fancy—the 'ideal', the 'evil one', etc.—or, if it must be like a blood relation, the lovely mother and the aggressive father of Freud's own infantile fancy. Just before, and during, a war, a large number of the citizens of the participating countries become acute neurotics in this limited but definite sense. The process goes further. An hysterical woman oppressed with fantasies of attack and seduction, screams. A man who has lost his temper shouts. An obsessional neurotic plays out his perilous ritual. All act foolishly and futilely, *because they cannot act appropriately to their real desires*. And all are afraid. I know a man of forty-seven, who was an artilleryman, an 'Old Contemptible' in 1914, who fought his gun through four years of active warfare, and came home with a deep war wound shortly before the fighting ceased. Throughout the war he lived keenly and doggedly, transformed fear into rage, and fired his gun. No doubt his nerves were frayed, and he himself was often afraid. But at no time during those endless months of hardship and peril of life were his nerves seriously upset. He never failed to sleep. And he spoke of his life in the army as being 'as happy as a sandboy's'. After twenty years of peace the war breaks out again. He is now a factory worker. A

bomb falls a mile from his home. His war memories are awakened.
But this time he has no active place to fill, no gun to fire. He
becomes disturbed by every passing aircraft, acutely apprehensive
of attack upon his country cottage, and wanders round the village
at night trying to detect betraying chinks of light round windows
or under doors. He has an acute war neurosis because his old
aggressiveness is aroused and he cannot hit back with effect as
was his wont when he was a battery sergeant in France. A man
in such a state falls a ready prey to prolonged hatred such as he
never suffers when he is an active soldier. I also know a skilled
psychotherapist, who well knows the Freudian mechanism of
obsessional group loyalty and hatred. But when war reached his
own country he became nationally and unappeasably aggressive,
and collected and recounted stories of enemy ' atrocities ' which
he made a reason for continuing in warfare. The screaming,
the shouting, the obsessional energy, the fearful caution, and the
morbid and unreasoning hatred—all these are due to the arousal
of primitive (not necessarily infantile) hatred *which cannot be
immediately and appropriately discharged*. They are all neurotic
reactions. And while conditions of group hostilities *expose* the
hatred of the obsessional because he *is* neurotic, the same conditions *create* hatred in the ordinary man by *making* him neurotic.
During a popular war, this war neurosis of delusionary hatred
becomes very widespread. The gulf is thus bridged between
obsessional and normal characters, by arousing in the latter new
' identifications ' with any primitive or infantile precursors of
obsessional hate that may exist with their minds. *In warfare, fear
and imposed inaction convert normal into neurotic minds*.

There is then a fluctuating line between the obsessional
character, whose hatred is always exaggerated and is stimulated
by facile adult ' identifications ' with infantile objects of abnormal
hatred and fear, and the normal members of society. The latter
are normally aggressive *ad hoc* to situations involving their own
welfare and interest, their own ' cause ' as they see it. But in
times of group hostility and the passion of war many normal
persons have hatred stimulated by ' identifications ' of their
enemies with certain fundamental ideals of evil which we all
seem to carry in our minds. Are these latter the same as the
infantile origins of the hatred of the obsessional ? I do not know.
But if they are, they have been dealt with very differently during
the whole long interval of development. In contrast with the
rich and morbid fantasy-identifications to which the obsessional
is always subject, the normal man finds only passing and occasional
need to identify any object with evil. When he does so, he loses
his temper, ' sees red ', and where possible attacks the object of
his rage openly. Warfare which involves whole communities
calls increasingly and infectiously upon men and women to
perform this identification of the enemy with evil. But it does so

in circumstances where only a limited number within the community can convert the answering and quite natural rage into action. This accounts in part at least for the acute and clamant hatreds shown by non-combatants in war-time. But the object of hate is not allied to the object of love unless there exists this obsessional element of Freudian infantile (parental) identification which appears to be intermitted between the primitive and instinctive idea of evil and the modern object with which it becomes identified in its peculiarly distorting manner. The sheltered upbringing by anxious parents from which many middle class children suffer, may engender or foster such obsessional identifications in infancy. The hard life and on the whole more normal emotional attention of the working poor for their children may militate against these persistent links between abnormal love and abnormal hate which can so often be shown to be the product of an abnormal infancy. Further, a physically active life seems to diminish the mounting and abnormal aggressiveness (whatever its origin) of the civilian adult alike in war and peace.

In the foregoing analysis of loyalty and its accompanying aggressiveness I have not attempted any differentiation between the sexes. All that has been written above applies to both sexes. Naturally the ' identifications ' formed by women are not precisely the same as those of men. But the deeper unconscious is more bi-sexual than the conscious life, and the essential identifications of ' good ' and ' bad ' run along much the same lines in both men and women. A comparison of the psychological case notes of Mr. C. with the excerpt of those of Mrs. B., will suffice to show the similarity of their obsessional neurotic mechanisms. Women have been thought more subject to personal loyalty (i.e. to a leader) and more violent in their hatred of enemies than men. The present war will probably show the effect of physical danger upon feminine hatred and in certain cases the effect upon it of active militancy. No reliable information has yet (December 1941) come my way upon any of these matters. In any event they do not separate women from men in any of the main responses of group loyalty with which we have been dealing.

V. SUMMARY : THE TRANSFER OF LOYALTY

We may sum up. Loyalty is grounded biologically in the need for unity, and for personal sacrifice for the safety of the ' herd ', psychologically in the social instinct which in most men at most times is stronger than the self-assertive instinct which opposes it. Powerful potential group loyalties are available in every normal human being. But the units destined to receive those loyalties are for most men very little predetermined in type. To secure loyalty societies have but to offer security and strength and ' rightness ', to be able to utilize certain ties of habit which are quickly formed, and to be willing to accept and to use a devotion which will be proportionate to their seeming need.

Man's awareness of his need of society starts shortly after birth. Links of varying strength connect the young child's concepts of what will bring him security and the love of parents or guardians with the objects of his adult loyalties. The means of linkage are unconscious fantasies, with the prototype characters of which unconscious ' identifications ' are subsequently formed. The mechanism is of peculiar strength and significance, and often operates with grotesque distortion, in the case of obsessional characters. But the process is one to which we are all subject.

Education and appeal are important factors in creating and in fostering loyalties, and particularly so are such appeals as excite ready identifications, e.g. with early father or mother concepts, or with inherent ideas of ' good ' and ' bad '. Loyalties may be formed by spontaneous association of individuals in groups (sharing their ' super-egos ', as Freud would say) or in response to the heroic and symbolic leadership of a patriarchal or ' father ' figure. In either event the loyalties of men are unstable. The identifications, and so the emotion, are readily transferable : they serve an instinct which has no determined object except that of the happiness of the individual through the satisfaction of his social conscience.

For the group, loyalty is biologically enhanced by danger or competition. Commensurately, for the individual, loyalty tends in the seeming presence of danger to engender a strong and unreasoning aggressiveness. In obsessional characters this aggressive defence of the group may be aroused by imagined and distant and intellectually conceived enemies. In such characters there also tends to be a link of similarity between the object of devotion and the object hated ; for in their prototypes of infancy they were often one and the same.

To-day the nation states still have our loyalty. With partisan prejudice, and without superior law, these units are compelled by their very nature to quarrel. But the actual aggressiveness of a national community against another nation is built up out of natural misunderstanding, to which is added the abnormal aggressiveness of artificially aroused loyalties, and the pathological aggressiveness which individuals of obsessional character contribute by their brightly burning hatreds. These last are the hatreds that rouse us from our happy lethargies of peaceful life and interest, and worry us with their increasing stridency of threat and warning through the quiet years when war is to the majority of all peace-keeping communities ' unthinkable '. The possessors of these passions win monuments to themselves by prophesying what they are in fact bringing about. In the end, their commotion and our own blindness allow us all to be laid by the heels by their infectious passion. We then reach the veri-similitude of ' inescapable conflict ' which is built up by the same methods of misunderstanding, distrust, quarrelsomeness, im-placability, angry threat, and self-righteous preparation for self-defence, which characterizes any tavern brawl when it is pre-cipitated by a few ill-tempered wretches among a group of normal men unrestrained by law.

Faced with these loyalties to conflicting nations, the problem before that Great Society of mankind to which we all belong is not to attempt to quench human loyalty, but to achieve its trans-ference. The nations of the world will have to be bound to law. A potent means to that end would be the alienation of the political loyalty of their citizens, without the transfer of which no world community can crystallize. Such a transfer need not disturb the affectionate strands of a thousand minor loyalties which bind a man to his nation, as to his village or his family. But we must not think that a transfer of loyalty to the World Community is likely to go very far in normal minds while all power organization remains national. Advocates of the World Community, such as Zimmern [1] and Lasswell [2], have canvassed such devices as the world postage system, and a world-wide hygienic union against germs to stimulate a sense of loyalty to a nascent world com-munity. Sir Alfred Zimmern puts into the mouth of Senator Root a sentiment well known to be his own when he says that ' the community of the world can be made . . . by the devising of suitable institutions with names pointing ahead to what they will ultimately become '. Such devices and activities would and do aid the imagination of man towards his total loyalty of the future. The enthusiasm and sympathy which were evinced for the non-political activities of the League of Nations and the International Labour Organization at Geneva are in evidence here. They prepared the way for a League success in the realm of power politics. But that was all. And as that success never came, those nebulous loyalties have vanished like morning mist before the sun of battle. I believe that the conception and firm advocacy of a transfer of power itself from the nations to their natural master, the World, will do far more to stir the imagination of men than any procedures of gradualness and attempts to create a preliminary courtesy authority have done. Certainly in crises power or a claim of power alone holds the loyalty of the masses true. Everybody greets the parson. But all obey the squire.

Above all, loyalty must be dealt with positively. Denial of loyalty is repudiation of nature. One might as well attempt to exorcise love itself. If, in 1933, the Oxford Union had resolved what it would fight *for*, instead of simply renouncing its easiest

[1] Zimmern, *League of Nations and the Rule of Law,* p. 234. (2nd edition. Macmillan. 1939.)
[2] Lasswell, *World Politics and Personal Insecurity.* (1934.)

and strongest natural loyalty, namely to ' king and country ', it would not have been so easy to foretell the subsequent breaking of that resolution by nearly all of those who made it. The problem of World Order is not one of abolishing a very tenacious emotion, but one of transferring a readily transferable emotion. That can be done either by directly bringing under the control of law those free and irresponsible national units which now receive man's loyalty, or else by creating the ideal of and demand for such a transfer within the minds of enough men to rally success-fully to its achievement. The change may come by wise public leadership, or by inspired public demand.

The minds of men are ripening for the change. The failure of the sovereign states to give security has been profoundly noted. We have to frame for mankind the new object upon which human loyalty can fix its gaze and revive its faith, a new unit which will not take its regular toll of human life, which will not hold us for ever down to the biological starting point of our loyalties, a desperate struggle to save *our* community in a world of com-munities. Men must be shown that their social enrichment depends upon a political organization of the world, and that that does in fact require the vital limitation of the present national states, which, while offering ' security ' can hardly find time to bury their dead, and in trying to maintain ' sovereignty ' so often achieve suicide.

VIII

THE MANIPULATION OF WORLD FORCES TO ATTAIN WORLD LAW

1. THE INCUBUS OF THE SOVEREIGN STATE

THE sovereign state is doomed and nothing can redeem it. In the first place it is not what it claims to be. In this world nothing and nobody is sovereign. To establish a claim to be above the law is to place yourself in a realm of force where there is constant strife and in which no one can for long remain the victor. Nor does it provide what a power group exists to provide, the best security available to its members. For to refuse to submit to law is to make oneself a slave, a victim of the passions of others and of one's own. And that is what the sovereign state does for us who are its members and subjects. Therein is the very reverse of security. Has it not proved so ?

To us as individuals the ' sovereign ' state gives a symbol of importance and a figment of security, while, through inefficiencies of organization so gross that they could result only from the operations of blind prejudice, it takes a toll of our total efforts so high as to leave us of this labour-saving, nature-controlling twentieth century, slaves to place and time, in labour and in drudgery, not less than our ancestors of any century which has preceded ours. Forty-five million English men and women, with artificial manure, motor ploughs, steam mills, electric ovens, and comparable advances of mechanical aid in every department of life, cannot feed, clothe and disport themselves as free men and women any more fully than their grandparents or great-grand-parents. Indeed for the majority of our citizens dare we claim that life by and large these twenty-five years has been so good, so safe, so free, so comfortable, so healthy even as it was for our ancestors between say 1715 and 1740 ? Ponder that, trade-unionists ! And do not think that it would have been better with more ' Labour ' governments—unless those governments had stopped the one leak that makes a sieve of national economy, the leak to armaments and your preparations to fight your enemies.

Collectively, the sovereign state first fosters, and then draws from us our worst passions. Avarice, distrust, intolerance, and finally self-satisfied rage, reckless and fearful lust to kill—these are the passions we show as national units, to those who look on without an ally's sympathy. And now, twice in a generation, the sovereign state is taking away, first throughout Europe and then throughout the world, our lives, our liberties, and our estates. And in the blindness of those partial views to which as men we are prone (and which it is the true business of government to correct and control and not to foster) in this our folly we allow it all to happen. Nay, we support its happening ; because through the partiality of the group (which is like that of a man who in blind temper attacks his employer) we see no other way of restoring ' honour and decency ' among men. But who, pray, two years before or twenty years after any great war that was ever waged could make a list of the honour and decency of the com-batant governments which would support for one instant our universal claims that a right lies so strongly with ' ourselves ' that we are free to kill our neighbours in the other camp, to wreck and destroy, until, like brawling drunkards, one of us is knocked out, or both of us are dragged off by the policemen of events, exhaustion, famine and pestilence, and handcuffed until we are sober again ? Ten years after this present war has ceased it will no more matter who ' caused ' or who ' won ' it than it did ten years after the last one. Such considerations will be irrelevancies for historians of the documents to ponder and debate. Politically, mankind will be crushed and burdened by the problems of an aftermath. Individually men will have forgotten all but the empty seats at table, the pensions, and the occasional fireside memories. What matters about a war to the men and women concerned is the starting, the waging, and the stopping of it.

Those and not the ' issues involved ' are the realities of our present life. Throughout the world, the ' sovereign state ' is a leader who has led his men to disaster twice running and in the shortest possible time in which it could be done. Loyal in the heat of battle its followers may still be. Loyal to balanced ' Powers ' nicely poised to bring gigantic ruin upon their peoples, those peoples cannot long remain.

The things that make intelligent men and women remain loyal to the myth of national sovereignty to-day are *prejudice*, *habit*, and *the absence of an alternative*. By *prejudice* I mean the whole system of conscious and unconscious misinformation by which every belligerent people is mentally bludgeoned into the first stage of loyal hatred, which supposes a malevolence and brutality to oppose the innocence and rectitude of ourselves, and so builds up and frees that very brutality against us. Compare any one-sided account of any long-standing personal quarrel! By prejudice I also mean that hatred of ' evil ' which is harnessed to aggressiveness, individual and collective, normal and pathological, and which is aroused by the plague of lies and half-truths, and for that matter the whole truths about the ' enemy ', faults comparable to which in ourselves we never hear, forget, or ignore. ' It is not the violent conflict between parts of the truth, but the quiet suppression of half of it that is the formidable evil ' [1] The *habit* that brings us into the line of an old loyalty again and again needs no further description. As a young Irishman once said to me : ' We must go on (against England), whether it is to the advantage of our people or no. For our fathers suffered in this cause, and we must not betray them ! '

The *absence of an alternative claim upon our loyalty* to that made by the nation-state is a very serious matter. For, until there occurs a transfer of loyalty away from the present nation-states of the world sufficient to bind those states to law, the present utter chaos of our world community will continue. I have said

[1] J. S. Mill, 1864, *On Liberty*.
It is easy to compile test questions of this fact. Four from the history of this present century will suffice.
Q. 1. The head of what great nation threatened a small neighbour struggling to maintain independence with war ' immediate and terrible ' unless it agreed at once to come into its empire ? A. (1) England 1921 *v*. Ireland ; (2) Germany 1939 *v*. Czechoslovakia.
Q. 2. What nation persisted in aggressive war against a small people in defiance of public opinion throughout the world ? A. (1) England 1901 *v*. South Africa ; (2) Germany 1939 *v*. Poland.
Q. 3. What Great Power broke its pledges to a lesser whose claims it had sponsored and guaranteed ? A. (1) England 1919 *v*. Italy ; (2) Italy 1935 *v*. Abyssinia.
Q. 4. What Great Powers whittled down and refused to honour obligations to the defeated enemy ? A. (1) England and France 1919–1932 *v*. Germany ; (2) —————— ? The very list arouses bitterness against the compiler. A rush of justificatory reasons for the action of our own side, whichever it be, comes to the informed mind. Reasons they are ; but the ' enemy ' never heard them. And what have *we* heard of *his* reasons ?

that we must not expect a world community to grow slowly, and slowly to solidify for itself a real law out of the ' pious aspirations ' of present ' international law '. That will not occur. *The prime requisite and firm creator of any community life is a law of order maintained by force.* For human nature is such that, in all its most necessary social relationships, it is subject to the permanent threat of the self-assertive impulse, which misinterprets facts, misjudges events, and then, through consequent self-justificatory passion, breaks the social bond, unless it be externally restrained. We may claim this as adequately confirmed. Nursery studies and family life confirm it. Social and national history confirms it. Modern psychology confirms it. And finally our common sense tends to confirm it—for all others except ourselves, which is in itself a final confirmation. Individual, group, or nation-state, we cannot judge our own cause. And if we try to do so we shall be reduced again and again to fighting for a supposed ' right ' against a supposed ' wrong ', for one set of illusions against another.

Now *force cannot operate far without loyalty.* Where men enslave multitudes, their rule is short and their power weak and weakening, unless they can arouse a widespread loyalty to themselves in the lands they rule. The evanescence of loyalty makes historians who chronicle the freeing of peoples from tyrants forget what held the ' tyrant ' safe upon his throne. The English and Germans who ' freed Europe ' from Napoleon witnessed in the loyalty of the ' Old Guard ' the last remnant of a force which had maintained the Emperor upon the shoulders of millions of devoted men and women. Whence springs that early power which enables a leader or a tyrant (he is often the same man viewed from a different angle) to start upon his career ? What but loyalty readily aroused by ' personality ' enabled the ' little corporal ' to capture the enthusiasm of that impersonal, Rousseauesque, French Revolution ? Recently a few Germans realized that a personal loyalty was far the quickest and surest way to convert a crestfallen people into a conquering power of gigantic force. Their success will be maintained at home and abroad as long as they can continue to attract a loyalty larger and more effective than any which can be opposed to it. You may call such a personal leadership with its suppression of opposition a tyranny. Every suppression of opposition, from the first institution of a press censorship onward, is a tyranny. But the source of power is not the suppression of the minority. It is the loyalty of the majority. Tyrannous force can only set up order if it can create and maintain sufficient loyalty. Some people think that the ' tyrannies ' of to-day differ from ' democracies ' because the former suppress opposition and the latter allow it. That is not so. Both suppress opposition directly it sets at risk the vital order of the state as they conceive it. And neither suppresses opposition short of that risk. A successful tyranny differs from a democracy in that it does not permit a division of loyalties by the presence in the field of any alternative governments. Both the great European totalitarian governments of to-day were born out of a chaos of conflicting loyalties which had threatened elementary law and order to a degree which no efficient government, oligarchy or democracy, could tolerate. It is literally true that it was two failures to set the necessary limitations upon democracy that made the introduction of fascism and national socialism both practicable and so widely acceptable. Psychologically it is a source of great strength to the totalitarian governments that they permit no rival objects to arouse the loyalties of their subjects. At a British election the citizen is asked to choose between two or three men or parties, each of which tries to blacken the other. The result often is that the average elector ends with no great opinion of any of the canvassers for his vote. It is not after an election, but during a war, when symbolism runs high even in democracies, that British governments become strong, popular—and if necessary tyrannical. At a modern German election the citizen is asked whether he still approves of his government or not : does his loyalty still hold ? If a government continues to hold such elections, and holds them under conditions of complete freedom of expression for the citizen, only very faulty government or a defeat in war is likely to produce disaffection so serious as to provoke a vote of no confidence from men at once subject to persuasive propaganda and without an alternative object of loyalty before them. Specific disaffections wisely remedied need never become election questions in the strenuous times for which these governments were designed. And only schism at the centre, or a massive ' landslide ' of popular feeling which put hatred in the place of love for the ' leader ', would be likely to replace such a regime.

The truth is that in easy times men are critical and lazy ; in hard times loyal and energetic. You may canvass the rising dangers to the League of Nations system, as for instance at the British Peace Ballot of 1935 ; but you will not unhorse a government of national selfishness and inertia thereby, despite any alternative loyalties you can present. In time of peace democracy had the means to create new loyalties, but could not muster the will. Perhaps too we were rather unfortunate in our total lack of leadership in any such direction. Totalitarian regimes, under the influence of the internal and external stresses which marked their inception and the growth of their power, have never admitted to their peoples the means of new loyalties. They have, hitherto, placed their own sovereign states in theory and practice before all other considerations. They have followed those interests with realism, skill, and determination, and also, whenever necessary, with the effective loyalty of their peoples.

II. THE LIQUIDATION OF THE SOVEREIGN STATE

There are some sixty sovereign states at present in the world. In 1930 there were twenty-seven in Europe alone. At the present time (1941) there are considerably fewer. The multiplication of states which followed the First Great War (of 1914–18) is being succeeded by a reduction at least in the effective number, as the ' Great Powers ' of to-day stretch every nerve to include their smaller neighbours within their economic and military control, and, where racial claims make it possible, actually to absorb or reabsorb them. But national and racial loyalties are such that though ' Great Powers ' may grow greater, and still greater temporary alliances may be formed, it is unlikely that a very great condensation, into say three or four stable power units, will occur in the near future of the world. Even if such an event came to pass the probability is that those units would have been formed as much by loyalty against as by loyalty to anything, and that our problem of world war would continue on a scale not less vast than hitherto. We will therefore exclude such condensations of sovereignty, whether regional, racial or ideological, from among the solutions of the problem of world government. Of the last of them, the ideological, we may say in passing that the devotee of world communism, fascism *contra mundum*, or an exclusive federal union of democracies, though he may be exercising his mind upon a novelty, is nevertheless expending his emotion in the old way, familiar to Mrs. Isaacs in her nursery school. Whilst shifting the object and altering the scale of his allegiance, as his ancestors have so often done before, he retains the two eternal groups, the *pro-* and the *contra-*, the white and the black, in which human loyalty delights. But to seek the association of those who are like us is to seek allies for a conflict. Therein lie wars interminable. *The object of world order is to find a means of associating with those who are different from and potentially hostile to us. The method is law superior to all groups ; the means the force that can create it. For that law and order to endure, there must be infused into the minds of men a loyalty such that most men at most times, and a majority of men at all times, will wish to maintain.*

III. REQUIREMENTS OF WORLD ORDER

No force of military victory *alone* will ever contain a preponderant dynamic sufficient to establish a world pax against the national, regional, and sectarian loyalties of man. But the creation of a new and world-wide unit of human loyalty, accompanied by an impartial law of elementary order, and the abolition of that national lawlessness called ' sovereignty ', could and would establish such a pax. We have considered the place of loyalty in the creation of a World Community. It can anticipate law ; but it will never go far or fare well without law. *The first and only requirement of world order is the binding of all men, individuals and groups alike, to law.* In practice to-day that means that the hitherto ' sovereign ' states of the world must relinquish their ' sovereignty ' in both senses of the term. They must relinquish first the claim— never more than a vain and foolish boast—that they are self-determining and subject to no external wills. They must also abandon their exclusive demand upon the loyalty of their ' subjects '. The maintenance, though not of necessity the creation, of world order requires the loyalty of mankind.

Political loyalty, as well as being an acquired and transferable habit, is nevertheless dedicated to the strong, for its biological justification is security. We shall find that an abrogation of their sovereignty will mean a great weakening in the power and in the significance of national states in the new real world. Security found elsewhere, the end of the claims of sovereignty and a weakening of power go hand in hand with the transfer of essential loyalty to the more effectual guardian. It may give us a pleasant and idle reflection to be a Man of Kent or a native of British Columbia ; but we do not attach to it such thoughts of heroism or of suffering either for our country or for ourselves as would create a passionate collective loyalty. The weakening and loss of significance suffered by the nation states of an ordered world will come accompanied by such an advance in the welfare of their peoples that individual regrets of a patriotic nature will probably meet with little popular support or toleration. The new unit will be all-powerful. For it will give satisfaction.

IV. METHODS OF ACHIEVING WORLD-WIDE LAW AND ORDER

In considering the ways in which the abolition of national sovereignty may come, we have to remember that force is required to set up, and loyalty is required to maintain, the world system of law in favour of which the old and partial loyalties and the old and incomplete legal systems of world administration to-day have to be superseded. There seem to me to be three main ways in which there can come about the creation of a complete human society to replace the partial societies of to-day.

1. *Voluntary abnegation of sovereignty.*—The first way is by voluntary abnegation of state sovereignty. In the past, governments and peoples have been known to give up self-determination and sovereignty for a greater good. It was the method which brought the North American states into their Union, and which transferred the seat of Scottish government from Edinburgh to London. Such a procedure is seldom followed except under pressing necessity. It is accompanied by much reluctance and

many misgivings.[1] Both the unions mentioned above were
nominally entered upon freely. But in both a very strong pressure
of events was needed to tip the balance against habitual prejudice
and pride. In both an effective union came gradually, and the
first alienation of sovereignty was minimal, i.e. for external
affairs, control of the army and finance in the case of the American
Union, a union of crowns alone in the British.

But we must still keep essential requirements in view. A
federation of partisan states in a partial community—a Pan-
America, say, or a United States of Europe—may offer great
attractions to anyone who is anxious to strengthen his own cause
against another's. Many advantages might be cited for almost
any enlargement of the present units of loyalty, the rigid nation-
states of our time. As these present states writhe and totter, no
doubt those advantages will be energetically canvassed. But
such enlargements are not solutions of the great problem of
human government to-day. As a judge of its own cause, a
federation of democracies would be no less partial than a union
of soviets. A combination of the two would but leave the world
under a new dominion, until a group of ill-treated antagonistic,
or ' have-not ' Powers succeeded in creating a counter union
capable of challenge. And that indeed, whether declared, or
realized, or neither, is the very implication and *raison d'être* of
any fusion of power in a world not ruled by law. The strengthening of the ' right ' against the ' wrong ' by A is a strengthening of
the ' wrong ' against the ' right ' for B. A world community
cannot be given its birth and its infant guidance by any union
which can be interpreted as directed against another unit of
government and power in a sense which is either discriminatory
or capable of challenge. For if it is discriminatory, the chances
are that in the end such a union will be challenged. Governments
who would abnegate their sovereignty in exchange for a world
security system must not do so in fear of attack by a superior, or
in order to attack an inferior, in strength. They must resign their
sovereignty without trying at the same time to retain their partisan
control of events. The world community will not be born to
save the British Empire, or to install the German. It will be born
to govern the world. And the prime ministers who ultimately
have the courage to abrogate the sovereignties of their own
countries to that end should not expect a place in the ' cabinet '
of a world order. A pension and their place in history should be
enough to satisfy them ! *To become a success a voluntary abnegation
of state sovereignty to create a World State (or a World Federation
of States) must either be world-wide, or alternatively two conditions
must be fulfilled. The first is that the power behind the new unit is*

---

[1] See e.g. The speech of Lord Belhaven in the Scottish Parliament in 1706
(*Everyman*, No. 714, p. 53) and note the bitterness aroused by the Confederation
issue in North America (*The Federalist*, Everyman, No. 519).

preponderant to secure world peace at the time of federation. And the second is that there is set up a truly impartial administration with world-wide opportunities of association. It will not then meet with any subsequent challenge. For permanent success is only to the strong and just : and, once it is established, no sectarian interest would ever set at risk the loyalty of mankind to an organization which truly expressed the needs of humanity.

The loyalty that would be required for the launching of a federal World State by a voluntary association of existing states could be created by an adequate canvass of the programme of the federators, with reassurances obtained from the personal integrity of the chief leaders in that, the greatest drama of world history. Excepting perhaps for nations which had recently incurred such suffering as a major defeat in war, public opinion could not be expected to plunge straight into an enthusiasm for federation. But with strong government and good leadership in countries in such key positions of power as, say, England and France enjoyed in 1930, an adequate proportion of that public opinion which we all now note as being ' different from 1914 ' might be expected to rally to the new ideal with great rapidity. In democratic countries federal leadership could come from outside the existing government : in authoritarian countries leadership from within could surely be decisive ?

2. *World law imposed through military victory.*—There is another way in which existing nation-states could be bound to the law of a world order. That is through the power of a victorious state or association of states which took advantage of a temporary but definite world ascendancy to impose law and order upon the world as a whole. This method deserves more attention than it has received. Wars usually continue until a definite military victory crowns the efforts of one side in the conflict. The victors of the Great War which started in 1939 may neglect all the lessons which are to be learnt from the mistakes of the victors of the Great War of 1914–18. But they need not do so. What was the chief of those mistakes ? The Peace of 1919 left the world in a state of peculiar instability because of an unusual circumstance, namely the withdrawal of one victorious belligerent, the United States of America, from the system set up to secure the fruits of victory. This withdrawal left an adverse balance of power which only unusually skilful statesmanship on the part of the ex-Allies could have prevented from forming an early encouragement to the defeated to renew the struggle upon more favourable terms. Nevertheless there can be no doubt that in the decade and a half which followed the war repeated opportunities were afforded to those ex-Allies to convert the temporary security of their unilateral armaments into a general security system, by utilizing a promised parity in disarmament to transfer sovereign power to a supernational authority, and to endow the latter at once with

collective force and a reassuring power of treaty revision and abrogation. This was publicly advocated in Britain in 1932, and there is abundant reason to believe that there would have been acceptance by France of the only part of such a scheme—namely treaty revision—which had not been put forward by the French Government themselves. The keynote of French policy which was sounded by all governments and apparently supported by most citizens from 1923 onwards, can be expressed in the phrase : ' Give us security and we will not quarrel about the method.' The lesson of the Great War was half learnt. I fancy the other half has often been in the hearts of Frenchmen : ' The method is incompatible with national sovereignty.' Unfortunately no English politician in office or in official Opposition supplied that answer. But does any delegate to the Disarmament Conference of 1932 now doubt that agreement between France and Britain upon the French plan of centralized force, with a British addition (not a substitution) of treaty revision, would have gone very far towards creating a hopeful starting point of a world federation ? If such a thing could have been done during that phase of Franco-British post-war ascendancy which passed rapidly away after 1932, it may be done in a similar or even more favourable phase in the future. From a national standpoint the greatest mistake of the peacemakers of 1919 may remain subject to argument. From a world standpoint it was that they did not utilize victory to establish a world security system. I believe that for simple men and for wise rulers everywhere the two standpoints are one. A wise victor may yet come to see them as one.

The form of a world state thus founded upon the victory of a nation or an alliance may differ at its inception according to the ideology of the victors. A totalitarian victor might be expected to impose his new World Order in a manner which, in form at any rate, retained sovereignty for national states or for whatever his ' total ' unit might at that time have become. But if it provided a legal system in which no conflicting units could ever judge their own cause and thus precipitate another conflict, it would earn loyalty enough from a war-ridden humanity to make a surer foundation than the world has yet had upon which to build its hopes of order and good government. A victorious group of democracies could be equally successful, if their federation also fulfilled the basic conditions of law and order—that preponderant force shall lie behind the system at its initiation, and that that force shall be placed behind impartial law, so that it is never again at the service of the partisanship of partial societies— even, hard thought, of our own ! The strong nation that can bind itself will free the world.

3. *Peace by revolution.*—There remains a third possibility ; a world-wide revolution of peoples against states as such. It is the Russian ideal of 1917, except that the conflict need not now

be a ' class ' one. Tsarist Russia was ruled by a social class which oppressed another social class. No Great Power can reasonably be said to be so ruled to-day. In England, with complete freedom of political association and expression in all times of peace, and also, and in consequence, a remarkable degree of similar freedom in time of war, there were less than half a dozen elected Members of Parliament who opposed the foreign policy of the National Governments of 1939 and 1940 except in criticism of their methods of waging war. If almost all the freely elected representatives of a whole nation agree that a war cause is their cause, they may all be in error, but it is difficult to believe that a suppressed class is very acutely conscious of its suppression by those that rule. Make them conscious ? But could éven a ' submerged tenth ' be made to regard the present House of Commons as a worthy object of social hatred and as deliberately standing in the way of their social welfare ? Let us regard the present House of Commons not as capitalist knaves but as the victims of a tragic delusion of nationalism ! And let us admit that in human loyalty to a partisan society we whom they represent have shared their delusions ! The public that then calls a halt is in a very powerful position indeed. Unlike all previous revolutions, such an attack must start and finish against a symbol and a policy derived from it, and not against the normal human beings who direct the policy and believe in the symbol. Such a revolution is no illegal revolution. For a democracy must abandon its title if its people cannot reverse their former policies. In Germany, again, there is no tyranny of class. The socialization of the nation has progressed greatly under the present regime. So thorough a people applies military rule in warfare to a higher degree than is customary in England or France. But that rule is no longer that of a socially privileged class in the way that military rule might well become in England. In peace-time there are restrictions upon opponents of the government which has become accepted by the majority. But whether it be the Reichstag, the ' S.S. ', the ' S.A. ', or a women's rural institute meeting, any such a modern German gathering can congratulate itself upon its breaking through of old distinctions of social class in the interests of the nation-state. The German delusion is the same as the British. It has been the same for all of us. And a world-wide revolution of peoples against the state unit as such would be a world-wide awakening, and a world-wide conversion. In particular, if national war is now persisted in to the point of exhaustion and a recurrence of the sufferings of twenty years ago, the peoples of the world may achieve a wisdom which can see through the heady passions of conflict, victory, and defeat ; so that the first is seen as the joint product of faulty human organization and normal human nature, the second as an illusion pure and simple for the mass of men who ' share ' it, and the third as the lot of all who suffer from warfare everywhere, whatever flag is flying on top at the end of the latest ' round ' of a hitherto endless contest. The place for the flags of national competition is upon the sports stadium, not upon the wrecked streets of neighbouring towns.

A peoples' revolution against nationalism could engender a world loyalty if it were wisely led. To be effective to a world order it would have to fulfil the same criteria as the alternative methods of self-abnegatory federation and a World State imposed by military victory. It would have to mobilize force adequate to maintain itself beyond threat of counter attack. And it would have to institute such law and such order as no effective group of peoples would subsequently wish to challenge.

V. A GUIDING RULE FOR WORLD LAW

Let us revise the requirements of the World Community in respect of law and force at its inception. World Law must secure from the very first moment of its existence two things :

First—That no unit shall be free to judge its own cause against another and attempt to enforce that judgment ;

Second—that the many and pressing problems which will come early before the first impartial courts of the world shall be judged expeditiously and by simple guiding rules of Equity, to which all men may be expected by their common humanity to give assent. That will be a modern ' Law of Nations '. The first guiding rule of that equity code should be to secure the greatest happiness of the greatest number of all mankind. But it must be combined with the recognition that the greatest happiness obtainable for him is rightly claimed by each.

Analogy, precedent, and codification will of course be used in the building up of world law appropriate to the World ' State ', or ' Federation ', or whatever form of association shall be formed. But give us first a skeleton of law to secure the ' good ' man against the ' bad ' and each of us against ourselves. Then the happiness and devoted loyalty of all humanity will give a support and a dignity to the first World Court which will readily secure to it the devoted services of high-minded judges. And their judgments will become the greatest boon which law has ever conferred upon humanity.

IX

CONSCIENCE AND SOCIETY

IN all the hubbub of embattled social theory by which we are surrounded to-day, the antitheses ' tyranny ' and ' freedom ', 'order' and 'anarchy' recur and resound. Hobbes told his contemporaries long ago that 'monarchy', 'aristocracy', and 'democracy' could become 'tyranny', 'oligarchy', or 'anarchy', by virtue of an altered viewpoint, i.e. an altered emotion. It is not what things are but what our emotions make them out to be that determines our attitudes to them. It is our own emotions, wayward and irrational, which are our greatest tyrants.

Freud spoke often of the stress and the pain of man's renunciation of self-will. There is no doubt that every individual does build up his conscience for himself with varying degrees of anxious apprehension of what he must do to be saved from the dire and fatal perils of social excommunication. In that long conflict within the mind between the claims of society and the assertions of self, concession after concession is made by the latter to the former. In more fertile and easier geographical climates a greater indulgence can be conceded to the self : in the cold dour north of Europe so much of dutiful effort has been needed to maintain life that in many of its sons the conscience is never stilled, the pleasures of self are snatched furtively at bed and at board, and the tyranny of 'I must' seldom or never gives way to the freedom of 'I may'.

Neither in the bleak north nor in the sunny south, however, does man ever succeed in his quest of direct self-control. Something of self-restraint must always be delegated to others. Law is the result. Without the aid of law, man's conscience works in vain. He perceives the disasters of his conflicts, personal and communal. But effort after effort, and lesson after lesson, prove unavailing. It is not that we do not obey our consciences. Many men do so to the letter. But, however severe it may become, our conscience only tells us *what to do in the light of what we can see*. And whether we repress it lightly and gaily, or heavily and sourly, there still exists beneath the surface that self-will of passion and desire which distorts our perception of what we see. In our conscious life our consciences may control us. In our unconscious life they never do. And so, whether we be Italian or Scottish, Spaniard or Russian, it is not lack of conscience which wrecks our societies in the absence of law : it is the false truths upon which that conscience has to operate.

We have finished with our theories of human nature. Human nature is a kaleidoscope of colours to its very centre. Of its two great moulding instincts, that of self-satisfaction through others generally wins at the executive level of our minds. But self-assertion in their despite is always at work within us, falsifying the 'facts' upon which our judgments are to be made. In such circumstances, can the human psyche be said to *want* a stable society ? *Consciously*, and with determination—yes ! Man has striven towards such an attainment with perennial courage and has always felt that 'after *this* struggle with evil is over, it will come!' But 'this' struggle with 'evil' is the very core of the problem which defies our unilateral solution! For our 'evil' is another man's 'good'. He is conscientious like ourselves. How should he be different? But his accounts have been progressively falsified to the same end, so that we, each of us, become convinced that the other is cheating. Then at last our consciences free us. And woe betide us all!

Freud thought we all *wanted* to reach that point of freed aggressiveness, and so to smash up our happy homes. We don't! —though for a number of obsessional characters there is a magnetic fascination about the idea, and for all of us there is something that is satisfied in destruction. But conscience is our safeguard there. It must be something evil that we destroy—or else a playful substitute, a penny shy at a fair.

Mankind wants, passionately and nearly all the time in these harrowing and critical years, to set up a secure society once and for all. He knows the value of law and order : he has experienced and delighted in them. He knows, or can foresee, the freedom that comes with good government, the easing of hard lives, the scope for adventurous ones, which it could bring. If national force and League of Nations mandates had been internationalized, and unjust treaties made readily revisable in 1932, unemployment, poverty, and drabness could have been well-nigh eliminated from Europe by 1942, and a spacious international life would be spreading around our great cities. As it is, their inhabitants are cowering and burrowing beneath their ruins, and millions of us are in dire uncertainty as to how our next night will end or whence will come our next month's food.

It is not our consciences that are at fault. They might usefully be more lenient here, stricter there. But on the whole they give society adequate security against the individual. On the whole we obey them. We have to! And there are no hidden springs of sadism in normal man, demanding blood lest they wreck all society. All society is in imminent danger of being wrecked : but it is not by man's conscience that it is being done. Our consciences are waiting to make us good and happy members of the world community the moment the ding-dong of aggressiveness and misunderstanding is prevented from perverting the judgments of men each within his own group. *It is our understanding which has been at fault.*

Partial societies always call for partisan evaluations and biased loyalties. Man is waiting, tired and anxious, to be loyal to his Total Society, directly he can organize it, or someone will organize it for him. The qualities necessary to maintain that Society are in us all—loyalty, conscientiousness, the peaceful pursuit of our duties, and the enjoyment of our pleasures. All that is required is for us to realize how and why it is that we have come by the law and order of our own nation-state, whichever one it is that we inhabit. It is because *we cannot live in peace without external law, cannot judge our own causes without its overriding guidance and correction.*

There is enough judicial ability and judicial integrity in the world to judge all the world's disputes. There is legal ability to draft codes for the World State. There is common sense to find decisions through the simple justice and right of Equity. Is there yet the enlightenment and the courage which will say : ' I submit myself to the Court. I submit the welfare of my fellows to a new and potent Court. Where I believe that settling things my way and my nation's way is right, *that* is where I now know I shall be wrong. Let a Swiss and a Danish and a German and a French judge settle our quarrelsome affairs, as we would were we private citizens and our quarrel lay in their lands.'

But first set up your courts, and charge them well from the highest integrity our communities can produce. And first lay down your principles : *No national sovereignty : People before states : Equality of race : Custodianship of backward peoples : All the aids to community that the economist, the politician, and psychologist can suggest.*

And first of all agree to do this, not with the friends who but turn your nation into an alliance, but with your enemies with whose aid you can turn the world into a community. It is you and they who share the force of your world between you. Make the great venture ! AGREE WITH THINE ADVERSARY—*QUICKLY ! And place the consciences of the world behind its Total Society.*

INDEX

Printed in Great Britain by Butler & Tanner Ltd., Frome and London